VIRAL

A True Story of
Epidemic Flu,
Fear And Faith

A.A.E. MURPHY

BALBOA.
PRESS
A DIVISION OF HAY HOUSE

Balboa Press books may be ordered through booksellers or by contacting:

Balboa Press
A Division of Hay House
1663 Liberty Drive
Bloomington, IN 47403
www.balboapress.com
1 (877) 407-4847

Because of the dynamic nature of the Internet, any web addresses or links contained in this book may have changed since publication and may no longer be valid. The views expressed in this work are solely those of the author and do not necessarily reflect the views of the publisher, and the publisher hereby disclaims any responsibility for them.

The author of this book does not dispense medical advice or prescribe the use of any technique as a form of treatment for physical, emotional, or medical problems without the advice of a physician, either directly or indirectly. The intent of the author is only to offer information of a general nature to help you in your quest for emotional and spiritual well-being. In the event you use any of the information in this book for yourself, which is your constitutional right, the author and the publisher assume no responsibility for your actions.

Any people depicted in stock imagery provided by Thinkstock are models, and such images are being used for illustrative purposes only. Certain stock imagery © Thinkstock.

Print information available on the last page.

ISBN: 978-1-5043-5343-4 (sc)
ISBN: 978-1-5043-5345-8 (hc)
ISBN: 978-1-5043-5344-1 (e)

Library of Congress Control Number: 2016904757

Balboa Press rev. date: 03/29/2016

Introduction

Before we became sick, I was a novice about such things as history, religion, health, human services or medicine. Learning about medical terminology and bodily processes was forced upon me by listening to and observing doctors, specialists and other medical professionals- including a family half-full of nurses - during my husband Joe's ordeal. I also learned to detest encouragement: "Be strong." "Stay strong." "You're so strong."

It has been a monumental challenge to put into words things which cannot be described. Words fall short when I attempt to explain the abrupt change to our lives and the slow transformation from health to illness to recovery to acceptance of permanently changed lives. As an example, the Hawaiian term *aloha* has several meanings depending upon the circumstance and the person using it; it can mean hello as a greeting, goodbye, a way of thinking (The Way of Aloha, Living with Aloha), it can mean peace, a way of life, an attitude, love, and much more. Likewise, the term *faith* has a multitude of meanings. Describing my faith in a higher power has been a challenge, yet faith was an integral part of my survival throughout the past two years. My intention is to portray the power and magnitude of my faith as you read about the events that have shaped my life, and my reactions to them. I don't feel I have to justify my faith, but I'm compelled to share what worked for me through an excruciating period.

I do not wear my heart on my sleeve. It is grueling for me to ask for help, to complain about or share my troubles, or to speak about what I truly think or feel when I'm suffering. I often present as protective, glib, flippant or tight-lipped. This book is the antithesis. Contained herein are my most guarded, intimate thoughts and feelings about the catastrophe that occurred when Joe and I became ill.

During Joe's illness and rehabilitation, I was also sick, yet I spent nearly every day, with few exceptions, at Joe's bedside advocating for him, watching every gauge, movement, machine, nurse, nurse's aide, even the rise and fall of his hospital gown as the ventilator breathed for him. When I arrived home at the end of a day, I was beyond exhaustion, with barely enough energy to take care of the pets, bathe myself, and eat before bed. There was no time or strength for email or phone calls explaining Joe's progress du jour, a cycle which continued for many months. As an alternative, I chronicled my thoughts via daily social media updates, finding it easier to summarize them as they occurred at Joe's bedside than to speak or write about them at the end of every grueling day. I've included selections of these posts as they appeared on my social media page.

Joe and I converted from lifelong Catholicism to another Christian faith in 2006. I ask that you forgive my Scriptural interpretations from the Bible, the Quran and other holy books. Despite, or due to challenges and doubt, my faith in God has grown exponentially. I can't imagine how I would have conducted myself without it. I know what I know as a result of what I have lived through. I know what I feel from the Spirit.

Through it all, I may have appeared composed and strong most of the time. I wasn't. I was numb, and in the privacy of my head and my home I allowed doubt, anger, remorse, regret and resentment to creep in, but not long enough for them to take up residence.

I'm filled with gratitude for family and friends who offered to review, revise, edit and critique much of this book.

> *But wilt thou know, O vain man, that faith without works*
> *is dead? For as the body without the spirit is dead, so faith*
> *without works is dead also.* ~ James 2: 20, 26

1 Though I speak with the tongues of men and of angels, and have not charity, I am become as sounding brass, or a tinkling cymbal. 2 And though I have the gift of prophecy, and understand all mysteries, and all knowledge; and though I have all faith, so that I could remove mountains, and have not charity, I am nothing. 3 And though I bestow all my goods to feed the poor, and though I give my body to be burned, and have not charity, it profiteth me nothing.
~1 Corinthians, 13: 1-3

Questions about why we got sick and survived, combined with faith in a higher power and the obligation of higher purpose directed my work. I'm sure I experienced twinges of survivor guilt; learning about the casualties of the pandemic H1N1 in 2009 and the epidemic of H1N1 in 2014 intensified my pursuit to document our challenges so that others could learn from them. The more I learned, the more galvanized was my desire to share what I knew about the flu, vaccines, faith and about how I handled difficult choices under extreme duress and illness. As a believer, I am compelled to translate my faith into action, so as not to be "as sounding brass or a tinkling cymbal". This book is the result.

Joe is living proof of miracles. Call it what you will; I credit my faith, and the faith of those who supported us, faith in God, Higher Power, Source, Great Spirit, Allah, Supreme Being, El Shaddai, YHWH, Elohim, Jehovah, Universe, Lord, Bhagavan, or Almighty as the source of my strength on this journey.

My intent is that you will find something contained in these pages that provides hope, inspiration, consolation, purpose, love and joy amid misfortune and doubt. If you are faithful, I hope this book is invigorating. If you are not a believer, I hope you'll be prompted to revisit the possibility of a higher power.

Although names, locations and occupations have been changed, this is our true story of epidemic flu, fear and faith, and a testimony to the divine inside us all.

Dedication

For NJS and FKS
That you will come to know perfect love, be inspired and
humbled by creation, and hold on to hope, always.
With all that is in my heart for you, Omi

Wherefore, whoso believeth in God might have
with surety hope for a better world,
yea, even a place at the right hand of God,
which hope cometh of faith, maketh an anchor to the souls of men,
which would make them sure and steadfast,
always abounding in good works,
being led to glorify God.
And now I, Moroni, would speak somewhat concerning these things;
I would show unto the world that faith is things
which are hoped for and not seen;
wherefore dispute not because ye see not,
for ye see no witness until after the trial of your faith.
~The Book of Ether, Chapter 12 Verses 4 &6

Chapter 1

"Endure to the end"

*Faith is the province of the defeated one who still clings to hope
as a nice idea faintly remembered.* ~ J.I. Abbot

After the Code Blue was called, hospital staff paddled Joe's heart back into rhythm. I received a phone call from one of his doctors: "Aoibhyann, your husband coded. You need to come to the hospital."

My husband Joe and I were diagnosed with H1N1 flu and pneumonia and admitted to the hospital January 27, 2014. He suffered a cascade of catastrophic consequences including peritonitis, diverticulitis, sepsis, burst colon, Acute Respiratory Distress Syndrome (ARDS). He was in the ICU for 33 days, comatose. He was placed on a ventilator because his lungs shut down due to ARDS, and administered a paralytic so that his lungs would allow the ventilator to breathe for him. (We humans are involuntary breathers, unlike cetaceans - whales, dolphins and porpoises- who must choose to breathe). Due to lack of oxygen, persistent high fever and H1N1 flu that mutated to H2N2, Joe suffered organ failure, total body fluid overload and cardiac arrest.

His abdomen was sliced open from sternum to groin during exploratory surgery; a portion of his burst colon was removed. The poisonous excrement from the colon permeated his abdomen and traveled to his lungs. He was septic, unable to breathe, and viral. Three people died from just H1N1 in that hospital in the month of February.

Joe's ARDS gradually cleared, his organs and brain woke up, and he came out of the coma. He was discharged from the ICU to a rehab hospital ill-prepared to handle his level of needed care; he had critical illness polyneuropathy- a sort of paralysis due to muscle atrophy. He also had a tracheostomy, colostomy, and stomach feeding tube. He had to relearn to use every muscle in his body, from his face to his toes.

In the first rehab hospital, Joe's catheter was removed while it was still inflated, and he endured a punctured bladder. He was rushed to a second emergency room with hematuria, nearly bleeding to death, suffering the agony of a swollen bladder and urge to pass blood clots through his urethra. Later he would tell me it felt as if he was "trying to pass a box of cereal" in his urine.

With all that we endured, it might be understandable if I became jaded, angry, resentful or bitter, but I didn't (for very long). I am a faithful person, but not one whose beliefs polarize, exclude or marginalize people, rather, I am one who believes that love, prayer, forgiveness and hope are the answers to every question, solutions to every problem and healing salve for every hurt.

Throughout this ordeal, I asked family, friends and others through social media, email and crowdfunding to pray for Joe. I knelt in prayer daily and asked God what His will was for me--what did He want me to do? How did He want me to handle this? What did He want me to say? I asked that He would be on my heart, in my eyes, in my words when I spoke, and when I wrote.

All the while, people from around the world were praying for Joe, and for me. People who didn't normally pray were praying. People who had given up praying and going to church were praying once again. Six of Joe's college football buddies and I held hands around Joe's bedside and recited the Lord's Prayer:

> "Our Father, who art in heaven, hallowed by thy name. Thy kingdom come, Thy will be done on earth, as it is in heaven. Give us this day our daily bread, and forgive us our trespasses as we forgive those who trespass against us, and deliver us from evil. Amen."

People on social media mentioned God and prayer and miracles. That in itself was a miracle to me--social media being used for prayer and the mention of God. I sought out prayer warriors, and they answered, in droves.

On the night Joe had cardiac arrest, I knelt in sorrowful prayer, pleading to God to tell me what to do, asking for strength to accept His will. I was overcome with calm. I felt the profound understanding of loss, and a portion of the agony that our heavenly Father must have felt as His innocent son Jesus was tortured and forced to die a criminal's death on a cross. I knew, without words, that God and His son Jesus understood my grief and pain, and I understood the true meaning of Christ's atonement.

The following day, I said goodbye to my beloved husband, whispering in his ear that it was okay to let go, that I didn't blame him for wanting to commune with angels. And I knew I would see him again. I began to prepare myself for his death, and was at peace.

Chapter 2

Island Hopping

February 5, 2012 Joe and I are standing on a jetty at Alehu Landing on Hapuna Bay just outside the airport on the east side of the Hawaiian island we called home, watching a mother and baby Humpback whale frolic in the ocean swells. We were photographing the anomaly and observing/documenting the whales' behavior. An escort appears, and joins the pair. We are in awe. We are wondering if mother and calf are demonstrating site fidelity – a regular return to the same site – similar to the whales of Stellwagen Bank off the coast of Massachusetts. Joe's cellphone rings. It is my son Patrick, telling us that his wife is in labor with our first grandson. We chat for a bit, exchange love and best wishes and then return to watching the whales. No more than a few hours later, mother whale, baby and escort line up and exit the bay, moving southward along the coast, past the airport, and remaining offshore in an area near the harbor.

Many stories and one month later, Joe and I are watching Alehu Landing and the island shrink and disappear out of the airplane window. Joe is sobbing like a sorrowful child, his huge shoulders heaving up and down.

Leaving is bittersweet for me; I'm sad, but thrilled to be returning to the east coast to meet baby and be with family again. We had moved to Hawai`i in 2008. Three years there, and one in the United Arab Emirates, was a long time to be gone. We missed many family events and celebrations living in exotic locations, places that many people can only dream of visiting. There is a price to pay to live in paradisiacal post cards and screensavers. We paid dearly.

The previous year (2011) we were in a car accident which left us both injured and our shiny new car a total loss. We weren't able to buy a new one, and refused to buy an "island car" as they had the reputation of being unreliable. Good friends Lidia, Big Ed, and Michaela loaned us their cars, tremendous blessings. But life in Hawai`i was never the same.

Fortunately, Joe was granted a transfer as an airport security agent back to New England. The only position available that was closest to family was an island thirty miles offshore of the mainland. He wanted to work at the airport closest to our home, but there were no openings at the time.

Island life was again sublime. We rented a few rooms in a house located one mile from the airport – within walking distance. Joe and I both worked there, and often enjoyed lunches together. Patrick, his wife and baby, and their friends visited us there, and our hearts leapt. Patrick's comment: "It's easier and quicker to get to the west coast than it is to come here." He was right. The island can only be accessed by ferry, boat or plane. Well worth the trouble and time.

If you have to leave Hawai`i, another island is a sweet place to end up. Once one of the wealthiest places in America, this island was built on the profits of the whale oil industry. Far from affluent or living in luxury, Joe and I would have been considered working class here, serving the public in the travel industry. The airport is the second busiest airport in the state. We worked long and hard through the summer of 2012, but we also enjoyed our time off, walking our Hawai`i-born kittens through the extensive rental house property, beaching, biking, swimming, photographing, touring the island and feeling that we had arrived home.

By June, I became ill. What first began as stiffness in my left hand pointer finger developed into a full-blown fever accompanied by sore throat, body aches, fatigue and violent, shaking chills. Thinking I might have the flu (working with the public at the busy airport?) I called out sick for the day, took some flu medication and tried to rest. Chills, sweats and fever worsened overnight. I nearly drenched the bed. Day two: Joe was preparing to go to work and I was sitting at the kitchen table, shaking and sweating with a terrible headache. I told him I needed to get to the hospital. I knew something wasn't right; I had never had this combination of symptoms before or with such severity.

At the tiny hospital, I was tested for Lyme disease, and found positive for *Erlichiosis*, a tick-borne bacterial infection originating from a bite by the Lone Star tick. I was prescribed a twenty-one day course of the antibiotic doxycycline and told to make a follow-up appointment with the island's renowned Lyme disease expert and doctor-of-all-trades. I took the pills, rested, and returned to work a few days later.

Island life resumed into normalcy through the autumn of 2012.

2012-2013

Joe persistently sought the transfer to our home airport, but there were no openings. Although life was pleasant, we wanted to move back to home to be nearer to our grandson, and to return to the original home which we had rented out during our years away. As luck would have it, in October, Joe's supervisor informed him of a need for a security officer at a mainland airport. The move would bring us closer to our goal of returning home, and seemed like the right opportunity at the right time. We vacated our rental, filling a passenger van with our boxes, bags and luggage. During the move-out frenzy, Max the male kitten bolted sometime while we were making trips up and down the stairs. We had to leave the island without him, returning the following day by plane – a perk of working for an airline – to retrieve him.

Joe moved in with my sister Therese, a nurse, who lived forty minutes from Joe's new airport, and I moved into our old home. Joe made the daily eighty mile commute to work four days a week and then drove home on his days off for nearly two years. The pace of life for Joe was taxing. Ten hour workdays, long drives to and from work and to home every week wore on him. He developed double bags and black circles under his eyes. Always trying to find humor, I teased him, telling him he was lucky he worked for the airport because he carried his own bags. The one hundred and seventy mile trip from work to home brought Joe across a heavily traveled turnpike. The area traffic is often congested and plagued by historically bad weather, and there is a ten mile stretch without exits, offering nowhere to go and nothing to do but endure the painfully slow ride and impatient drivers.

Joe would arrive home most Saturday nights about 11PM, crash into bed, awake early for church on Sunday, try to rest on Sunday afternoons, put on his best face for date night on Monday, and then pack up and head out early Tuesday to return to work. There was little time for us to do much of anything significant, and he was often so fatigued on Mondays that our lives fell into a beige, tired routine. Tuesday schedule: I'd help him carry his bags to the car, lean into the open window, kiss him goodbye, and tell him I loved him and remind him that this too shall pass, then watch him drive away, both of us waving.

He often cried before he left. I steeled myself. We had so many other worries. We were barely making ends meet financially, living paycheck to paycheck. Our church and my Dad helped us financially and spiritually. Joe sought out financial assistance from the town other charitable organizations. We were always astounded that a full time worker was living at poverty level. I had done some research and learned that in approximately twenty-four US states, a full-time job at minimum wage barely affords rent. So many of us living in financial slavery.

In Joe's absence, I had taken on all the responsibilities of home, including yard work: mowing the lawn in the summer, raking the leaves in the fall, snow shoveling in the winter, caring for the plants outdoors and then digging the tender ones up and bringing them in for the winter. Cat care, duck care. I sorted and paid the bills – a task at which I had historically failed. Living in exotic locations like Hawai`i and the Middle East had taken a huge financial toll on us. I tried to find the joy in small things. By necessity, I had grown a thick skin. True, I was closer to grandson and family, able to begin teaching again and living in our home, but I was alone. And lonely. Joe had the companionship of my sister, but they both worked similar hours and rarely saw each other. The winter of 2013 was brutal. Typical four-hour drives between the home and work grew into six hours or longer, in blinding snow and slick ice.

The commute from Therese's house to the airport was not a day at the beach either. In September, October and November, Joe started his 5:00 AM shift after riding in on his touring motorcycle through dark of night, fog, rain and cold. December was too cold and snowy to ride the bike safely, so Joe borrowed a friend's Explorer until he purchased a brand new Honda Fit in January, 2013. Joe worked on Super Bowl Sunday after switching days with another security officer so he could attend grandson's first birthday party the prior Saturday. Sadly, the party was canceled because of a fierce snowstorm throughout New England, so Joe had Saturday off, but had to work on Sunday. He opted to stay at Therese's that weekend instead of driving home.

Super Bowl Sunday brought more snow and freezing rain, so Joe set out at 2:30 AM, two hours earlier than usual. Security guards are held to strict attendance and punctuality standards, and Joe wanted to maintain his meticulous record. Driving was treacherous that morning. Traveling thirty miles per hour on the deserted route, he was making decent time and feeling confident that he would arrive in time for the 5 AM shift. At the top of a small sloping hill seven miles from the airport, Joe encountered a patch of snow-covered ice. The Fit started to slip. An experienced driver, he knew not to panic. The slip turned into a slide. He tried to steer out of it, but the car spun, eventually turning completely around once, flipping over and landing upside-down off the road in a ditch. There he was, on the side of the road, in darkness, in blowing snow, cold, hanging by his seatbelt, thanking God that he was unhurt. He reached into his jacket pocket, pulled out the cellphone and prayed for a signal. He dialed 911 and reached the police department. Meanwhile, the driver of a newspaper van passing by saw the car lights off the side of the road, stopped, got out of her van, approached Joe's car, and shouted.

"Are You Okay?"

"Yes, I'm fine, but I can't get out of the car."

"I'll call the police."

"I already did, they're on their way."

Joe was brought to the hospital by ambulance, miraculously sustained slight injuries and released. The Fit was declared a total loss. Another auto accident, another car totaled, another stressor on an already-stressed out, tired man.

Joe continued to fight to be transferred to our home airport, and after nearly two years, his request was approved. The official first day on the job was New Year's Day, January 1, 2014.

Chapter 3

Breath and Prayer

Part of every misery is, so to speak, the misery's shadow or reflection: the fact that you don't merely suffer but have to keep on thinking about the fact that you suffer. I not only live each endless day in grief, but live each day thinking about living each day in grief. ~ C. S. Lewis

Two weeks later, mid-January 2014, Joe developed a cough which started as an irritated tickle, transforming into a phlegmy hack accompanied by fatigue, body aches and intermittent low-grade fever. When he wasn't coughing while lying down, he wheezed and "crackled". He visited the walk-in clinic, was swabbed for flu (negative), diagnosed with bronchitis, and called out sick from work a few days.

Sometime during the span of the following two weeks, I caught whatever Joe had. We'd be awake, coughing into the wee hours, unable to lie flat in bed. Doing so would induce a coughing spell or wheezing to the point of breathlessness. My cough was dry and deep, unlike Joe's. But like Joe, I wheezed and crackled upon exhaling, and had severe body aches and fatigue. I also visited the walk-in clinic where I was swabbed for flu (Type A and B - negative), diagnosed with bilateral pneumonia and prescribed the standard drugs and course of treatment. We ate very little, had no appetite, forced fluids and took our $100 prescriptions as directed. One for cough medicine came in a teeny tiny bottle, with a tiny eyedropper. The recommended dose was one *milliliter* – a droplet. I thought for sure this was a mistake. Under protest, I took the precious nectar as prescribed anyway.

Neither of us improved.

I was amazed that Joe was able to return to work, as sick as he was. His co-workers didn't appreciate his return. I called out sick also and languished on the couch, upright, feverish, weak and disgusted at myself for not being diligent about disinfecting the air and surfaces of our home. I coughed incessantly.

At home, Joe and I would pass each other, or sit together on the couch, coughing and wheezing, looking at each other, horrified. *Are we going to die?* we'd each think, feeling poisoned by some invisible, undetectable contaminant.

On Friday night, January 24, instead of date night, Joe and I could stand the coughing and fevers no longer. More concerned about me than himself, he drove us to the hospital emergency room. I was taken to one of the treatment rooms where I was swabbed for flu for the second time; the results were again negative.

Joe sat beside me in the chair. He was pale and feverish, coughing. We joked with the good nurses attending to me that Joe really needed to be seen also. One nurse whispered, "I'm really not supposed to do this, but let me take your temperature." She did, and confirmed his fever. She agreed that Joe could go back to admitting so he could be treated also. We asked if we could be in the same room, and she told us she would see what she could do, joking "Hey now, it doesn't look good when my patients double!"

Joe returned to the emergency room admitting clerk, was given the hospital bracelet and walked back to my room.

We were both dehydrated and put on IV fluids. Joe was swabbed again for flu - negative. Our vitals were monitored. We were given medicine for our congestion, cough and fever. X-rays were taken of our chests. The radiologist didn't find pneumonia on mine, but the nurse disagreed. Joe was diagnosed with bronchitis. Hours passed. I took a selfie of us in our hospital gowns, with our masks and IVs. We tried to be cheerful, sharing this horrible illness together.

With drugs and intravenous fluids, our fevers subsided, and we improved slightly. Negative for the flu, we were discharged to home after midnight. We were famished, having been given only a few cups of water to take our pills. We couldn't remember when we had eaten last. We asked the hospital if there were any pizza places that delivered to the hospital. A nurse was nice enough to give us the phone number. We waited for the pizza, and devoured it on the drive home.

We took another $100 worth of prescriptions and tried to rest and heal through the weekend.

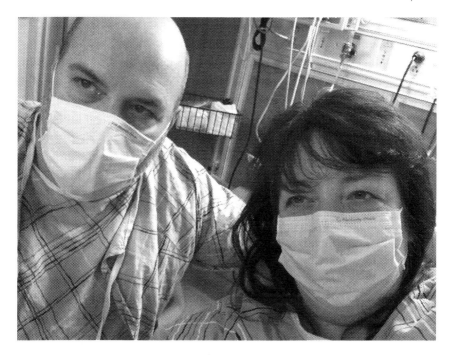

JANUARY 27 New symptoms

During the night of Sunday, January 26, 2014, sicker than I, sweet Joe sat on a stool beside me and rubbed my head and shoulders. Another day and night of misery for us, three weeks since Joe became sick, and two weeks for me. Nothing had changed despite numerous medications and the visit to the emergency room on Friday night.

Mid- morning, Monday, January 27: We were both still feverish, coughing our fool heads off, dehydrated again, frightened for, and worried about each other.

January 27

Social media post:

> Feeling poisoned. Pneumonia, bronchitis, high fever for over a week. Going back to the emergency room. Now new symptom: vomiting.

I had forced myself to eat a tangerine for breakfast, became nauseous, ran to the bathroom and vomited. I returned to the couch, propped myself up with pillows and wrapped the blanket around me up to my neck. Joe wandered like a zombie past me to the kitchen where he stood rubbing his belly just below the navel. His face was bright red.

"What's wrong with you honey?"

"Aggggh, I have this pain, right here," he said as he rubbed his lower abdomen.

"Oh NO Joe. Don't even say that. Does it feel like diverticulitis?" (He was hospitalized for diverticulitis ten years prior).

"I don't know, but it really hurts. How are you?"

"Same, except I just threw up."

"What? How is that possible? You haven't eaten anything."

"I know, right? I ate a tangerine and threw it up a few minutes ago. Maybe it's all these stupid useless meds. Are you nauseous?"

"Kind of, but mostly it's this pain in my belly. And I have watery diarrhea."

"Oh no, Joe. This is not good."

We stared at each other. I knew that something was horribly wrong.

"We need to go back to the hospital. You don't look good at all. Get dressed. I'll drive."

"Are you sure you can drive?"

"Yep. Let's go. Right now. We're getting worse. There must be something else wrong. You probably have diverticulitis. I don't want to die here in this house. Get dressed. Right now! Let's go! Hurry up! Do you need help getting dressed?"

"Nah. I'll be out in a minute."

Joe waddled back toward the bedroom.

Driving to the hospital, I took the wrong exit; at the end of the exit ramp is a stoplight where one must take a right or a left. I had driven these roads hundreds of times and knew them well. We had just driven this route on Friday night when we went to the emergency room.

I sat there, idling at the end of the ramp, dazed.

"Woops. I don't even know what to do right now. I have no idea how to get us back to the highway. Sorry, honey. Hang on. I'll get us there."

Joe said nothing. He was hunched over in the seat, red-faced and whimpering lightly. I turned right, then left, then left, eventually finding my way back to an on-ramp to the highway.

When we arrived at the emergency room, I parallel parked downhill from the entrance. By the time I unbuckled, grabbed my purse and locked the car, Joe was already semi-sprinting up the hill. Conversely, every one of my steps seemed to take forever. I'd take a step, stop, and breathe slow, shallow breaths. *Why can't I walk?* I thought to myself. Step. Stop. Breathe. Step. Stop. Breathe. I was only three steps away from the car. I thought I might not make it to the entrance. The air was frigid. I must have looked like death in a woolen coat, staggering up that hill. By the time I made it to the entrance, Joe was checked in. I took the seat next to him. I gave my information to the admitting clerk.

"What brings you here?"

"My husband and I were both just here on Friday night. We've been sick for weeks and taking medication, but this morning I threw up. I'm having a hard time breathing. And I have a fever. And I was diagnosed with bilateral pneumonia two weeks ago."

We waited to be called. Joe sat with his head between his knees, rocking gently. His face was beet red and he was still whimpering. I placed two chairs on both sides of an end table, and laid myself across them.

Joe's name was called. He needed a wheelchair. I took his coat and his phone, told him I loved him and reclined again.

Someone in white came to me shortly thereafter. I had no recollection of time. It could have been ten minutes and it could have been thirty.

"Are you Joe's wife?"

"Yes."

"He is going in to surgery. Something burst inside his abdomen. We don't know what's wrong with him, but we have to operate."

"When?"

"Right now." The man in white let out a little snicker. "I just wanted to update you on his status. Can you sign this form?"

"Sure. Can I see him?"

"No. He's being prepped for surgery."

"Can I call him?"

"Yes, does he have a phone?"

"No, I have it. Can you bring it to him?"

"Okay, give me a minute."

The man in white took Joe's phone from me and vanished. I fumbled in the great abyss called my purse for my phone, waited a moment and called Joe's number.

"Hello?"

"Hi honey, it's me. What is going on? You're going to surgery? How bad is your pain?"

"It's bad, Ave. They gave me morphine, but it isn't even touching it."

He was barely whispering.

"You're going to be fine, honey. I love you. I love you. You'll be okay. I'll see you in a little while."

I heard him breathing, but saying nothing.

That conversation would be our last until the end of February, our lives forever changed.

I had been sick with respiratory illnesses before, and hospitalized with pneumonia as a child. Still, I had never been this sick. Not when I endured sixteen and a half hours of hard labor beginning with pains five minutes apart, not when I was sedated with a spinal, labor stimulated by Pitocin but not progressing past two centimeters, not after I was rushed to emergency Cesarean section still overwhelmed by labor pains when my son began to experience fetal distress, not even then had I felt so near death.

Before Joe and I were admitted to the hospital, I envied angels, thinking they had the better deal. I can't honestly say that I had any volition to live; I had been drifting in and out of a medicated stupor, during which

I visualized myself floating around in the heavens, at peace, comfortable, light and airy and free to fly, free from the sickly skin suit encumbrance anchoring me to earth. I told Joe I dreamt that I was an angel and that I wasn't sick anymore.

My memory of the admission to my room in isolation on the "flu floor" was foggy at best. I don't remember much until I saw two men sitting at the foot of my bed. Doctors St and R, replete with gowns, masks, and gloves: "Your husband is out of surgery. He survived, but he is a very sick man." I remember thanking them and asking them when I could see him. They reminded me I was very sick, and told me I needed to ask my doctor.

Breath is underappreciated. The first few days I was hospitalized, with every breath, I felt close to death, as if all I had to do was choose not to inhale, and I would just slip away. I understood how captive dolphins who allegedly choose not to breathe simply sink to the bottom of their enclosure, and die.

On the second day, I was heavily medicated, with low oxygen leading to total exhaustion, struggling for every single painful breath, and still coughing up bloody sputum. My desire to see Joe was so compelling, I pulled myself up out of bed, dressed in the clothes I was wearing when I was admitted.

A nurse entered my room and found me sitting up in bed, contemplating how I was going to get to the third floor.

"Ms. Murphy, what are you doing?"

She, like so many, couldn't pronounce my name.

"Ave-yin. My name is Ave-yin. I'm going to see my husband."

"You get right back into bed. You're not going anywhere! You have the flu, and you really can't leave this room."

Was my desire to see my beloved the reason I continued to fight to breathe?

January 29 social media post

> Update about our situation: Joe and I are both in the hospital since Monday. I have bilateral pneumonia, type A flu H1N1. Joe has pneumonia, type A flu H1N1, sepsis following diverticulitis and an emergency colonoscopy, and now has acute respiratory distress syndrome (ARDS). He is in the intensive care unit breathing with a ventilator, and now has a feeding tube because he will need nutrition. They have him sedated and he has not been allowed to wake up since Monday. Thank you for your prayers and all your help.

From Therese:

> Aoibhyann, Prayers are being said for you and Joe. Please rest, also have you told the MD about coughing up blood, please do so and maybe they need to do a portable chest X-ray to see how the lungs look, and if you have effusions, you may ask about a chest tube. Love you, talk to you tomorrow. Xxxooo

My reply:

> Thank u sis... I feel prayers. Yes they have taken sputum samples daily. I ate today, had a bm and actually had the blinds open and lights on. I was awake more than I slept... and took a look in the mirror. Oh how I need a headband!! Xoxoxoxoxo thank you for everything.

January 30

> For those of you who know someone with the #H1N1 flu, please don't blame them for not getting the (hashtag) flu shot. Joe and I both swabbed negative for flu twice, but our bodies were wrecked by pneumonia and bronchitis before we caught it. The nurse said the whole floor is filled with pneumonia patients who got the (hashtag) flu. Many had flu shots! If you are flu-free, count your blessings, bite your tongue and put

on a mask. This (hashtag) flu is random and merciless. Let's love one another, shall we?

Early in the morning, peering through the blinds of my hospital room, in isolation, on the "Flu Floor":

> Good morning happy, warm sun! 40 - something days till spring...

From daughter-in-law:

> Hi Omi, I know I can't come visit you, but I just wanted to let you know we are all thinking of you and Poppie Joe and hope you both get better soon. This is me enjoying some oatmeal at the table you guys got me for Christmas. I miss you and please let my Mommy or Daddy know if you need anything. Xoxo

My confusion about whether or not to get a flu shot, or the efficacy of doing so was searing. I was terrorized by our illnesses and knew very little about the flu other than regular people were catching it and dying as a result. I knew Joe and I were very, very sick. I defaulted to relying on the strength of my faith, and hope that we were going to live.

> Update: I am warmed by everyone's compassion and concern. I must say that even though all the odds are stacked against Joe right now and he is in critical condition, I do believe in the power and healing that comes from prayer. An army of angels is coming to his side today. I know God's loving arms are around him. Thank you everyone keep praying!

> Yes, get a flu shot. No, don't think you're safe even if you do. Wash your hands as much as possible and wear a mask in public. I am not kidding. This will kill you.

While in bed, I read about a young north Texas woman being among the latest deaths in the 2014 H1N1 Flu epidemic.[i]

The news reported that the prior week the flu season reached "epidemic" status, with 7.5 percent of all U.S. deaths in the second week of January due to flu and pneumonia illnesses, surpassing the CDC's epidemic threshold.

Thursday night update: So many of you have offered prayers and comfort and asked if there is anything that you can do for us. I am overwhelmed and unable to answer everyone privately so here is my public request: please get a flu shot type A H1N1; Spread the word about H1N1; Wash your hands as often as possible; wear a mask and don't worry about looking silly; keep praying; and if you are currently displaying any symptoms of the flu, get checked right away. H1N1 kills in as few as four days. Don't fool yourself into thinking because you are healthy, eat right and take care of yourself, you are immune. This is what matters to me right now: stay healthy and prevent yourself and your loved ones from catching this. Love to all.

Last update Thursday night: Liza, Joe's nurse came down to speak w me...he had a very rough night last night but this evening his fever is down to 101, and she was able to reposition him without spiking his BP. He is still septic and his pneumonia is a little worse, everything else is the same... This is good news everyone. Keep those prayers coming! Thank you.

Took an ER selfie last Friday during visit #2 when we both swabbed negative for H1N1. Happier times! Wanted you all to have a pic of Joe so you can focus on his sweet face when you pray. In a weird kind of way, I'm thinking his perforated bowel may well have saved our lives because if he didn't have that pain we would have stayed home like good patients. But when we came back on Monday, we both were positive for bilateral pneumonia and the nightmare that is #H1N1. Scarier still is that so many people think they have a cold, take something to bring down the fever and are dead within 4 days.

January 31

Joe's doctors came to see me just now, he is still septic caused by the poisons from his perforated bowel which settled in his lungs already weakened by flu and pneumonia --all his systems are holding for now but their concern is the kidneys which do not tolerate these chemicals very well. Sometimes there are abscesses following the perforated bowel. His lungs deteriorated this morning a bit, so they had to address that. 7 to 14 days of this is not unusual, if the other systems hold, they said. They are going to allow me to see him sometime today. Keep praying! Now more than ever, he needs prayers.

Update Friday. I spent time with my honey just now! And will get to see him again this afternoon before I am discharged later today. Must bring oxygen home but at least I'll be home. I don't want to leave here without Joe, but he is in excellent care. PRAYERS ARE WORKING...KEEP THEM COMING, DOUBLE, TRIPLE TIME SHARE SHARE SHARE.

I am struggling to breathe, on oxygen, pale as death and worried about Joe. My doctor tells me that since I have been fever-free for twenty-four hours, I am going to be discharged. The hospital is full of germs and I am vulnerable, he tells me. Home is the best place for me, he assures me.

I had no idea what I was facing, but I remember being concerned for our pets, and wanting to be able to sleep uninterrupted. A hospital is not conducive to rest with staff poking and prodding and checking vitals and taking blood at regular intervals even into the wee hours, with the noises in the hall, announcements over the intercom, phones, intravenous alarms, etc. I call friend Rita and ask if she can pick me up when I'm discharged. She agrees to bring her husband Mike with her, drive me home in my car (left in the ER parking lot after I drove us in on Monday) and then return to her home with hubby in their car. I phone friend and retired nurse Skylor to update her, and she is shocked. She comes immediately to spend time with me and assess the situation. Rita arrives. They ask me repeatedly if I am sure I want to go home. I affirm my need to be home with the pets, in my own home so I can get some rest. They aren't convinced, and look horrified. Quietly, I wonder if they are right.

The nurse shows up to remove my IV, and Rita and Skylor confront her: "How can she go home? *Look at her*! She's not ready! She can barely breathe or stand up!" The nurse asks if they would like her to call the doctor. They approve. I repeat that I really need to go home; the temperature outside has been in the single digits, and even though Rox and Rita have been caring for the ducks, I'm worried. Rox, an independent, sturdy 80-year old vegetarian, lives only a few miles from our home, and has cared for our ducks before, though not like this time in the dead of a brutally frigid, snowy winter and not trudging through waist-high snow over solidly packed ice path to the shed. Rita, our original pet-sitter, is hearty, capable and willing to share duck sitting with Rox, but ironically she lives a block away from the hospital, a twenty minute drive from our home. It has snowed nearly every day. The roads are packed with ice due to the freezing temperatures, and driving in these conditions has been hazardous.

Ducks (and cats) are creatures of habit; they have certain expectations. Ours don't like strangers, they don't eat when they're upset, and they are not fond of the cold. Worrying about them was silly because ducks are equipped to survive quite nicely in sub-zero temperatures. Think: down - the perfect insulator. But the helplessness I felt in the hospital, the combination of inability to help Joe, to care for cats and ducks and home, to care for myself or breathe without assistance was stunning. I'm not an anal, control-freak, but I needed to regain some semblance of purpose and independence.

Skylor and Rita hemmed and hawed, lovingly concerned.

When the doctor arrived, he spoke to me gently and firmly, providing instructions for follow-up care. I didn't hear much, but I remember Skylor and Rita asking him if he really thought I was ready to go home, alone, to a cold house. He insisted that I was, reminding us that a hospital is full of sick people, no place for me.

February 1 social media post:

Home last night. Will call ICU in the AM

I was hospitalized for five days and unable to visit Joe. When I was discharged, I was still sick and unable to drive or see him regularly. My poor husband lie there in the ICU, a lump of flesh, bones, tubes and machines, with few visitors.

Once I was home, I called the ICU several times a day for updates, and gave family and friends his location so they could visit. I was feeling powerless and frustrated, but trying to be optimistic.

Bright lights in my life: family, and the necessity for humor.

Stepmom Pearl offered to bring me to the hospital on Sunday, if I was feeling up for it. Barely able to care for myself, stand or walk, I mustered the energy, bagged up my portable oxygen and slid into the passenger seat of her car. We planned to stay only an hour or so, enough time for the thirty minute drive each way before my oxygen ran out.

Pearl dropped me off at the main entrance, parked the car, walked back through the icy parking lot, met me and walked beside me as I drove the motorized wheelchair to the ICU. We dressed in the gown, gloves and masks, (me awkwardly adding my mask over oxygen tubes), and entered Joe's room. The nurse looked on through the glass wall.

Unsteady by his bedside, overwhelmed by the sight of the tubes, the gauges, the wall full of machinery, his swollen, pale face, arms, hands, his closed eyes and motionless body, I began to feel queasy. I leaned in and spoke to him, told him Pearl and I were there, told him he was very sick but was doing great, that he had to fight, that I couldn't stay long but promised I'd be back. I told him I loved him and missed him, apologized for not visiting sooner, explaining that I was sick, and lied, assuring him I was healthy now.

"Remember when we drove to the emergency room last week?"

I spoke to him with a certainty that he could hear me, and that he was taking mental notes, summoning the wisdom and courage I gained from watching my comatose mother suffer:

"You became very ill and you needed surgery, but you haven't woken up yet. I was admitted also, on the second floor, just below you. We both had the flu," I explained. "That's why we were so sick. You're in the ICU. You've been asleep for a week."

I rolled myself to the edge of the bed where I lowered my head, wanting so much to be near him. I rubbed his feet and massaged his calves and thighs, being careful not to move the catheter tubing. I told him he was in good care, that heavenly Father was with him, that He held him in the palm of His hand. I reminded him that he survived the surgery and needed to rest and heal. Pearl told him she loved him, and that she'd see him soon.

We peeled off our protective gear and placed the pallid blue bundle in the trash.

The nurse spoke to us about Joe's condition and vitals, then Pearl and I rode the elevator down to the main entrance lobby, where Pearl left me so she could retrieve the car. Lightheaded and queasier now, I plugged in the wheelchair to recharge, and shuffled toward the chair near the main entrance revolving door. I was unaware that my oxygen tank was empty.

Thinking I was weak and weary from just visiting Joe, I tried to breathe through the nausea. Inhale slowly to the count of eight, exhale to the count of eight, I calmed myself, all the while searching for someone to help me in case I keeled over. Breathing in, breathing out, walking at a snail's pace, my nausea increased tenfold. I froze in the middle of the lobby, looked toward the two volunteers manning the admission desk and let out a feeble "Help me, I think I'm going to be sick."

They didn't hear me. Louder and more desperately, I warned "I'm going to be sick!" One of the women at the desk gestured toward the wastebasket at the coffee station. "Over there, over there!" she urged, waving me away.

Too late. I gagged and heaved, leaving an acrid puddle right there on the lobby floor. When I caught my breath, I staggered toward the wastebasket at the coffee station, plunked down on a chair, dropped my head between my knees, and puked again.

Meanwhile, Pearl had been waiting for me in the car at the valet entrance on the other side of the revolving door. Concerned for me, she came in to find me slumped over in the chair, a yellow Wet Floor sign in the middle of the lobby, and a puddle of puke between my feet. I hadn't eaten much since my discharge two days ago, but was vomiting a good amount of clear liquid. I didn't think there was anything left in me.

"Oh my God, Aoibhyann, what happened?"

"I don't know, Pearl, I'm so sick. I threw up. Twice. I couldn't make it to the door."

"Let's get you home."

Pearl (a vibrant septuagenarian, if you please) escorted me and my bags to the car. The heated seat was warm, cozy and luxurious, and I relaxed in the moment, feeling somewhat relieved that the episode was behind me. We talked about what happened in the lobby, and shared our thoughts about how Joe appeared. We agreed that seeing Joe in that condition was difficult; I could tell Pearl was upset, too, but she concealed it with her typical calm and pleasant demeanor.

Halfway home, the nausea returned with a vengeance. Stifling the urge, I asked Pearl if she had a bag.

"I don't know. Why? What's the matter?"

"I think I'm going to be sick again."

All I could picture was vomit all over the interior of her pristine car. "This cannot be happening again," I thought. I didn't think I had anything left in my stomach. I never thought to roll down the window. Pearl handed me an empty cup, and a moment later, I leaned forward, heaved and retched, and filled the cup.

"Oh Aoibhyann you poor thing!"

I don't know how she wasn't sick herself, hearing me heave, sharing the same heated air, the images of Joe still lingering.

We were quiet for the rest of the trip; fifteen minutes felt like an hour. I was woozy, nauseous, embarrassed, holding my cup o' vomit, pressing my head on the cold window.

When we reached the driveway, I burst from the car, down the sidewalk, up the two steps, through the front door, and headed like a junkie toward the main oxygen tank. I pulled the portable tank tubes off my mask, plugged in the home tubes, sat, and waited to regain breath and life.

Minutes passed. Pearl asked if I was better and if I felt comfortable about her leaving.

"I'll be okay now, Pearl. Honestly, you can go. You've done enough. I don't know how to thank you. I'm so sorry I was sick in your car. It's late. We had a long afternoon. You can go. Please drive safely and give my love to Dad."

Convinced, she hugged me, asked me if I was sure I didn't need anything, said goodbye and left.

More time passed. I wasn't feeling the burn of the raw oxygen flowing through plastic into my nostrils, so I checked the machine to see if it was turned on. It was. I followed the snake of tubing from my cannula back to a coil on the floor. It was unplugged from the machine. In my haste for breath, I had plugged in the wrong tubing.

Oxygen is underrated.

More trials ahead for Joe and me, with Pearl and others sustaining and supporting us.

February 2

> What a spectacular day it is today! Update about Joe: he had a bad night last night, having some respiratory issues and not tolerating being moved. He has a new fancy-schmancy air bed that that looks like a spaceship! They are trying to wean him a tiny bit from the "cocktail" (Propofol) that is keeping him in a coma. And they have given him a little nutrition through his central line which he seems to be tolerating. His oxygen levels are low so they're going to work on that today. I noticed yesterday when I was with him that when I touched his knee he seemed to wince. Even on his best days, his shoulders and knees are shot from football, so I told the doctors that he could be uncomfortable because of the way that he's lying, and the way his legs are stretched. They are going to work on giving him more morphine as they decrease the cocktail. No one will say, but I believe he is starting to turn the corner. Please understand Joe is in a medically-induced coma and he is unable to talk to anyone, unresponsive, sleeping. I am home on oxygen and talking is a challenge for me so forgive me if I don't answer the phone or talk for too long if I do. Love and prayers and thanks, Aoibhyanne

Wishful thinking. Doctors continued to tell me Joe *wasn't* "turning the corner".

Therese calls to tell me that she's coming to stay with me. She's worried about me being home alone, sick, unable to care for myself and worried about Joe. I don't refuse her. It's a three hour drive from her home, the same trip Joe took weekly on his days off. When she does arrive, I finally feel the comfort and solace of my sister's love, care and expertise as a nurse. She firmly asks questions and observes my condition. I've been on the couch, unwilling to sleep in our empty bed. Sleep is difficult, and napping doesn't happen, even though I'm beyond exhaustion. The house is in shambles. I've had the ducks indoors, crated or in the bathtub at night; feathers and seeds and dust in every nook and cranny. Dirty dishes in the sink, clutter everywhere. Therese starts to scurry, scrubbing and cleaning in silence. I protest; she tells me to rest. She is wearing sterile gloves and wiping all surfaces with disinfectant. Her presence is tranquilizing. I drift off to sleep on the couch for the first time in several days.

Later, Therese and I visit Joe. She's stunned and admits she can't handle seeing her brother-in-law in this condition. Even though she's a nurse and deals with sick patients every day, they are awake and expressive. Joe is neither.

It's wonderful to have my sister with me; I swear I'm feeling better because of her.

Therese would return to home and work; ironically she was assigned to cover in the ICU. She reacted terribly, breaking down in tears, reminded of Joe. By lunchtime the first day, she asked her supervisor to be returned to her floor.

Social media post:

> Just saw Joe. I think he would want me to share this. Asking a favor: if you know of someone who is alone, sad, sick or suffering, call them. A few words...a kind gesture...do it for them, do it for yourself. No one should be alone. Say the words you need to say. Heal your wounds. Forgive yourself. Forgive somebody else. We are all flawed, but nothing is beyond the heart of our Savior. Love knows no limits! All is forgiven. Don't hesitate, not even a minute. There are no guarantees for tomorrow. We only have this moment. Open

your heart. There is joy in this life. Your job is to find it and share it. Do it now. Do it today. You'll be amazed at the burden love lifts. Thank you. Love you! PRAY.

Later that night:

Update Sunday evening. Joe is worse. His fever is up, he is not tolerating the ventilator so they had to paralyze him so that the machine breathes for him, and he is not tolerating food though his tube. Kidneys are failing. If you want to visit him, now would be the time. He needs to hear you.

Posted happy pictures of us, in happier times. Angels watch over my hubby...heaven will have to wait. Expecting miracles.

Monday February 3

When Joe first arrived in the ICU, church friend and CNA "C" (who happened to work there) recognized Joe by name only. She couldn't step into his room, having a difficult time coming to terms with his status. She was eventually able to perform her CNA duties, but was more comfortable when I was there.

Update Monday: Just got off the phone with Joe's nurse, his fever is down to 100.4. It was 103 yesterday. They did not talk about dialysis. He is putting out 750 Ml per hour, that's good. They changed the settings on his ventilator today and he is holding at 92. Surgeon is ordering a CT scan of his belly to make sure there are no abscesses. They had him off food yesterday and last night, but after his CT scan if all looks good they're going to try food again.

They want to wean him off the vent. It is a slow and delicate process. He is off the blood pressure medication as of this morning. It sounds okay today...keep praying. Thank you! Miracles on the way.

Monday February 3 evening

> Update: Joe is still hanging on. Keep praying! Thank you for
> your love, comfort and support. Joe's children: please go visit
> your Dad while he is still with us. He loves you and needs to
> hear you. It is difficult but you can get through it.

I was feeling supported by friends, family, church family, social media
family and yet abandoned by Joe's adult children. Fearing Joe's death, and
the possible regret that would follow if they didn't visit him, I first called
Joe's childhood friend, Big Cosmo, to update him and ask him if he would
contact Joe's three adult children. He did. Knowing that, I expected to see
them in the ICU. They never showed.

February 4

> Update Tuesday; Joe is holding...no change...still positive
> for H1N1. Sons and daughter: your father is critically ill. It's
> hour by hour. WHERE ARE YOU?

Some of Joe's family eventually did come to visit him. Some relationships
were mended. Some would require more stitching.

Church friend D B asked," What can I do? My response would be repeated
throughout the month, encouraging any and all who wanted to see Joe
while he was still alive:

> "I wish I knew. It might make you feel better to visit him,
> talk to him; some say it is very hard to see him this way, but
> worth it. I think it's more a matter of letting him know he
> is loved, talking to him, supporting him, saying what you
> need to say to him, reading Scriptures to him, playing music,
> keeping him here with us. My fear now is that he's had a
> glimpse of heaven."

I meant it when I wrote that I feared he's had a glimpse of heaven, for
sure. I fought back, massaging him and performing Reiki on him daily,

whispering in his ear that he was in control of his body. I repeatedly told him to send health and healing to every cell, every fiber and tissue, every muscle, bone, joint.

"Health and healing, God's love and light and strength," I'd whisper. "Every cell. You can heal yourself."

I resurrected more photos from happier times to post on social media.

Wednesday February 5

> Mexico 2004...one our favorite places on earth. Look at his smile! He had just touched a baby gray whale in Magdalena Bay.

Started a crowdfunding campaign. The first social media post about it:

> So many people have asked how they can help us. Thank you for even the tiniest donation. The last thing Joe needs to worry about is how we are going to pay our bills when his sick time runs out. Bless you!

> Update: Temperature is up, but his kidneys are working, and his oxygen levels are rebounding more quickly than yesterday. CT scan to check for abscesses may be soon, but the surgery site is healing well. Flu meds are done. One day at a time. Prayers for his caregivers are welcome.

Thursday February 6

I posted a picture of Joe and me on Maui. The caption:

> Joe and I volunteered hundreds of hours on Hawaiian islands babysitting for precious Hawaiian Monk seals. They are critically endangered, so it was an honor to be in their home, educating the public and protecting them from harassment and harm. How blessed we have been.

This morning, Therese and I were sorting out medical forms, bills and mail that I had been unable to handle on my own. The phone rang.

"Ave, this is Dr. Eb. We called a Code Blue on your husband. You need to come to the ICU right now."

I repeat to my sister, "Therese, the doctor said Joe coded. What does that mean?"

"Oh my God, Aoibhyann, hang up. Let's go. *Oh my God, oh my God, oh my God.*"

"Okay, doctor, we'll be there in thirty minutes."

Standing at Joe's bedside, I could see colors of near-death trauma; his lips were swollen and blue, his face ashen gray. He looked more dead than alive, without the benefit of undertaker's artful disguise. Doctors beckoned me (and Therese) into the conference room to deliver the message no spouse can bear to hear.

"Aoibhyann, your husband's heart has been running a marathon for two and a half weeks now. All of his other organs have failed. There is no sense resuscitating him. If this were my family member, I would make him a Do Not Resuscitate and let him go."

Therese is sitting to my left, sobbing. I can see her in my periphery, and I hear her, but I don't understand what is happening - or why she's crying.

Still sick, on oxygen and medication, I stared blankly, thought and replied, "I don't know how you can ask me to do that. I *can't* do that. I believe we have a merciful heavenly Father who will either take Joe, or bring him back, but I will not make that decision."

Doctor told me he respected my wishes and assured me they'd continue to do all they could to keep Joe comfortable.

I contacted Joe's friends from Hampshire Christian College to inform them of his decline. Six huge, grown men, former college football players rushed to be by his side. We encircled Joe's bed and recited the Lord's Prayer. Two had to leave the room, in tears.

Joe is so loved. What an incredible, sweet, powerful moment: six strong men of faith reciting the Lord's Prayer today at his bedside. Thank you guys for coming to be with your Hampshire Christian teammate - the Warrior! We love you! So thankful to you.

Saturday February 7

To (Therese's friend) asking how Joe was: Not better, not worse. Nothing to report, just another day inside this tornado that will not end. Doctor told me to start thinking about what to do if his heart fails again. How does one possibly make that call? My heart may fail me too. I don't know how to navigate through this.

Texts from friends KTrain and CB arrived daily. Joe's situation seemed to stir many to action. Train mentioned his very good friend, a Benedictine monk, was going to meet him at the hospital at 10:30 the next day. He offered to anoint Joe, bless him, etc. and asked me if I wanted him to give Joe last rites, too. He told me Father and his fellow monks had been praying for Joe since hearing about his illness. He mentioned that he had spoken to their friend Gonzo, studying to be a Reverend in the Catholic church, about the strength of Joe's faith, even though Joe was no longer a Catholic.

Last Rites are administered by a member of the clergy prior to bodily death. In Joe's case, they were unnecessary because there were no such traditions in our church, but the expressions of love and concern were tender, and moved me to gratitude and humility. Father came anyway, and spent hours with Joe.

February 8

Former missionary Charles posts a copy of a story told in the voice of a currant bush who laments that s/he has been cut down, eventually growing into a healthy and strong bush.

February 9

Note to Dane's wife after she asked how I was. I had begun to practice a standard deflection when asked how I was feeling:

> So, how about them Red Sox? wink I am trying not to think about the gravity of the situation. Nights are hardest for me, so I decided to sift through my 16,000 digital photos and extract all of those with Joe. It helps to lift my spirits to relive happy memories.

People told me to hope and pray for a miracle, and for a while, I did. Now, I wanted to tell them to shut up. They are not standing over Joe's body, or hearing doctors tell me all his organs have failed. They are not the ones who, so desperate for a sign of life, lifted Joe's eyelid and saw flat, dry, yellow death.

Inspiration was welcomed and appreciated, but anemic. I was in despair, losing hope. Needing more, I asked and received.

> Request: So that we can uplift one another, post your favorite inspirational verse on my social media page. Here's mine, for you: "A new commandment I give unto you: that ye love one another; as I have loved you..." John 13:34.

> "For God so loved the world that he gave his only begotten Son, that whosoever believes in Him should not perish, but have everlasting life." John 3:16.

> "Fear not, for I am with you; be not dismayed, for I am your God; I will strengthen you, I will help you, I will uphold you with my righteous right hand." Isaiah 41:10

> "One thing I ask of The LORD, this is what I seek: that I may dwell in the house if the LORD all the days of my life, to gaze upon the beauty of the LORD and to seek him in his temple." Psalm 27:4

> "Neither height nor depth, nor anything else in all creation, will be able to separate us from the love of God that is in Christ Jesus our Lord." -Romans 8:39

> "...faith, hope, and love....The greatest of these is love."

> D&C 78: 17 Verily, verily, I say unto you, ye are little children, and ye have not as yet understood how great blessings the Father hath in his own hands and prepared for you; 18 And ye cannot bear all things now; nevertheless, be of good cheer, for I will lead you along. The kingdom is yours and the blessings thereof are yours, and the riches of eternity are yours.

Philippians 4:13 "...I can do all things through Christ who gives me strength"

1 John 3:16-18 "This is how we know what love is: Jesus Christ laid down his life for us. And we ought to lay down our lives for our brothers. If anyone has material possessions and sees his brother in need but has no pity on him, how can the love of God be in him? Dear children, let us not love with words or tongue but with actions and in truth."

"Trust in the LORD with all thine heart; and lean not unto thine own understanding. In all thy ways acknowledge him, and he shall direct thy paths." Proverbs 3:5-6

"Abide in Me, and I in you. As the branch cannot bear fruit of itself unless it abides in the vine, so neither can you unless you abide in Me." John 15: 4

"Come unto me, all ye that labour and are heavy laden, and I will give you rest. Take my yoke upon you, and learn of me; for I am meek and lowly in heart: and ye shall find rest unto your souls." Matthew 11:28-29

Sunday February 9

Tomorrow Monday the doctors will perform a tracheotomy so the ventilator tube can be removed. Joe will suffer more insult to his already-weakened body. It will be two weeks tomorrow since this all began. I thank you for your continued prayers and ask that you enjoy the photo album I shared so that you can keep the images of a healthy, happy Joe on your heart and in your prayers. Love to you all and thanks, Aoibhyann

Our first moments with grandson, one month old. We had just returned from Hawai`i.

Our team had just successfully rehabbed and released a hooked Hawaiian Monk seal

First week on the job. Joe created the floral arrangement in the background. Bird of Paradise grew wild in our yard.

My guys... Ireland

Whales could be seen right off shore, Hawai`i

Joe was amazed that there were palm trees in Ireland

Dubai 2010. How blessed we have been

The world's most expensive Christmas tree Abu Dhabi, UAE

Forestville Quebec, our first Blue whale!

The seal is molting, and the only reason we were that close is because we were authorized to take photos, Hawai`i. It was the volunteer uniform but yes we probably would have dressed the same anyway...we were "that" couple

Joe's birthday- we snorkeled with manta rays! Hawai`i.

Joe was such a tremendous Cub Scout leader--sweet kiddos.

Green sea turtle #788 had to be lifted on to a truck, flown to Oahu. She died the next day.

Yes, proof he kissed the Blarney Stone!

Joe braved the waves, no matter what. He's a beach boy. We were at Polihale ("Happy place") on the island's west side, fierce winter surf.

Poppi Joe so in love with grandson.

We made it from the UAE to the Philippines!

Joe would not look good with a toupee. Hawai`i. Half of a coconut husk on his head.

Waimea Canyon, the "Grand Canyon of the Pacific", Kauai, Hawai'i.

Mauna Kea, 9000 feet elevation, Big Island, Hawai'i

Aloha. We were delighted to have son Patrick with us. South side, Black Sand Beach, Hawai'i.

February 10

"Health and healing to every cell, Joe", I continued to repeat. My social media update:

> Many of you have been so sweet to ask how I have been. Thank you for your concern and prayers. It is so difficult to handle this, I know. But for me to live in a state of yearning and prayer is agonizing. I've come to surrender. I must take care of myself, still on oxygen. Pneumonia is still present. Going to my follow up with my doc today..first time driving. I've been physically weak, sick and overwhelmed. Joe has probably been communing with angels and you know what they say about seeing heaven and being with God: people beg to stay! His will be done.

> Update: 1:40 PM the team just took him down to surgery. Three anesthesiologists at his side. He tolerated being taken off the ventilator and is getting oxygen manually. Before he left, we prayed and listened to his favorite songs and all his numbers were stable. One hour or so and I'll update you as soon as he is back. Thank you for constant prayers.

> This is Joe's room while he is in the operating room...keep those prayers coming...

> Surgery done...all went well. Thank you Lord.

We can see Joe's sweet face again instead of that alien tubing coming out of his mouth! His numbers are "holding" and he is being weaned off the paralytic so tomorrow they may try to feed him nutrition through his tube to get his bowels moving. Pray, pray, pray..keep the healthy loving thoughts coming. It's working.

Okay everyone I learned today that evidently everyone at the hospital knows of the bizarre-o case of Aoibhyann and Joe surviving pneumonia and H1N1 and the disaster that followed for Joe. And we have been dubbed the "Poster Children for Flu Shots". So noted. Now GO GET YOUR FLU SHOT!! H1N1 reached epidemic levels the second week of January. Love y'all. YOU DO NOT WANT TO GET THIS. #H1N1 is a merciless killer, taking lives in as little as four days. It's a major miracle we are both still alive. I am not kidding.

Crowdfunding

I created the crowdfunding campaign originally with a $6000 goal, believing if Joe lived, he would be in rehab for a few months, and then return to his "normal" life. We had no savings and neither of us could work, so I figured this would cover three months of our typical bills. How naïve.

Ultimately, the campaign raised $33,575 from 167 donors and was shared 627 times on social media. Here is my first post:

My beloved husband Joe has been critically ill since Monday 27 January; in a medically induced coma with H1N1, pneumonia, Acute Respiratory Distress Syndrome (ARDS) and sepsis due to a perforated bowel from diverticulitis. He is on life support. Doctors say he is critical and are considering his situation "hour by hour".

Prior to his hospitalization, Joe and I were both sick with pneumonia and bronchitis. He exhausted all of his sick time. He will have only ten weeks of paid time off. Since I tutor, I am only paid when I work. I missed a few weeks prior to my hospitalization for pneumonia. I don't know when I will return to my part-time job and haven't had a paycheck in two weeks.

We do have health insurance, but our financial needs are overwhelming at this time. If Joe does live through this, we are facing massive time out of work with no pay after ten more weeks. He may have to go to a Long Term Care Facility and face extensive rehab. We live frugally, but living expenses, car, insurance, copays, prescriptions etc., exceed what we are bringing in. We have no savings or assets on which to rely.

There has been an incredible outpouring of love, support, comfort and prayers and everyone has asked how they can help. I thought I would provide a vehicle for financial support to those who wish to help in a very concrete way.

I set the goal of $6000 which is our bare minimum expenses for three months with no pay coming in. I know if Joe lives through this, the last thing he needs to be worried about is how we are going to keep our home and pay our bills.

Your help, love, concern, compassion, prayers and support have helped me to face this nightmare with hope and appreciation. Thank you from my heart, Aoibhyann

Almost immediately, my nephew, CJ, was the first to donate. Again, the demonstration of support and love comforted me. Supportive notes and donations started flowing in; some gave as much as one thousand dollars, and some sacrificed to give what they could. Cash gifts came; friends handed me envelopes filled with small amounts, hundred dollar bills, or checks from those who were unwilling or unable to donate online.

February 11

Crowdfunding post:

> To our dear friends and supporters: Your generous gifts are already at work. I'm home now recuperating, and the bill collectors have started calling! I want you to know how grateful I am for your donations. Joe has had three "good" nights so far and tolerated his tracheotomy surgery yesterday. The plan is to eventually get him off the ventilator once his lungs clear, and to gently de-medicate him out of the coma. It is so wonderful to see his sweet face now that the alien ventilator tubes have been removed! Today I think he has "turned the corner" the doctors said he had not turned. I do believe recovery is now a possibility. He will have much rehab ahead, but at least we can pay our bill for a few months. For that I am appreciative to each of you, what a tremendous burden lifted.

> "I lift up my eyes to the mountains—
>   where does my help come from?
> My help comes from the Lord,
>   the Maker of heaven and earth…" Psalm 121

Later that day: Skylor, stalwart companion, friend from church, retired RN is here again with me through another episode. She tells me to be calm and reminds me to breathe. At first I stand and watch while Joe's ventilator alarms. The nurses who had been assigned to him 24/7 check in occasionally, manning the station behind the glass outside of his room. Skylor and I wait. I ask her if this is normal, and she looks at me and tells me she doesn't know. More waiting and alarming. We are monitoring his BP, heart rate while listening to the alarms. Bing bing bing bing beep beep beep beep. Bing bing bing bing bing. Watch Joe's heart rate, BP, ventilator still alarming. Repeat.

My stress level is off the charts, heart pounding like I'm trying to enclose a firecracker. I move to Joe's feet, alternating between massaging them and laying my torso across them, hugging whatever I can wrap my arms around. I sob. I'm thinking this is the end. Skylor rubs my back and shoulders. This would not be the last time Skylor comforts me while I'm in desperation. Here is my post:

> Setback today. Student didn't hook up Joe's ventilator tube correctly, and he was alarming all afternoon. He is stable now, but it took several hours. My poor honey, suffering... **Someone *** is going to hear from me tomorrow morning. You can take that to the bank.

> The doctor (who was absent all day until we paged him, I was distraught) arrived. He asked me if I'd like to transfer Joe to another hospital. Then he told me I have to "look at the big picture," explaining that my husband is "no longer the most critically ill patient on the floor." Before he left, he offered: "If you have any questions, page me anytime." Ya think?

> Sister and RN Therese told me to insist tomorrow no students will touch my husband.

> Supervisor guy telling the student or whatever she was what to do..we watched, she fumbled here and there...hours later, Joe's vent is alarming (no nurse to be found, I had to go to the desk and ask for someone, they paged the nurse in the room, when they answered I said *NO ONE is in here*) the supervisor and the student spend another 45 minutes fumbling around with numbers, settings, they wiggle his trach, move his head, numbers are low low low...they turn off the alarm while they're working..but I know what's going on, so does Skylor. Finally the supervisor says "Hmmm let's check to see if everything is connected properly" (following a humidification treatment that he oversaw the student do) and clicked one tube, and numbers were immediately back where they should have been in the 500s.

The direct Respiratory supervisor was right there in the room, watching every move of the student. It was like watching a cyclone hit, in slow motion. And the nurses were treating me like I was annoying them by asking (politely, all the while weeping at his feet) to *please tell me what was going on*! The supervisor is the one who eventually said "Let's check all of the connections..." and voila! Snap, and his numbers started to rebound instantly.

Thank you, Lord, he's stable again. Good night.

February 12

Social media update:

> Joe is stable today but running a fever. Meeting held. I politely request that no students work on my husband. My wishes were respected. I am truly grateful to everyone who has cared for Joe and helped him live. We will press on, he is a "fighter" so they say, and we will continue to support everyone and pray! No students will be touching my hubby. All is well for today. Thank you, heavenly Father, for guiding my words and thoughts. Thank you everyone for your concern and support. Please know how much I appreciate you.

> Just got an update from his doctor; he told me something I did not know! Joe is making tiny baby steps in the direction of healing--however, he said the ARDS (acute respiratory distress syndrome) is still his critical problem. I asked what the treatment was for that and he said "to keep the patient alive--there is no treatment other than time--the lungs will heal themselves if the patient lives". I gasped. I knew Joe was critically ill these past two weeks but I had not understood the main reason. If you can't breathe, you don't live. So I am grateful for all the staff has done to get Joe to this point. Amen.

Thoughts and prayers going over the pond to Ireland, suffering from bizarre major storms, hundreds of thousands without power. Peace and health and strength and warmth to you all.

February 13

How do I thank my sister for being an angel? How do I let her know how much her support means to me, how important it was that she took vacation days from work, drove three hours to be with me, nurse me, pray with me, love me, comfort me, push me, encourage me, cook for me, fill my cabinets with food, clean and sanitize my house, pay my bills, complete ridiculous paperwork, take care of my ducks and cats, buy food for the birds, rescue Cyrus the cat who is being tormented by the Hawai`i cats, drive me to the hospital to see Joe, cry with me, hope with me...endless sisterly love. "Thank you" seems so cheesy and lame. Can you see the halo over her head? Love you

Friends and family had suggested that I find something else to focus on so that I do not burn out from caring and advocating for Joe and dealing with the associated issues. I had no problems with that, as I had been caring and advocating for my son, my students, animals and the environment for the better span of my life. Healthy distractions were mainly related to what was happening outside my little traumatized world in the ICU, and beyond the walls of the cold, lonely home I retreated to each evening.

So cool: counting whales via satellites. This is critically important to saving them. Thank you, JJ, for the link. Thank you Lord, and all of Joe's caregivers for another day.

I also found it helpful to find and share humor wherever I could, and maintain a grateful attitude. But Valentines' Day was challenging.

February 14 Valentine's Day thoughts in lieu of my visiting Joe:

The stars have lost their luster
The sun and moon mean nothing to me
I need you back
Need you to open your eyes and smile again
When you were away
I was in a perpetual state of longing, but I wouldn't say
Not healthy or positive to yearn
But here I am
What is it all worth if you're not with me?

Second week: Morning: I am groggy today but okay. Hard time going to sleep, I usually take a half of a Xanax and one melatonin. I had weird dreams last night of playing the guitar and writing songs for Joe. My bishop and our home teacher came over yesterday afternoon to give me a blessing, told me they do not feel Joe is going to die. Bishop and his wife then went to see Joe and called me on the way home, he told Joe to wake up! There is work to be done!

Just got off the phone with K the receptionist and she told me Joe's BP was 116/64 and his ox heart rate was 86...all excellent...yesterday his BP climbed to 146/74 and his heart rate was up to 105 at times. I had asked Rose his nurse yesterday what she could do, she gave him some Dilaudid and the numbers came down.

By this time, family and friends were rallying to my support. My Dad, his wife Pearl, my sister Therese, my only son, Patrick, his wife, nieces, nephew, aunts, cousins, near and far were steadfast. Groceries were bought and delivered, church friends brought home-cooked meals regularly. Joe's Hampshire Christian teammate and friend, KTrain, initiated an email chain consisting of many of Joe's roommates, teammates, dorm mates, and friends. K-Train texted, emailed and called me regularly, then sent out a summary to the group. Greeting cards, both hand-made and store bought were sent. Family members who were nurses educated me about "peep" and all functions in the ICU. These regular calls, emails, gifts, offers and check-ins were the fiber of a caring network that sustained and uplifted me so I could function. Still, I didn't function well. I didn't always return calls or emails. I wasn't cheerful or articulate when I did, robotically reporting Joe's condition at that time.

Patrick offered to take me to the hospital. He had been an upright stepson to Joe, remembering birthdays and holidays and Father's Day, even though he was close to his own father. He has always been my joy, and I cherished every moment I could spend with him, now busy with his own family and life.

> Patrick's bringing me to the hospital; he is coming at 10:00 and I have been praying that the conversation in the car is inspired. This is about all of us, not just Joe, not just me.

Prayers answered: the conversation was inspired, but it took place at lunch, over the clamor of plates and conversations, after Patrick saw Joe and perhaps understood the severity of his condition. Sometime mid-salad, Patrick asked me what my plans were.

> "What do you mean?"

> "What are your plans, Mom, in case, you know, Joe….. doesn't… make it?"

> "I'm praying."

> "That's great. But have you thought about making arrangements?"

Picking over the croutons, I chewed on his words.

> "What kind of arrangements?"

> Awkward pause.

"You're not going to be in any shape to write his obituary or make funeral arrangements if it happens. You should work on that now."

Profound silence.

I was so impressed at his courage although I didn't tell him so.

We chatted about how the obituary should be organized, what to do about the funeral, and what we would say to those who came. Or didn't. The challenge came when considering what to do with Joe's body, and where to place his remains.

I had to decide if I wanted Joe buried, or cremated. He was a stubborn ox about such things when I asked him about it through the years. He didn't prepare a last or living will. He wouldn't commit to telling me what to do with him if he was ever incapacitated. He refused to talk about it, giving me the standard response: "I need time to think about it." He was apparently out of time now, leaving the hard decisions to me. I couldn't decide where he would want to be laid to rest: with me? With his mother and father and family? What is the name of that cemetery we visited? I remembered the name of the street was an alphabet letter, like A or B Street. Did I have to contact his family to ask them if they would prefer to have Joe buried there? To be fair, I hadn't chosen a permanent resting site for myself, either, but I was considering having my cremated remains become part of an eternal reef.

Patrick and I grew closer that day – something I never thought possible. We had, as he would say, a "good talk."

To my niece (Therese's eldest daughter) following her email:

> Hi Bella you a so sweet. So much going on in your life! And you take time to write. You have always been so thoughtful just like your mom. I had a bad day today, stayed in bed all day never got out of my pajamas. I wasn't feeling well and I was so sad that I couldn't see Joe today on Valentine's Day. I

wrote my thoughts instead. I'm really tired, Bella, and I miss my husband, my friend. So many times I think of something and grab the phone to call him. It's as if reality hasn't sunken in yet. My life is upside down. I'm grateful for family, friends, church, and social media contacts for holding Joe and me up in prayer.

However, I'm still not 100% and I have no idea what to do, say, think. There's everything and nothing on Google that I can read up on to know how to handle this. The doctor went from giving me little to telling me all the news...in graphic details, (because I asked) and now I wake up at 2 AM with anxiety, crying.

It's a mess.

I don't even know what good can come out of this. Life is for the living..even though this is a part of living no one likes to think about. There's no way to prepare for this except to give thanks every day for what we have...knowing it can be taken away! Thank you for asking. I know it must be frustrating, unable to do anything! I'm sure you just want to fix everything! Me too. Love you, hugs to everyone and a happy Valentine's Day

To Therese's friend:

You are a peach, thank you so much. I'm not a good patient. The weird thing about this situation is because I can't control what happens with Joe, I've become kind of meticulous about my private life and time...it's the only thing I can control...I think I'm going through the Anger stage of grief right now. I had the conversations about transferring Joe to another hospital this week, but decided not to, as my Grandma used to say [the classic] "The devil you know is better than the devil you don't know." I think it would be too traumatic for Joe--he is still critical and on life support. I trust his care, I just know it's up to him...he shouldn't have survived to this point, any of the four things he has can kill. The docs told me yesterday the treatment is keeping him alive. And they have done that so far, so I'm eternally grateful to his caregivers.

Valentine's Day update on Joe: appropriately he may require a blood transfusion. His recurrent high temps are indicative of an infection, so they are going to change the site of his central line, thinking that this may be the origin. Another day...Please keep prayers coming.

In response to a post "Relax, Nothing is under Control" from M B, I wrote:

I was thinking the same thing but if there's anything I've learned from this, it is surrender--and the funny thing is--it came with *no* effort. It just overtook me. New meaning of the term "brought me to my knees".

Thank you Lord for another good day; Joe's fever is down, his heart rate is better, BP is good, oxygen is being tapered, coma medication is being tapered, he finally looked peaceful and restful today--and--(wait for it) he actually tried to open his eyes! Miracles, miracles. This is a pic of his life support equipment, the wall full of Valentines and cards and pictures he will see when he does open his eyes, and the collection of angels from Skylor hanging over his bed. Thank you everyone for your prayers, keep them coming...so grateful to you all.

February 15 After I quoted Psalm 121, our friend and former missionary Charles posted a quote:

Much as I lament the gathering storms, there will be some usefulness in them. Events will help to draw fresh attention to God's higher ways and His kingdom, which is to 'become fair as the sun, and clear as the moon'.

(Doctrine & Covenants 105:31) ~Neal A. Maxwell

To Charles:

Thank you Charles...this came at the right time. I am fatigued. Had a less than sparkling day yesterday, sick again, had to stay in bed all day, never got out of my pajamas. Bummed because I couldn't spend Valentine's Day with my hub. Of course on some level I know it's just a silly day...but on a different level it was another punch in the gut of this boxing match.

Yeah, I see a bigger picture. I see that I can use this situation for good. My choice...most days there is no question about how I will react. I pray, I pray to know the right thing to say, to do, to think...and the inspiration comes. Makes me think of all those in history who were blessed according to their faith. Thank you for finding us and blessing us with the gift of the church...don't know where I'd be without it.

Bottom line: I realize that many many many out there watching this all unfold have little to no idea of exactly what Joe and I are going through - how could they? They are witnessing my reactions...and perhaps at some time they will encounter a similar test of faith, God forbid, and remember.

Going to see Joe today, yay! Already my spirit is brighter just anticipating. Who would have thought all those eight years ago that this is the trial we would have to face? Again, without the church and without our faith, I am certain there would have been a different outcome.

Keep those wise and spiritual comments and prayers coming... they are helpful when I'm sure you don't know what else to say or do. Big whale love to you, Aoibhyann

Sunday February 16

Today Joe opened his eyes half way again and the nurses said it looked like he was trying to say something. I had to warn him not to do that so as not to hurt his throat. I want to be here tomorrow when he opens his eyes again, clinging to any bit of hope or change.

> Dr. Eb ordered two units of blood to help Joe's tired blood, and I learned his blood type. One bag each three hours and thirty minutes then Lasix to help his fluid, followed by the second bag of blood. I prayed that they would pick healthy blood for Joe. Have heard some stories about people developing allergies after having transfusions. We don't need any issues with his blood. Perfect healthy donors-- that is my wish.

> Respiratory therapist checked his lungs today. She said they are better than last Monday, still yucky and full, but better, and she agreed with my observation that the sputum is now a dark brown and much less in volume. I recall when I was hospitalized with pneumonia and H1N1 I would cough up a lot of bloody mucus, and by the time I was discharged the mucus was much less and the same dark brown color as Joe's.

> Su is his nurse again today. She is wonderful. She is ON IT! She knows when his heart rate and BP are up and is sensitive about giving the Dilaudid. He rests so comfortably after the Dilaudid and I'm amazed at how quickly his BP and heart rate decrease...it only takes a few seconds. I've been singing Meredith Andrews' song *You're Not Alone*.

> *...You're not alone, for I am here,*
> *let me wipe away your every fear,*
> *My love - I've never left your side,*
> *I have seen you through the darkest night,*
> *And I'm the one who's loved you all your life,*
> *all your life...*

Monday February 17

In addition to all that was going wrong, Joe now suffered another ailment: nasty phlegm appeared overnight, grossly greenish yellow, gunky globs oozing out of both nostrils. Hard to miss. I asked the nurse if he thought the phlegm should be cultured. He told me that he thought it would be, but the antibiotics that Joe was receiving should take care of whatever was causing the discharge, so the nurse wasn't too concerned. I thought it odd that he would develop something viral or bacterial. Different nurses had different opinions.

Tuesday February 18

Met infectious disease specialist Dr. A. He discontinued the doxycycline and did a CT scan for sinusitis. He quizzed me about the administration of our flu swabs, asking me to describe how they were performed, and how they felt. I told him the first time at the walk-in clinic, the swab was uncomfortable. The second time, at the emergency room, the swab was higher in my nasal cavity, and it hurt. A lot. The third time, at the emergency room, it felt as if my brain was punctured. The depth of the third swab, Dr. A posited, may be the reason I tested positive for H1N1 flu. Perhaps I had the flu prior to January 27th.

Dr. Eb told me that he wants to remove the nasogastric (NG) tube and put a percutaneous endoscopic gastrostomy (PEG) tube in his belly.

Wednesday February 19

CB, wife Kat and friend came in this morning on their way to the boys' hockey game. Joe tried to open his eyes, lots of stories about the good old days at Hampshire Christian. Dr. Wa rounded with Ananda, the respiratory therapist Sonia, Sara the nurse (in traditional nurse whites and hair wrapped in a netted bun) who is very sweet and super competent. Strangest thing is I understood 80% of what they were talking about. Dr. Wa always leaves me saying, "Keep praying". When they finished rounds, Dr. Wa asked me, "You got that?" I nodded affirmatively. Wow: the perk of being the wife of a critically ill patient – learning medical and bodily terms, functions and processes, although I'd not have chosen to do so. I'm a teacher, not a medical professional, but I'm learning regardless.

Social media update:

> Orders for today: changes: Dr. Wa wants to be conservative and not put Joe through another procedure, so he ordered removal of the NG tube. YAY! Sara discontinued the tube feeding this morning at eight o'clock, and doctor does not want to put the PEG tube in. Joe can go a day or two without the tube feeding milkshake, says the doctor. Sara may decrease the Ativan to 1mg today. Dr. Wa lowered the ventilator oxygen to 49% from 50% and is attempting to have Joe accept a 1:1 ratio, meaning he is taking in as much as he is exhaling. For the past 3 days he had been "breathing above the ventilator"...a good thing. Today he has been breathing at the mid-20s to as high as 24.

> Sonia said tomorrow they will try phase one of aggressive therapy to get him off the vent[ilator]. She explained it but I didn't really catch it all...just that there will be periods of time they will have him breathe unassisted by putting something on the trach. Big day for Big Joe. Thus far he has responded positively to everything they have done to get him off the vent, the Ativan and the coma meds. Prayers.

The culture from the nasal discharge came back positive for three things: sinusitis, staph and candida yeast infection. They added a new antibiotic with anti-fungal, and re- started the doxycycline. The sinusitis has to hurt. His temp was 101 at 3 AM and down to 99 this morning. I told Joe this new drug should give him some relief today, combined with the removal of the nasogastric tube he will be making great progress very soon. I am certain of it. Big step as I have not been certain of anything for over a month, with the exception that my faith has doubled, tripled even, and that God is at our side, angels are here, and prayer works.

More Reiki today, especially on the "occlusion" on Joe's left forearm, feels like a hard subcutaneous lump. His feet are less swollen today, his right forearm still looks like it belongs to Popeye, not Poppi Joe.

February 17 Sparrows and Surrender

Having surrendered to the probability of Joe's death, I found peace. Even though he appeared to be improving, I searched for inspiration. It came in several unlikely places such as a New York Times editorial. I commented "YES" on the social media post entitled *Alone, Yet Not Alone* by David Brooks, published on the very day we were hospitalized – January 27, 2014. Brooks examines the "yawning gap between the way many believers experience faith and the way that faith is presented to the world."[ii] Brooks' words echoed deep inside me. He suggested there was a "silent majority who experience a faith that is attractively marked by combinations of fervor and doubt, clarity and confusion, empathy and moral demand."

Brooks applauds Christian music artist Audrey Assad, and I delight in her songs, especially "Sparrow"; the title resonated with me. Assad transformed the slow, soulful, gospel hymn "His Eye is on the Sparrow" from the early 1900s into an upbeat, rolling melody and rhythm that carries the listener from doubt to comfort.

> *Why should I be lonely,*
> *long for Heaven and home,*
> *When Jesus is my portion,*
> *and a constant friend I know?*
> *Why should I be troubled*
> *when His tender voice I hear?*
> *His eye is on the sparrow,*
> *and I know He's watching me.*

In 1991 I wrote and published an article featured on the cover of the state newspaper's magazine; the story, entitled *T-11/91* described my experiences with job loss. Recently unemployed, I hammered out the story in a few hours, submitted, began job hunting again and forgot all about it. I earned *The Pink Slip Prize*, a contest "for which it is better to be ineligible".

In the second paragraph, I alluded to the popular biblical verse from Matthew 10:29 to illustrate my doubt about God's care for me.

> "Allow me to enlighten you about what you can look forward to should you find yourself in my position, with a lack of position. First, there is no alarm clock blaring at 4:30 a.m. I now wake with the birds. If it's true, as it is said, that God sees each sparrow fall, maybe that explains why he was too busy to see me the day my desire to get out of bed died."

> *29 Are not two sparrows sold for a farthing? And one of them shall not fall on the ground without your Father. 30 But the very hairs of your head are all numbered. 31 Fear ye not therefore, ye are of more value than many sparrows.*[iii]

To understand these biblical verses, it helps to couch them in history. The sparrow is a tiny bird that is not considered to be of much value, but of great value to God. These were common in the time of Jesus, and often caught, skinned, roasted and sold for food. I believe the reference to God's seeing each sparrow fall signifies God's omnipotence, and the unfathomable magnitude of His care for us. How great is His love and attention for us, if He knows the number of hairs on our head, and notices the falling of every sparrow? I wrote *T-11/91* twenty- five years ago, burdened with angst, doubt and a heavy dose of insignificance. Audrey Assad sings sweetly with her lyrics about doubt, faith, joy and the comfort of a constant companion.

February 17

Popular inspiration from Olympic athlete Scott Hamilton:

> *The only disability in life is a bad attitude...God is there to guide you through the rough spots...*

Social media post:

> Funny Story: My back went out again this morning (car accident 2 years ago, L4 L5 protruding disks and fractured

SI); stuck on couch, can't turn the way the physical therapist taught me because I would have fallen on floor. Prayers. Panic. Reiki. Yoga Breathing. Prayers. Screaming. Crying. More Prayers. Willing myself to get up...failing. Call my neighbor to help, she fetches my visiting nurse's phone number. Call visiting nurse--they suggest calling 911. Hang up, pray some more, fear of wetting myself on the couch motivates me to suck it up and call 911. Takes five strong men to gently twist and move me to a standing position. No screaming. I ask them to please stand by while I use the toilet; sometimes I get stuck there when my back goes out, and Joe usually helps me. Success- and out I walk from the bathroom with Donald the Muscovy duck following me, Pegasus the Pekin also waddling into the kitchen after jumping out of the tub where they stay at night. The EMTs are laughing, taking pictures, telling me I made their day. HA! I made their day! What a hoot. Here's to angels in the form of helpers: EMTs and neighbors and pet ducks who lightened my spirit.

After that episode, I decided I should probably not sleep on the too-soft couch. I returned to bed, and that first night was less than fun. Complain, complain about my first world problems:

My back rules me and everything I do! Yesterday it wanted to humble me. Humbled. Helpless once again. Others who rule: our very jealous cats, who have not appreciated Joe's absence, or mine when I'm at the hospital all day, every day. Last night, after crawling into bed ohhhh soooo sloowly, fixing the covers, leaning back sllooooooowly and carefully (so as not to upset the back further), I finally found a comfortable spot. Impish Felicia decided to push my jewelry box off the dresser, (the size of a breadbox, quite impressive) then proceeded to bat everything around on the floor- as cats do. *You have got to be kidding me*! I raised my voice and body...out of bed slooooowly I crawled, bent over slooowwwwly, picked up every piece of jewelry....crawled back into bed. (Repeat sequence above). Settled, I begin to work on my laptop and realize the power cord had become disconnected. OY! Out of bed again, bending down to retrieve and plug in power cord... repeat sequence again. Thankfully, back cooperated, wish I could say the same for the cat. Funny story to end a day that started with a funny story.

February 18

Crowdfunding post:

Friends, family and angels near and far--- an update on Joe's status: He continues to show tiny signs of improvement, headed in the right direction as opposed to even one week ago. Hospital staff has been fantastic. Joe has been trying to open his eyes now that his coma medication is being decreased. I can't wait to see his eyes and see his sweet smile again. It has been a slow recovery, he is still critical and "not out of the woods yet" as the doctors say, but he is still with us, and he is still fighting. I am grateful for every day, for being able to hold his hand and talk to him, knowing he hears me. I have communicated all of your get-well wishes, all of your generosity. I'm sure he hears and appreciates you all. The nurses say his heart rate increases when he has visitors. Just wanted to tell you how much we appreciate you and how important your help has been, and will be, in Joe's recovery.

February 19

Social media post:

More get well cards and prayers for Joe! Many thanks to all of our young ones at church who sent these hand-made cards. We love you and are so grateful to have you in our lives. Your prayers are powerful, and are working.

February 20 11ᵗʰ Anniversary of the day we met

Update:

> Good morning, Happy "Aggressive Ventilator Weaning
> Day" for Joe. Blessed troubles. Happy Anniversary to my
> love-- today marks eleven years since the day we met- a frigid
> Thursday also. Cannot have imagined that Joe would teach
> the Ice Princess how to open her heart, knock down those
> bricks and love again. I love you Joseph, keep pushing...we
> will be there with you today...you can do this!
>
> ...even the doctors say this is difficult. But they wouldn't
> do it unless they thought Joe was ready. Keep praying!!!
> Especially today.
>
> 2:43 PM: Joe tolerated about 15 minutes of the ventilator
> weaning. More blessed baby steps. He's tired, sleepy and
> only receiving the coma medication as needed. Vent settings
> were lowered again today which means he has to work harder
> for each breath..but he is doing it --- and stable. Saw a few
> grimaces today, and some silent "coughing" behavior – (sorry
> honey but I was thrilled to see them.) Still opening his eyes
> for scant seconds..not responding yet but I am hopeful that
> will come. Thank you everyone for your prayers. I am one
> blissful, grateful girl today.

From our mutual friend, Ellen, who has known Joe since childhood:

> When I think of Joe, the words that come to mind are gentle, kind, strong and lovable. Hoping and praying that he continues to fight to live and come back to us.

Later that afternoon, I posted:

> My honey opened his eyes halfway for a few seconds today on and off...very groggy, uncommunicative, and the most heart- wrenching part was when a huge frown and grimace came over his face...and he wept. Absolutely unbearable. Can you even imagine what is happening inside? If I could trade places with him, I would in an instant. Hang on, sweetie... you're getting better every day.

On the Wednesday of week two, I asked Dr. St what the treatment was for ARDS. He said bluntly, "Keep the patient alive." When I asked him what else we can do, he replied, "Play the waiting game and hope his lungs begin to clear on their own." He went on to suggest that maybe we could start to look for signs of improvement that next Monday. Miraculously, Joe started to show signs on Friday: better vitals, beginning to open eyes, tolerating his rolls nicely, and his fever was lower.

I posted:

> Meds this week: Piperacillin, Zosin, Micafungin ordered by Dr. Ab, Infectious Disease specialist, to attack the fungal infection and candida, Zosin for the sinusitis. He discontinued all the antibiotics in the middle of week two because he ruled the fever to be a "medical fever" wherein the body actually begins to fight the medicine that is intended and prescribed to help it.
>
> Dr. Ab also prescribed a "cousin" of what he had discontinued last week and was watching Joe's reaction closely. He apologized to me for prescribing another antibiotic after he had discontinued them. Imagine that: a doctor apologizing to the wife of the patient. Certainly the prescribed drugs have worked, yet the combination of antibiotics may be contributing to his three-week fever. Dr. Ab stands by his bedside sometimes and looks puzzled.
>
> The nasogastric tube was removed Wednesday of week three. He went nearly three days without food, so they re-administered IV fluids (TPN). Dr. Wa was in; I was told there were three options at this point given the infection: (1) do nothing, (2) insert a gastric (stomach) tube, or (3) reinsert the nasogastric tube. He admitted he would prefer the gastric tube as the obvious choice as they did not want to reinsert a nasogastric tube considering why they had removed it, and the IV TPN was a another "playground for yeast and other infections", unsuitable and not as nutritious as the milkshake that he would receive through the gastric tube. Yummy.

February 21

Update Friday:

> Joe held his eyes open for quite a while today (although not really focusing on anything) and actually smiled at Abby, his pretty blonde nurse, K Train, Skylor and (Pearl's daughter) Julie -- Thanks for coming today; means the world to me and helps me through these days. PRAYER WORKS eternally grateful for all of you holding me up when I couldn't do it myself.

> First the tears, then the smiles.

> Successful ventilator weaning today-3.5 hours (ventilator breathes 12 times per minute, he does the rest on his own) with coaching "Breathe, Joe, Breeeeeath. Deeeeper. Breeeeeath." Because he was paralyzed and in a coma, his body has kind of forgotten how to do certain things...so he has to work through this and be re-trained e.g. breathing without assistance. I can tell you first hand that just with pneumonia and H1N1, breathing is underrated and every breath is painful and difficult. I can't even imagine how much work Joe is doing, and yet he is living up to his Hampshire Christian nickname: "Warrior". Successful ventilator weaning today-3.5 hours *and* he had the stomach feeding tube put in today-only necessary until he is off the ventilator and eating on his own....tolerated everything well, stable, fever is nearly gone, everything working as it should, resting peacefully when I left him tonight - His NG tube (nasogastric feeding tube through his nose) was removed this past week due to a severe sinus and yeast infection in his upper respiratory tract--kind of a catch-22--can't feed him unless he has the tube, but the tube is a playground for bacteria and virus and fungal infections. He is weak beyond description, no response in his hands, fingers, arms, legs, toes. It is as if he is waking up muscle by

muscle, starting with his eyelids and his tears and his smile and his lungs. So grateful for your support and prayers; I feel the strength of them.

Let's keep those prayers coming that he can get off that ventilator and sustain his alertness ..this would be the number 1 and number 2 goal and milestone on the road to recovery.

February 22 Saturday

Doctor St, one of four on his team, called me and said Joe is in Phase 2 of the recovery; first phase is critical and the goal was to keep him alive. Phase 2 is plateau and recovery. "He has a long road ahead of him" said the doctor, and he "does not want to celebrate a success until he's home hanging around with you." But we did agree that he is on the mend. All the drugs (paralytic, coma meds, pain meds, antibiotics, antiviral, etc.) do tend to linger in the body for a while but Joe opened his eyes when the doc called his name -- an excellent sign.

Can you believe what Joe has been through? In the last week alone I've spoken to three people who have lost loved ones to H1N1 --just the flu. There is yet another epidemic predicted for March. Please, please please, unless you have a good excuse, please--stop in to your local pharmacy and get a flu shot..it takes one second, there are minimal side effects and you will spare yourself and your loved ones the agony that we have experienced.

Obvious here that I was concerned about others catching the flu, unvaccinated. I was thinking if there is even a slight chance that the vaccine would prevent infection, it would be better than remaining open and vulnerable. After what we had experienced, I thought the flu vaccine was a no-brainer.

"I stand all amazed" -- God is great and His mercy is endless and beyond our comprehension. That's why it's called FAITH. Love and thanks.

More blessings: My Dad met me at home that night and brought a present-an electric fireplace/heater.

> Thank you Dad and Pearl for the warmth and comfort ...no firewood to lug, no fire to tend through the wee hours, no smoky house. Aaahh. Now all I need is for Joe to be home by my side, enjoying this with me.

February 23

The blessings and healing continue:

Dr. St came in on Sunday. He mentioned the word "rehab". Friends, Dad and Pearl and I all heard him say that he felt Joe might be ready in one week. When we asked him to repeat how long until he can be transferred, he backpedaled and said "Let's see how he does." He is rarely one to be positive or give encouragement or hope.

> Blessed Sunday update on Joe: I can't believe I'm writing this, but Dr. St said the word "rehab" today! Joe is doing well on the aggressive ventilator weaning which means he is closer to removal of the ventilator, and once that is accomplished we can think about his next challenges out of Intensive Care. Blessings and miracles abound. Thank you for your continued prayers.

Re-posted this from a social media meme:

> Nurses are being scorned for being late with medicine, and yet they are holding their bladder because they don't have time to use the bathroom, and starving because they missed lunch. They're being peed on, puked on, pooped on, bled on, bitten, hit, yelled at and are missing their family while they

are taking care of yours. They may even be crying for you. The minute you read this, nurses all over the world are saving lives. Re-post if you love a nurse, are a nurse, appreciate a nurse or a nursing assistant. Thanks to all the nurses.

February 23

Crowdfunding post:

> Update on Joe: One month tomorrow this all became our reality. Doctor was in with us today and mentioned "REHAB"--so our directional lights are on, and we have begun to "turn the corner" that eluded us for four weeks. Doctor also mentioned that Joe is officially in Phase 2 (of 2 phases) of recovery. Phase 1 was staying alive. Phase 2 is plateau, and improvement. Joe's nurse told us today that for every day a patient is in a coma, count on three days in rehab, and if a patient is on a paralytic (Joe was) then add another day or two. Altogether, it appears Joe may be facing at least three months in rehab. He will have to learn to use all his muscles again as they have atrophied. At this point, Joe is waking up muscle by muscle; I watch his face and his body every day to see which one will move next. First to move were his eyelids, then his tear ducts (he cried) then his mouth--a smile, a grimace...more grimaces...today he moved his left toe and by the end of the day he was moving his left forearm and both knees oh-so-slightly. He is experiencing extended periods of half-opened eyes; he will open them if asked and he can respond to a question by blinking e.g. "Blink once for yes--do you hear me?" When he answers, his blinking is deliberate and different than normal blinking. Doctor says there are two categories of response--the brain, and the body. He said Joe seems to be aware and responsive--an excellent sign.

The respiratory team began "aggressive ventilator weaning" this past week: periods of time when the ventilator is adjusted to allow Joe to breathe on his own and exercise his atrophied lungs with the ventilator only breathing 12 breaths per minute. Joe has to learn to breathe again on his own. His lungs were shut down for a month and the paralytic and coma medications linger in the body long after they are discontinued. He endured only fifteen minutes the first day and required medication to calm him, but the past three days he has gotten stronger and today he did well through six hours total with zero medication required to calm him. I think Joe deserves an Olympic Gold Medal for his effort. He has earned his Hampshire Christian nick name - "Warrior"! I honestly cannot believe what he has had to endure, and can't imagine what is coming, but I am so blessed that Joe is alive, and grateful to everyone who has supported us through this. Thank you for your constant prayers and love and good energies and well -wishes. Stay tuned for more updates and please share this with anyone you think might be looking for ways to support us--we are going to need it!!!! Much love, Aoibhyann

Response to my niece, Marie, who said she can't wait to hear Joe's laugh again, and cautioning me to care for myself:

Thanks Marie. You are right--I miss his laugh and his hugs. I'm falling in love with him all over again, one muscle at a time. I cannot believe his strength and determination, his will...the fight in him. Unbelievable. Our cousin said that I am taking care of two people by taking care of myself. Great advice. I have been trying to rest and stay calm and eat healthy and hydrate--and my faith has quadrupled through all of this. Strength I didn't know I had comes from Above, and from everyone here. Love you!

Back to the miracles: Received a social media post from R, Patrick's darling former classmate. She came to Maui and lived with us for a short time before moving on to Oahu. We love her like a daughter.

> I am so glad that Joe is doing well. I am not a prayer person, but I gave it a try for him. I hope a speedy recovery is to follow *Sending you continued good fortune*

When speaking of the name of God, I think of the classic example of the question: what's in a name?

> *...'Tis but thy name that is my enemy;*
> *Thou art thyself though, not a Montague.*
> *What's Montague? it is nor hand, nor foot,*
> *Nor arm, nor face, nor any other part*
> *Belonging to a man. O! be some other name:*
> *What's in a name? that which we call a rose*
> *By any other name would smell as sweet...*
> ~ Romeo and Juliet Act II Scene II, Wm. Shakespeare

My response to R:

> Thank you for "giving it a try" R. It's in the humbling that the prayer is most powerful. I found myself a hundred times stronger when I was on my knees in surrender and humility. There are no logical explanations for what happens through belief and hope in something greater than ourselves. That's why it's called faith. A leap beyond our understanding, a step out into the unknown...oh so scary! But undeniably The Source of all of my strength and hope.

> Powerlessness is spectacular but there is a remedy. I could have succumbed to the pain and grief; the way I see it, we have two choices--we can be bitter, angry, agnostic, apathetic or unapologetic, or we can be faithful. Most of the human race chooses faith in something. My opinion only: One God, different names and prayers.

I appreciate your message and hope that things have settled for you. Just me, not judging, just telling my story about what works for me.

February 24 More blessings, more learning, and a party

Received this from cousin and her husband, a "Catholic medical kit" including Holy Water from Lourdes and the Jordan River, rosary beads, rosary book, miraculous medal and prayer cards. What a blessing. Joe received the water first thing this morning.

I had a ridiculously horrid day today. Ironic because Joe had a good day--although he was racked with pain and grimaces and such all day, awakening a little more, muscles waking up a little more, tolerating six hours total breathing on his own, but also aware of his limitations and pain and tears--big tears --and the saddest face. Must be horrible for him! And now that he can communicate by blinking, I have begun peppering him with questions...

His face today was classic. I asked him if he knows where he is, and he shot me a look like "Of course! You've been telling me for four weeks!"

It floored me-- even with his few facial muscles working, his personality comes through loud and clear. I was humbled, and by the end of the day watching him struggle just took me over. I started at his feet, saying "Do your feet hurt? Blink once for Yes." No response. "Do your ankles hurt?" No response. "Do your knees hurt? Blink once for yes." No response. "Do your thighs hurt?" No response.

This continued up to his chest. I was frustrated and sobbing "I want to do something for you, I feel so helpless."

I felt badly about feeling badly and feeling useless, I wanted nothing more than to run away. For the past four weeks, I had a purpose. That purpose was my motivation to get out of bed every morning, and to carry on throughout the day. I felt I had value and worth. But now that Joe seemed to be waking up and healing, I thought there was nothing for me to do and no way to help or serve him. I gathered my bags and hurried to his side.

"I'm going to go home now, baby. I'm so sorry."

I left in tears and didn't want to go back. I'd have to suck it up and put on a happy face tomorrow.

Listen to me--I'm so blessed my husband is alive, and I'm complaining about what a bad day *I *had. This marks the end of Aoibhyann's Pity Party, February 24, 2014.

Social media update:

> Joe's facial expressions are totally Joe. He's back. Yesterday, Monday, he gave me quite the look when I asked him if he knew where he was, as if to say "Do you think I'm stupid?" Even more expressions and movement today. What a difference from even this past weekend. Eyes are open and bright, more movement in extremities, he can move his head left and right for "yes" and "no". Today he mouthed "water" so Christina the nurse brought me a cup of ice water and green sponge-tipped swabs. Joe seemed to enjoy them and likes to bite them, even holding tightly between his teeth when I attempt to remove one. That's Joe. He is staring out more toward the opposite wall today, briefly nodding off. Joe has been fever-free for three days!

> Morphine was administered about 10 AM; it seems as if he doesn't want to sleep, but can't stay awake either. He fights. I wonder if he is petrified to sleep again. Twelve hours off the ventilator today beginning at 10 AM. Yesterday, he was off the ventilator at 3 in the morning, then rest, then three more hours from 6-9 PM. Nurses said he was comfortable all night. Sunday was a trial also, about six hours with assistance "A" meaning assisted breathing by the ventilator 12x per minute and "S" meaning sustained. He did well again, with stable vitals. On Saturday he did not have any aggressive ventilator weaning because it was the day after the placement of his stomach tube, and on Friday he was supposed to go off the ventilator for six hours but only went four because he had the gastric tube surgery at 4PM.

Week Four

We can lift ourselves, and others as well, when we refuse to remain in the realm of negative thought and cultivate within our hearts an attitude of gratitude.
~President Thomas S. Monson

Yesterday Joe was given the flu and the five- year pneumonia vaccines because he was fever- free for more than twenty four hours. I declined them when I was hospitalized; felt too much like a pincushion and couldn't bear one more needle. Plus, it didn't make sense to me to take a flu shot if I already had the flu. I couldn't understand it, and I didn't have any energy to figure it out. I thought if I had the virus, my body had built up an immunity to it.

> Today Joe is even making the face that he makes when he exhales through pursed lips like his mother used to, a "Pffffhewwww" sound, even though he is breathing through the trach.

February 25

> Guess who? Bright eyes wide open. Breathing without the ventilator. Smiling, mouthing words ("water" to me, and "We love you" to Skylor), and wiggling toes, turning head. Waking up muscle by muscle. If you guess Joe, you'd be correct. He's coming baaacck ! Rehab on the horizon..maybe this week. Whooooo hooooooooo!!! God is great and His mercies are endless. PS Not too many people can believe Joe's progress since two weeks ago. Miracles? You betcha

> Yes, after H1N1 epidemic predicted to return in March, we really *do* need to take precautions against tick bites. Tick-borne illnesses are legion...and Spring is nearly upon us, hard as that may seem to believe being 17F degrees outside.

February 26

From BC, one of our friends from church:

> So happy to hear Joe is doing well. We continue to pray for him - even my kiddos pray every night without a reminder from me "please bless my Primary teacher to get better." Love you!!

JJ, a student in our church primary class, asked her Mom and Dad if she could visit Joe. Parents forewarned her about his condition; she didn't relent. We always allowed her to lead our class in song, and she had an adorably sweet voice. Mom brought her to the ICU, and she stood in the doorway (disallowed from entering his room) singing children's church hymns. She could be heard throughout the hall. Nurses would later comment on JJ's angelic voice and the change in the mood on the floor after she sang.

More examples of the miracle of the prayers of children: JG, a student in our primary class, told his parents that he had been including Joe in his prayers, and was certain that he wasn't going to die. (Mom revealed this to me only after Joe and I returned to church many months later.)

I was told by the case manager that a representative of the rehab hospital I'd chosen (on the advice of the team) would be visiting Joe to assess his candidacy. She came, interviewed me, asked Joe a few questions (to which he nodded his head) and approved his admission. Little did I know this would backfire in the most egregious way.

February 26

> Our dear Dr. Wa giving Joe the news that he will be released to the rehab hospital tomorrow! May be just another day on the job for this man and the entire team ... But I am forever humbled and grateful for their care, kindness, excellence and expertise, and for doing everything in their power to keep Joe alive when the odds were against him. Joy.

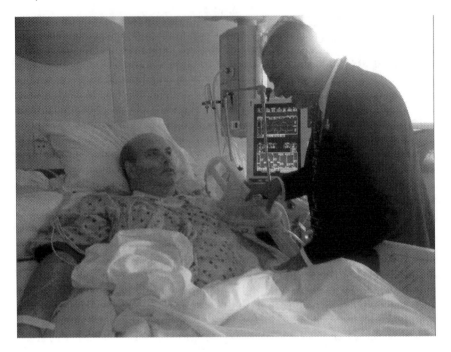

Chapter 4

If Wishes Were Fishes: Get Whale Soon

February 27

10AM: EMT and ambulance personnel arrive, ready to transfer Joe to the new rehab hospital. I try to counsel Joe about what is going to happen. Nurses who were his lifeline come in to say goodbye and wish him well. He appears to be listening to them, but I wonder what he'll remember. One male nurse tells the story of how sensitive he was to Joe's ordeal because he suffered a similar fate a few years ago. A motocross racer, he had an accident, breaking several bones and suffering head and spinal injuries. He too was in a coma. He too fought valiantly in rehab to recover. Doctors told him he would probably never walk or work again. He said he remembers wanting desperately to recover and not wanting to believe that he would be as limited as the doctors predicted. He eventually went on to become an ICU nurse.

The ambulance personnel strap Joe into the gurney and wrap him tightly, like a newborn, with his head sticking out of the top, bobbing to one side. I tuck a rolled-up towel under the left side of his head, as I had done for the past many weeks, so that it wouldn't flop sideways. I ask him if he is okay, and he gazes at me and indicates he is, but I don't think he has a clue. All the better.

I follow the ambulance out of the hospital parking lot and on the highway (they sped at 75 mph-why?) to the rehab hospital. The roads have cleared, and although it's cold, it's not snowing and there's no ice on the road. The grey skies threaten, but I'm happy to have the ICU in my rear-view mirror.

> On our way to the rehab hospital. Joe needs prayers now more than ever! -- Prayers for peace, prayers for strength, prayers for the courage to face the long, hard road ahead..Thank you.

The Discharge Summary included these discharge diagnoses:

1. Respiratory failure
2. Multiorgan failure
3. ARDS
4. Flu with influenza A positive, H1N1 positive at the time of admission
5. Prevotella loscheii peritonitis
6. Staph coagulase negative and Candida from nasal mucosa
7. Pansinusitis
8. ARDS
9. Total body fluid overload
10. Multilobal pneumonia
11. Electrolyte imbalance
12. Anemia
13. Occluded thrombus in the left cephalic vein below the elbow which does not need any treatment
14. Poor nutritional status
15. Acute kidney injury with development of acute renal failure, status post tracheostomy placement for ventilatory management

16. Status post gastrostomy tube placement

Upon admission to the new rehab hospital, four things irked me, the last of which put me over the edge. Can't recall names, won't be able to. One nurse or therapist asks where Joe's boots are. Huh? She explains that he should be wearing boots so his heels don't get bedsores, and to protect his limp foot muscles. When I tell her that he never wore them, she makes a face, and sighs, "Oh we'll have to order them. It might be a few days before they arrive." Then someone took a look at his ostomy and said "Okay! We will have to order these supplies." The last straw was the nurse's aide or CNA coming in and telling Joe "Here's your call button in case you need help" and then slipping it under his flaccid and limp hand.

Think of al dente pasta and you can imagine his body draped on the bed.

I flipped, inside.

I left Joe's room and went to the visitor's lounge – a windowed room the size of a closet with a couch, a chair, an end table with a lamp and some old tattered magazines and a phone, and one wall which held the door to the bathroom - to call the woman who did the assessment at the ICU in the original hospital. I explained that it appeared the team was not ready for Joe, or didn't read his records; she confirmed that she had sent a copy of her complete assessment and records to the case manager who emailed her to say she received it, (obviating her from any liability)? I then spoke to the case manager about my concerns and she went flying around the floor to find answers. I told her the call button incident just broke all confidence I had that anyone was ready for Joe or knew his case. Frazzled, I called Therese, who was equally outraged and advised me to politely ask for a *Nurse to Nurse* report. She confirmed that nurses don't really have to give me anything and that I was probably already labeled by them as a bitch because I was advocating for Joe and making their jobs difficult.

Shortly thereafter, the head nurse, another nurse and I met in the hallway; I explained calmly, politely but directly that this man had been in ICU for thirty- plus days and I had been with him every day, watched every movement, expression, gauge, tool, machine, chart, etc., and he had been under 100% watchful care, as opposed to being lumped into the bed here and then left.

They tried to assuage my concerns by saying I should have faith in them. I chuckled a little and not in a happy way. I asked for the Nurse to Nurse Report. Was there one? (yes) Had everyone read it? (no)...

I met the admitting doctor and really liked her and her manner. She told me the plan was to wean Joe off the ventilator, maybe put in a cap on the trach so he can speak, and if he does well, wean him off the trach altogether. Tomorrow the goal will be to move him into a sling so he can be in a sitting position.

Had a powwow with everyone, just a sulky day; went home and cried and prayed on my knees for a better day.

The staff who greets him talk to him as if he is fully functioning. Initially I thought they were incredibly friendly and positive.

Another nurse visits and tells me that the team will be assessing him, so I'll have to leave and wait in the patient waiting area. I'm floored. Do they have any idea that I've been with him every day for the past month? Do they understand I've been his advocate, his masseuse and his constant support? What are they going to do to him that I've not already seen? I'm a bit perturbed, but I comply, and as I leave the room, I hear the swish of the curtain as it obscures any view.

I re-plastered Joe's wall with creative "Get Whale Soon" from niece Shelly, from students of CJ's mother in law, and church friends. Sweet masterpieces, each one.

February 28

Joe lit up and became very anxious when he saw me today.

Boots came, OT, PT, warming treatments on his forearms.

Stalwart Hampshire Christian buddies Fern, Gook, Digger, Doc and the dark haired Bumble came to visit him in his new home. He can open his eyes, most of the visible tubes and gauges have been removed, and his meds have been reduced so he looks as if he's awake and aware. He still has the trach and can't speak, only mouthing simple words. But he is still a limp noodle in a bed. Good visit, much better than the first time the guys saw him in early February, critically ill, near death, in a coma, when they and others held hands, circled his bed and prayed the Lord's Prayer. I told them I loved them and thanked them for bringing some light into Joe's life.

Joe mouthed "*Help*" to me, and then again within the same hour "*Av help me*". So I started at his feet, asking, "Does this hurt?" No response. He smiled at me...the second time I asked him if it was because of the boots on his feet, or because he couldn't move (yes) so I explained the situation to him (read: lied) and told him he's in the right place and making progress.

Joe breathing all day without the ventilator, exhausted: he was restless and in pain. Catheter incident overnight- a bloody mess that no nurses want to touch. They called the APRN and he arrived Saturday morning to replace it. Joe asked for pain meds and was given Dilaudid, Morphine, and Tylenol. Later that evening I asked the nurse why they replaced his catheter, and why there was blood in the tube. She tells me with authority that it's standard procedure, that it had not been replaced since last month, that 30+ days is too long for a catheter to be in place, and that the blood is just from the catheter "sticking to the mucous membranes", assuring me a little blood was normal and would eventually stop. What did I know about catheters? I believed her.

Saturday March 1 Stork and Seagull

Arrived at Joe's room and saw no one in his bed (?!) And the legs of someone in a reclining chair bed. Could it be that Joe was moved, or is in the hall somewhere, or got a roommate? Moving further into the room, I see it's Joe, dangling in sitting position in a sling, like he was delivered by a stork.

Julie, Dad and Pearl came and stayed until 3- ish. I walked out with Julie hoping to spend a few hours at home, laundry, and grocery shopping, and just being normal again, a state I had forgotten. Instead, I found a seagull standing on the sidewalk by the McDonald's, holding its wing in its beak. I turned the car around to find it had hobbled across the road to the other side. I swung the car around again, turned on the car emergency blinkers, grabbed a blanket to cover and pick up the poor creature, drove to a parking lot, readjusted and put the bird in a box I had in the trunk for just these occasions.

I drove home, checked on ducks and cats, googled wildlife rehabbers, called a few, finally found one who lives in a shoreline town who handles these birds; she affirmed that she handles seagulls and would be happy to care for it.

I drove forty-five minutes like an animal ambulance. The moment the rehabber held the seagull she said, "Aww I can feel the bone is broken... doesn't look good."

No kidding, I think to myself. *I told this to you when I called you.*

She showed me her owls, a single one in a kennel on her porch, and a pair perched on a limb in a shed-sized shelter in the yard. I tried to catch my breath while I witnessed these majestic creatures, sitting like stuffed, feathered statues, staring into my eyes. If I had more time, or if this was another day in a different life, I might have lingered there, absorbing the owl's essence, speaking with my heart to theirs.

I explained to the rehabber why I was in a hurry. She appeared concerned, and she indicated she would give the gull some pain meds and check out his wing, but "because the bones are tiny and thin, there is no way to set them." So frustrated, disappointed and bewildered at what had just occurred, I gave her a twenty dollar bill and asked her to try everything she could not to put the bird down. Deep down, I knew she would, and felt a great sense of waste.

Had I not collected the poor thing and tried to find care, my conscience would have nagged. If I drove on, like so many had been doing, and left the bird on the side of the road, another driver might have run it over and put it out of its misery. I did what I thought was best, understanding now that I really didn't change the outcome. I suppose we act according to the dictates of our conscience, believing we are doing what is best.

I realized two things since this whole situation with Joe. 1. We have very little control over anything in life. 2. A life is a life is a life. Each is valuable and precious. I can't control Joe's recovery. Yes, it helps for me to be there but when he is doped up and sleeping he really doesn't need me, and even though I thought my afternoon was going to be different, God had other plans. The two hours I thought I would have to myself to be normal again was spent driving a wounded seagull to a rehabber who probably euthanized it anyway.

While I was in route to the rehabber, HC friends King and Elisabeth came up unannounced from several hours away. They tried to call me a few times but I couldn't find the phone in my purse while driving, running out of daylight. I needed to find the rehabber's house and was unfamiliar with the roads in town.

I returned to the hospital where they were waiting for me; we had a quick visit, they left a framed picture of King and Joe from last year's reunion, and a note for me. This was the third time they had visited Joe; I had missed seeing them the first two times.

Social media post:

> Yes, maybe most people would keep driving if they saw this gull in the middle of the road with broken wing..but I've learned two things lately (1) nearly everything is out of our control, and (2) life is precious..life is fragile..and if I can help, my answer is always yes.

Found a fan for Joe's room as it was boiling hot. We needed to keep his blinds closed to the afternoon sun. He likes it dark and cool. Ice chips are still making him cough. Nurses and RT like the sound of his cough, say it's productive.

Spent the evening until 9:30. Joe was restless again, so I stayed. I kept telling him I'm going home now, honey, but he didn't want me to leave.

Sunday March 2

Arrived at 10:30 so I could spend some good quality time with Joe before his visitors. I helped the CNAs wash him, saw his wounds all healing nicely, decubitus on his back is still good, and while this was happening he mouthed "*Help, help, help me.*" We went through the twenty questions again, starting at his feet, but he didn't tell us what was wrong. His heart rate was over 130; I didn't even need to see his blood pressure.

Every day since I started being with him, his heart rate spoke for him. He was very agitated, moving legs and arms in spasms, but we asked if those were spasms or if he was doing it-- and he indicated it was him. I tried to calm him, then told him sternly that he was going to stroke out if he didn't relax and get himself under control. He mouthed "I want to stroke out." I told him we had come too far for him to give up now, and warned him lovingly I would smack him if he spoke like that again, then tried to calm him a little again. Grace his nurse brought four vials of something to flush his catheter and then urine came out so she thought maybe that was the cause of discomfort and anxiety. He received 2 mg Dilaudid again, which settled him.

We joked that he was going to run out of there! We have a runner! Grace tried to encourage us, telling us he has gone up two segments on the recovery scale since he arrived on Thursday. That's Joe, the Warrior! Fighting, fighting.

When he was lucid I asked him if he remembers what happened to him, I told him the story, asking him if he remembers the beginning. He whispered that he did, up until the surgery. I repeated that we had already lost him once, cautioning him to relax, urging him not to push so hard.

A routine procedure upon admission is a chest X-ray. This was performed by a perky woman named Torrey who appeared to be about my age. I mention that she is perky because I'm not. I struck up a conversation with her and was surprised to learn we had similar backgrounds. We both worked at the same aerospace manufacturer in our 20s, we both were Christians, and we both had a slightly alternative view of life. Torrey and I talked over Joe's bed for much longer than she should have remained. Another instant connection which I would later discover to have significance.

K- Train and his wife Gillian visited with Joe. I posted on social media that I was appreciative for everything they had done for him, and that their constant presence and communication with everyone was so very helpful and inspiring.

Social media post:

> Feel the love, Warrior. Feel the love.

So many friends and family members had been hugely supportive since Joe was in the ICU. They seemed to take a special interest in taking care of me and visiting Joe.

Monday March 3

Met with Nurse Manager. Some items were resolved: Joe's anxiety will be addressed with Selexa starting with 30 mg in tube daily 9 AM. APRN was on the phone with me briefly this morning, but was called away for the day. Joe will be given 1 mg Ativan in the morning and every 4 hours as needed for anxiety. Oddly, Morphine was discontinued. He'll be given Dilaudid as needed for pain: 2 mg for moderate, 4mg for severe. Seems they are managing his pain, but not looking for the source. Psychology consult was scheduled for this week. Foley catheter irrigation as needed. Speech therapist may be in to assess his swallowing. Dietician will be in to address sugar in his food.

I asked what the plan was for this week; Nurse Manager replies that she will talk to APRN during Wednesday rounds. Admitting or some other doctor will see Joe on Thursday.

Tuesday March 4

I am told there will be a meeting on Thursday at 9 AM with a doctor. IV was removed today.

Joe was given 4 mg Dilaudid because he asked for it, suffering 7 on the pain scale of 1 to 10. What is causing the recurrent pain?

Friends from church came to give Joe a blessing at 2 PM. Brother P said Joe's "suffering would be long but rewarding and that he would learn and be able to comfort others because of it."

I've had a week of disappointments and confusion, very little evident or appropriate care for Joe and loads of frustration. I ask the case manager if we can call a Family Care meeting to address my concerns.

Social Media post:

> That moment when you understand the difference between medical care and marketing....
>
> "Obviously there is nothing we can say to regain your trust.... If you don't like our facility you have two options: bring him to an emergency room and have him re-admitted, or call the original hospital and see if a doctor will take him back..."

Through daily updates with family and friends, I asked for help and prayers. Abundant support came quickly. From my sister Therese:

> For my sister, I am so sorry that you are carrying such troubles on your shoulders. God has a plan for you. I wish I could be there in a blink of an eye. You need an advocate with you on Thursday at the Care meeting for Joe. Stand your ground,

don't let anyone suggest that you can go elsewhere-how dare she! Maybe the Warriors need to be with you,ha,ha, maybe DPH [Department of Public Health] needs to know how staff is speaking to family members at such a[n] Acute Care Hospital. It's so maddening- love you xxxx

Wednesday March 5

Speech therapist did a clinical swallow test; gave Joe some pudding and asked him to swallow. He still has some oral incoordination. She tried nectar; he did cough, but spit it up, and the suction showed he is still aspirating. He is still too weak. Therapist said she was in on Monday to do the clinical swallow test, but Joe he politely refused, saying he was too tired.

He is instructed to practice swallowing and pharyngeal exercises. Although he cleared oral swallowing, this doesn't rule out mild oral weaknesses.

We are told there will be "spontaneous improvement." Exercises are (1) squeeze the throat and swallow hard. 2. Hold tongue, bite gently and swallow without pulling tongue out. He is very limited with pitch range. He tried to mimic the therapist's squeak, but didn't do very well. We are told to make this the third exercise to practice.

I receive a phone call from a teaching recruiter with whom I'm registered. She offers a job coach position, pay is in the low $20,000s. I tell her I have to think about it and will get back to her.

K Train called around noon time; he is concerned with the quality of the care Joe is receiving. We talk about the possibility of moving him to another facility. I tell him that I think the move will be too traumatic for him. Train will call some friends to see if he can pull some strings or get some answers. He warns me that Fat Dog, Rip and maybe someone from administration will be coming tomorrow.

Joe sat up at edge of the bed, and was moved to a wheelchair. He is losing weight: yesterday was 103.3, today 102.2 kg.

I'm watching Joe's health decline in a hospital where he should be rehabilitating. For every advance, it seems he suffers another setback. I share some of this with KTrain, who calls every day, but I am basically alone now in the room with Joe. The nurses only come to check on him when I call. Since he is off the ventilator and IV, it seems he is making good progress, but his elevated heart rate, pain and catheter bleeding are a puzzle. I seek out help from friends and family. Ellen tells me she knows the hospital Patient Advocate and gives me her phone number. I called and asked for the woman, but I'm told that hospital is not with the one where Joe is, and suggests if I have issues I should direct them to the hospital Director.

Exhausted, I make a note to call the next time I have a moment to myself. I try not to leave Joe's bedside when he is awake and lucid. He is struggling moment to moment.

March 6

Family Care meeting held to address a distressing list of questions and complaints I've had since Joe's admission. Complete disaster.

I needed some time to process what occurred during the Care meeting. Three days later, I was able to articulate some of my thoughts and reactions. Days and nights were blurred into one long string of stressful sorrows. Joe's versions of reality were also altered, but they were medically induced.

Meeting notes from Thursday:

> Joe had some "trauma", and he was put back on the ventilator. The main doctor said all patients come from ICU - and asked if Joe was better today than he was yesterday. He suggested that I see if I could take Joe back to the ICU at the original hospital seeing as I'm dissatisfied with the care he's receiving there.
>
> Skylor advocated for me and told story about her experience with hospitals, and said we can we do better...

The APRN said he takes pride in his work.

Doctor told us the Nurse to Nurse report said nothing about polyneuropathy, admitting when he first saw Joe, he thought he had a spinal cord injury.

Friday March 7

Flurry of attention today. Curious.

The admitting doctor suspected apnea could be affecting Joe's breathing and oxygen levels.

Met another doctor who was friends with HC friend A-bear. He told Joe the plan to do his respiratory therapy first. They shared stories about Hampshire Christian, and doctor asked Joe where from because of the way he said *fo-ah* in the word *fourteen*. Doctor introduced the cough assist and spoke about the Passy- Muir valve.

Earlier today I had records faxed to another rehab facility. Dr. was aware of this and asked Joe if this is truly what he wanted. Joe said he wasn't sure.

Social media post:

> The eight days Joe has been mouthing "Help me, help me, help me"...

> Still waiting for the Friday "I'll call you every day" call that was promised yesterday at our Family Care meeting...

Saturday 8 March

I posted a photo of another happy memory with Joe at the Fish Fest 2013 talking about New Zealand's critically endangered Maui dolphins. Who doesn't love him?

Crowdfunding update:

> Friends, family, angels--update from Rehab--Joe has "congestive heart failure" from all the meds; nurse said this is reversible, but it's another challenge on his long list of challenges. Good news is that he is a fighter and has already progressed through two steps of progress on his recovery chart. (Don't know how many there are...) He's fighting hard and has been moving his legs and arms, fingers and toes. Yeah, Warrior! Thank you for your continued support--very much appreciated and needed.

March 8

Skylor's post on my social media page:

> Joe looked great today! He's getting a little, cheeky pressing his call button every 2 seconds, just so I will have to turn it off. On-off-On-off-On-off-On-off. Then I looked squarely in Joe's eyes and said,

> "Yo, you touch that call button again, and I'll smack you!" He pulls a face at me, and pushes the button AGAIN!!

> Ah, it's great to get a slight handshake, his wonderful smile, a wink and a few words in his Mafia voice! We Love you Joe and Aoibhyann!

March 9

Trying to project hope, I posted this rant:

> Blessed Sunday! Happy thaw! This week marks six weeks since Joe and I were hospitalized and eight weeks since we became ill.

Joe is awake and speaking this morning; nurses had him looking at the sports section of the newspaper, and he is again wearing the Passy-Muir valve on his tracheostomy. He is brighter and making great gains, moving his muscles, shifting himself in bed, suctioning himself with the Yankauer when he coughs. Pain meds are still messing with his versions of day, night, time, and reality. Yesterday he was in Dubai, this morning he was in Ras al- Khaima (we visited there when we were living in the UAE).

I am grateful and blessed for all of the help and prayers and nonstop concern, support, monetary and spiritual assistance you have all provided, especially Skylor, who had been at his bedside regularly while he was in the ICU, and who has made incredible sacrifices for Joe, and for me.

Please do not misconstrue this next narrative. My intention is to illustrate the disparity in quality of health care for those who are incapacitated. It is not an indictment of health care providers; we have been blessed with superb doctors, nurses, CNAs, specialists, etc. I understand American (western) medicine is imperfect, and provided by people who put their pants on just like the rest of us. I understand that with complicated cases such as Joe's, there are no absolutes. We have been living in the gray area of healthcare.

This is not about me-it is about Joe and other patients like Joe and their caregivers. This is about a flubbed - up admission to a rehab hospital, and eight days that followed when he was unable to speak, move, or advocate for himself. This is about a meeting that was called to address my questions on day seven of Joe's admission during which I felt victimized, abused, badgered and bullied-and during which I asked questions that were not answered - questions that were suggested to me by other healthcare professionals who understood that those questions were my right as Joe's advocate, questions that I asked at the fifth hour following his admission, such as why, during his admission, was Joe handed a call bell and told to press the red button if he needed help. Huh? He could not speak and was paralyzed. When we did discover during this meeting that Joe's condition of critical illness polyneuropathy was not indicated in his discharge summary, the rehab hospital threw the other hospital under the bus.

Five minutes into the meeting, I was asked if Joe was better off since he was admitted or not? I hesitated. The doctor blew a gasket. This is about a doctor who was so distracted by the television on the wall in the room that he made little eye contact with me as I spoke, and who stood up in the middle of the family meeting, walked away from the table and tried to turn the television off. He was told by one of his minions that it doesn't turn off and he proceeded to frisk the television to find the off button. He returned to the table and then appeared distracted and preoccupied by something down the hall, so distracted that I asked him if there was an emergency he had to attend to, at which point he managed to finally make eye contact and shout *WHAT*? This is about a doctor who disallowed anyone from answering my questions, such as *May I see the Q15 chart?*(documenting nurses checking in on Joe every 15 minutes)-- finally throwing his hand across one of the nurses like a driver protecting his passenger from an imminent collision--and said "NO-we have been here for an hour and a half you are twisting all of our answers -- we are done" and proceeded to stand up (followed by his minions) and leave me and my two witnesses, Pearl and Skylor, sitting at the table.

Traumatized, I couldn't calm myself using any of the defaults I'd practiced. I fumbled around in my purse to find a Xanax (prescribed for me for stress and sleep); the bottle had opened and the teeny- tiny pills that had spilled out littered the bottom. I fumbled and cried, blubbered something about how abused and puny I felt. I fumbled and sobbed some more, until

Skylor could take no more. Gently, she asked, Aoibhyann, *what* are you *doing*? We dumped the contents of my purse on the table; Skylor found and recognized the unmarked pill, handed me one and refilled the bottle. I remained in my chair waiting for the medication to kick in.

> I only wanted to get answers about why Joe had to suffer lack of care-- I only wanted to advocate for him. I only want what's best for him --this is not about me, but about a wife acting on her husband's behalf.

During the meeting, I pointed out some glaring discrepancies, although there was no admission from the hospital staff, merely an indication that these issues would be addressed. Finally validated, I was told that I should forget about those first seven days, and move on. How can I forget about the first seven days of "healthcare" and "move on"? During the meeting I asked what the improved care would look like; how would it be different than the first seven days? No answer. I was promised the physician's assistant would call me every day; she has yet to call.

> This is about arrogant, absent doctors and overworked nurses, long spans of time during which Joe looks at me and mouths "Help!" after which the help doesn't come for more long spans of time. This about short- staffed weekends, waiting for forty minutes to get repositioned, receiving medications that are "as needed" when he finally has regained some flexibility so that he can ring the call bell-and then no one comes, or someone calls to ask what he needs but he is unable to speak or describe his discomfort, impaired by the trach... a patient who finally is able to hoarsely whisper one or two words at great expense of energy and so medicated that his thinking is fuzzy at times. How is he to articulate or advocate for himself?

> I wonder about other patients who do not have advocates, and I worry about what happens to Joe when I am not present. People ask me how I am feeling, how I'm I sleeping? How

am I handling this? I ask about the Red Sox. People remind me that Joe is improving, that the very fact that he is alive is a miracle, that he is showing great gains. All of this is not lost with me-I am keenly aware of the miracle of Joe's life and his improbable swift recovery. This is not about that. This is about looking forward and trying to discern if the quality of care that Joe is receiving is consistent throughout our healthcare system with other incapacitated patients.

This is about my husband who has mouthed *Help me Help me Help* me every day since his admission to this rehab hospital. One of the nurses at this hospital told me that Joe would not remember any of this. I will.

My task is to look my husband in the eye when he does have periods of apparent lucidity and convince him how great he's doing, how hard he's working, how proud we are of him, and deal with the look on his face that only a spouse can understand. He mouths the words *Get me out of here* nearly every day. I've been with him when he is frustrated by his inability to explain himself, identify his pain, or describe his needs. This is not about me, but I'm the one who can document this, and I thought you all should know.

I thank you for your guidance, help, prayers, suggestions. I consider them all. Please know I am doing what I feel is right, what I understand to be best for Joe, given the current set of circumstances. I'm working on this like a wet hen on steroids! Stay tuned.

March 11

"But sanctify the Lord God in your hearts: and be ready always to give an answer to every man that asketh you a reason of the hope that is in you with meekness and fear..." ~1 Peter 15

"...yes must press forward with a steadfastness in Christ, having a perfect brightness of hope, and a love of God and of all men..." ~2 Nephi 31:20

"Angels speak by the power of the Holy Ghost; wherefore they speak the words of Christ...I said unto you, feast upon the words of Christ, for behold, the words of Christ will tell you all the things what ye should do." ~2 Nephi 32:3

March 12

Learned what "Foam In, Foam Out" meant, and learned how to do it properly, sterilizing hands when entering and exiting a patient's room. A task analysis: rub palms together, interlock fingers and rub, cup fingers together and slide back and forth, swipe palms up and over thumbs. I was providing hands-on care for Joe, and didn't want to be responsible for spreading germs and making his condition worse (if that was even possible).

I was with him during the day his catheter was removed. Standard procedure, they explained, saying a catheter shouldn't be in for longer than a month or so. The nurse removed his first catheter, the original which was inserted on January 27th, in place for more than thirty five days, and inserted a second one. Shortly after the second one was inserted, tiny blood clots appeared in the tubing, so small they might be easily missed. I observed a thin red line of blood flowing through his tubing, along with those tiny clots, and blood at the external urinary opening (called the urinary meatus). Again, I was told this was normal, and when I pressed the nurse for an explanation, she told me (in almost these exact words) "sometimes the catheter is in for so long that it adheres to the mucous membranes...when it's removed, these membranes tear a little, so blood can be expected." I asked her to repeat what she had said, as I couldn't imagine the process.

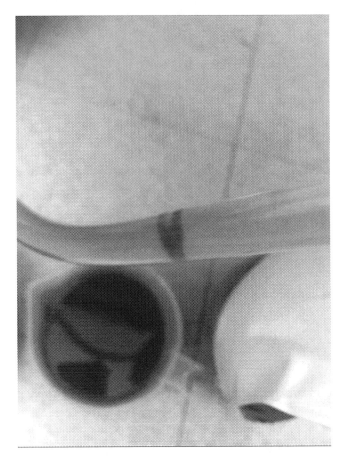

The thin red line of blood, clots and bleeding from the meatus area worsened over the next few days. Joe complained of pain in the general low abdominal area, and at the area where the catheter had been inserted. We asked the nurses to request more pain meds, and finally a prescription for lidocaine was approved and applied for some relief. The lidocaine tube was locked neatly in the medicine cabinet between administrations, a strange routine. I wondered why Joe just couldn't have access to the lidocaine gel whenever he needed it. Rules, I understood, but still, they appeared ridiculous. Not as if Joe had a hangnail and was asking for morphine.

During this ordeal, physical therapists had goals for Joe, and were eager to assist him with sitting up in bed. He had not done so in over a month, being comatose and then flaccid with polyneuropathy. He had been out of bed in a sling, but not of his own volition or ability. One day, the two therapists arrived and informed him the goal for the day was to sit him up and allow him to hang his legs over the side of the bed. Seemed innocuous enough. These two waifish women prepared Joe, lifted his torso and then pivoted his body, and swung his legs over the side of the bed. He had no muscle tone. For the first time, I observed his upright body, his feeble chicken legs and arms, his neck so limp that his head fell forward. Therapists asked him to keep his head up, to lift his toes on one foot, then another, to hold his arms stiff so he could balance. I took a picture, with one therapist wishing not to be included. She can be seen hiding behind Joe, in the pink shirt.

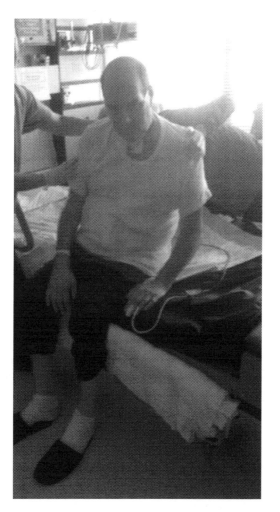

As successful as this first sit-up was, the therapists expected more in the following days. Their next goal was to assist Joe in a standing position using a contraption that looks like a stair climber in a gym, without the stairs. The Sara (Standing and Raising Aid) device was wheeled in and placed in front of Joe's bed. He was moved to a sitting position and then strapped into the device, with a diaper-like sling wrapped between his legs and around his bottom and hips. The diaper was connected to the device. Therapists placed Joe's hands and arms on the handles, feet on the footrests of the device and activated the remote control which hoisted Joe from a sitting positon to standing by lifting his bottom up (via the diaper sling) and raising his arms at the same time. It looked awkward and uncomfortable, but what did I know? The therapists were the experts, and Joe did need to start moving again. Joe could only "stand" for a minute, maybe less, before he grimaced and his body shook.

I thought he was making progress.

I did notice his bloody catheter tube sticking out from between the material of the diaper sling and his leg. I noticed when the diaper sling was removed, his urinary meatus was bleeding again, and the blood in the tube seemed to be increasing. I don't recall anyone anchoring the tube to his thigh, a practice that I would later learn is fairly standard so the catheter doesn't move when the leg does.

A day or two passes, and the blood, clots and bleeding and pain in the abdomen and urethra are somewhat better. A decision is made to remove the catheter altogether. We rejoice that he is one tube less and one step closer to recovery! We await the first pass of urine, and at last, at about 8PM Joe tells me he has to pee, so I happily hold the plastic urinal under him to catch a glorious 125 CCs of dark golden liquid. It's the celebrations of little things that make a world of difference. I don't notice red blood, and don't see any blood at the urinary meatus site, so I'm confident I can go home. I'm comfortable that he'll have a better night than he has had the past week.

Later in the night, Joe rings for help because he has to urinate. No one comes. He fumbles with his plastic urinal, attempting to place it between his legs, and pees. He feels relieved, and leaves it there because it's easier than trying to pick it up and place it somewhere. The liquid he peed felt different than urine. He brings his hands up to his face and sees blood. He rings the bell again. No one comes. No one calls into his room. He has no idea of time, newly wakened from over a month of medicine-induced coma.

When finally one of his favorite nurses comes to check on him – the only nurse on duty for twenty four beds- Joe tells her to look at his hands. She sees the blood, pulls the sheets back and gasps "Oh my God! What happened?" She gets on the phone to call for assistance and is told to call the ambulance.

The ambulance EMTs arrive, and ask where they should take Joe. They are told to take him back to the original hospital, a thirty- five minute drive. One EMT shouts, "No Way! If you want me to transport this patient I am taking him to the nearest hospital that has a doctor on duty!" The nurse tells the EMTs that they have to take him to the original hospital, and they argue back in forth while Joe lies on the gurney in the hallway, bleeding.

Social media update: (here we go again)

> Joe in emergency room. Clots in bladder. Brought in some time before midnight last night. Prayers....

I posted the photo of the clot in the tube, explaining:

> Just one of about two dozen clots Joe has passed today. He is excruciating pain when these "bladder spasms" occur, lasting for about forty minutes. He could use a visit from happy friendly faces...10th floor, orange elevators, main hospital. Thanks for your prayers.

Joe was brought from the seventh floor (for general care) to the "higher level of care" respiratory floor. The admitting nurse collected information from me and from Joe, suggested I find an advocate, and told us she would recommend he be moved to the respiratory floor, as she deemed him in need of more care than what would be provided on that floor. Why did he need respiratory care? I wondered. He was bleeding through his urethra. It seemed no one could look at the big picture, reminding me of the story about people holding different parts of an elephant and not recognizing which animal it was. Someone held the tail, another the trunk, another a leg, etc. Later in the day, I hit the proverbial wall of despair, frustration and grief.

My social media post:

> My turn: *Help me! Help me*! I have no idea what Joe needs... case manager talking to me about making referrals to other places. She determined Joe needs a consult with a physiatrist (?) who can oversee the big picture. We don't need more of the same. Why is this so difficult??? Heaven help us.

A pair of urologists, a male and a female, checked in on Joe in the new room on the new floor, and asked us questions. I explained the origin and genesis of Joe's issues, starting with H1N1 flu, organ failure and cardiac arrest, ARDS, rehab, ending with the current problem, paraphrasing what the nurse at the rehab hospital told me: bleeding is normal when a catheter is replaced, that the tubing sometimes sticks to the mucous membranes. The urologists glared at me as if I was speaking in tongues. They didn't have much to tell me.

I would repeat the explanation of how Joe's bleeding began. Doctors continued to look at me uneasily. I knew something was not quite right, and I knew they knew. I understood that doctors do not want to implicate other doctors or nurses, but I wanted to push the issue because I had a feeling something was wrong. I was beyond my limits of patience and way outside of my wheelhouse trying to comprehend how Joe survived death and appeared to be rehabbing, only to wind up in another emergency room and another hospital, with another emergency, apparently bleeding from his bladder.

Had been sleeping in the hospital chair the nurses provided for me, needing to stay with Joe during this period of waiting and watching and continuous bladder irrigation (CBI). A gallon-sized bag of sterile saline had been flushing Joe's bladder. He was experiencing painful spasms, the frequency of which depended upon when the drainage bag was more than half full, leaving the fluid nowhere to go but to fill his bladder. I learned this through observation. When the nurse emptied the drainage bag Joe would feel relief. But whenever the nurses were busy and the drainage bag was nearly full, the spasms and pain began. I watched the nurses empty the bag and measure the urine output enough that I felt confident to do the same whenever the drainage bag was reaching half full.

I was leaving the three measuring cups of bloody urine under the bed near the drainage bag so I didn't accidentally kick them over. Nurses would usually say nothing to me when they finally did arrive to record the output, as if we had a silent and mutual understanding. It was apparent that Joe's nurses were overextended and had other patients who were needier than he.

Through the nights, I slept when Joe slept, but remained vigilant to monitor the bag so he wasn't awakened by pain and spasms. I monitored his medication bags too, so to prevent them from beeping when empty, I'd go to the nurse's station and tell them. The hospital chair was hard, and the room was freezing. I shivered through the night, in and out of sleep, inches away from Joe.

Days seemed to be slightly better staffed, so I was able to go home for a few hours, take care of business and shower before returning. Since Joe was wearing the Passy-Muir valve over his trach, he was able to speak for himself and express his needs.

Two days and nights passed as the continuous bladder irrigation produced bags and bags of bloody urine. By the afternoon of Thursday the 13th, Joe was giving up. He had only been on an insufficient dose of meds to take the edge off the pain, but his condition had worsened and no one reacted. He may have been seen by a doctor or urologist while I was home, but I never saw one when I was there.

His urine drainage bag was perpetually clogged, so nurses fumbled with his catheter to see if they could restart the flow.

Communication about Joe's progress was poor. Nurses were pleasant enough, and seemed to be trying, but we were getting nowhere. Nurses who tended to Joe were constantly being paged, or called on their mobile phones, so while they were dealing with him, they were assessing the situation with another patient. Joe was a patient patient, but after two days he reached a point of exhaustion and breakdown.

I didn't know what the plan was, and didn't understand why my husband had to suffer. Flashbacks of watching my dying mother ran through my head. Why was this so complicated? Was Joe dying? What was causing the problem, and why wasn't anyone doing anything for his pain? Why weren't we solving anything? The situation was definitely worse than when he arrived. If a patient can't receive proper care at an award-winning hospital, where can he?

I was holding Joe's hand, standing over him, coaching him to breathe through the spasms, as if he was in labor.

> "Look at that picture of the lighthouse. Focus on it. Breathe with me. Close your mouth. Smell the roses, blow out the candles.
>
> Breathe in...one...two....three...four...five...six...seven... eight...Now exhale slowly...eight ...seven...six...five... four...three...two....one. Great Joe, hang on..."

We did this for hours. Joe was quivering, and white as a sheet. I called nurses who would eventually arrive. I asked them to please increase his pain meds and get a doctor. They said Urology was called. But no one came.

> "I can't do this anymore. I want to die. I want to give up. I can't. I can't. I can't. Help me, Jesus. Help me. Where is the doctor?"

Joe squeezed my hand at the start of another spasm. Then, he let go and began to writhe, throwing his arms around and slamming them against the bed railings so violently, he ripped out his intravenous line. Focused on his face and trying to coach him, I didn't notice the pool of blood on the floor.

> "HEY! LOOK AT ME! You are NOT giving up. You haven't come this far to die now. You're NOT going to die. LOOK AT ME! Get control over yourself. You did this before and you can do it again. Breathe with me, honey. It's all in the breath. Sssshhhhhh…Slooooowwww your heart…You know how to do this…Breeeeeethe…One…two…three…four…"

As Joe's advocate, coach and eternal partner, I knew what had to be done. I prayed a more fervent prayer than I'd ever prayed.

> "Heavenly Father, your son Joe has had enough. Please help us."

And at once, I was inspired to call upon Joe's mother, a stern Emergency room nurse who had passed away in 2010:

> "Catherine, I know you're watching. I know you're here. If anyone can help us now, you can. We know you can get things done. We need to you kick some butt downstairs and bring a doctor up those ten floors to this room. Joe's done. Please, inspire someone to come here and help him. Please. We know you can. He needs you."

I returned to coaching and breathing with Joe. A nurse arrived again and saw the bloody floor. She called a phlebotomist to re-insert an IV line. I continued to monitor Joe's urine output and drainage bag. It was still clogged.

Within minutes, a urology team marched into the room. (Thank you, Catherine. Atta girl!) The young doctor wore his coat draped across him arm, as if he wasn't planning to stay long. He asked Joe what was happening, but Joe was too exhausted to explain, begging.

"You gotta help me, Doc. Don't leave me! Don't leave me."

The doctor doubled the doses of pain meds for Joe, rested his coat on the chair, and rolled up his sleeves. He attempted to adjust Joe's catheter, pushing it just millimeters further into the bladder, and then watched and waited to see if urine would flow. It didn't. He asked his assistants to fill syringes with saline, and told Joe he was going to remove the plugged catheter, drain it and manually extract urine (instead of allowing it to drain into the bag). Once the doctor removed the catheter, we could see the bloody clots and understood why there was no drainage. This was not good news, but at least we knew the cause. Using the syringe, the doctor flushed the catheter, reinserted it, slipped a syringe onto the drainage end of the tube, and began to manually extract bloody, clotted urine through the tube into the syringe. A brilliant idea, but no simple job.

Doctor pulled hard on the syringe, filled it with blood and clots, and then gave it to one assistant who emptied it into a plastic bucket. He took an empty syringe from the other assistant and completed the cycle. Pull hard, empty into bucket, pull hard, empty into bucket, remove clogged catheter, flush, jam and plunge catheter back in, pull hard, empty into bucket...

The doctor grunted with every extraction. He was sweating. Two half-full buckets of bloody clots, syringes and bloody gloves on the bed made it look more like a crime scene. One assistant left the room, saying, "I'm going to have to step out, doctor. I'm not sure if it's the blood or the smell, but I have to leave."

The grueling process of pulling clots from Joe's bladder through the catheter continued. Joe was quiet and relieved from a combination of increased pain medication and a somewhat empty bladder. I was thankful for angels like Catherine and the Urology team. I can only speculate who else was watching over us.

March 14

Social media post:

Good morning everyone- Update: Rushed to his third hospital early this week due to problems with his catheter. He has been receiving continuous bladder irrigation which is like an IV only through the catheter. The urologist worked on him last night for several hours because he has been passing clots which clogged his catheter and caused a distended and spastic bladder – horribly painful. They performed an emergency CT scan last night as they suspected a perforated bladder, hernia or prostate problems, but everything checked out fine. (Really?) Nothing found except the clots in his bladder and constant bleeding. They suspect this is because of the length of time the catheters had been there - since January 27 for the first one, and then February 28, and then another last week. Nurses tell me that no organ likes a foreign body - and tries to reject it.

He received two more units of blood last night because of the amount of blood loss.

Urologists will perform a cystoscopy today during which his urethra and bladder will be scoped and any tissue, fibers, cysts can be removed or cauterized to stop the bleeding.

Despite it all, Joe has tried to rebound, joking with the nurses and smiling when he's not writhing in pain. Staff here is excellent and all shifts have kept on top of his care, vitals, discomfort etc.

Thankful and grateful to our heavenly Father for keeping Joe in His arms, and to all of you for your prayers and constant support. Will post another update following surgery. You can rest assured he is in the best place now for his needs. I'm at his bedside as I write this and he is resting comfortably. He has been speaking with the Passy -Muir valve on his trach and has become more and more lucid and aware of his circumstances as the heavy meds are being reduced.

He is so grateful to you all; please know how much your prayers mean to him (and me).

Along with Catherine, the young urologist and the nurses who stayed with Joe, other angels arrived. Dr. N and another urologist greeted me the following morning to explain the surgery. They were patient, tender, kind, thorough and comforting. An old high school friend sent me a note to inform me that Dr. N was the best; her father was a urologist and worked with him. She told me I could have complete trust in him.

As Joe was being prepped, a representative from another rehab hospital interviewed me. She told me her hospital had just lost a patient who succumbed to H1N1 flu. He arrived through the same airport where Joe worked, fell ill, was brought to the hospital and died four days later.

The cystoscopy was performed; the perforation in Joe's bladder was cauterized, and he tolerated the procedure well. Orders were for him to rest in bed for seven to ten days, to move him back to the seventh floor. The following day, he acquired a fever and began coughing again.

March 16

Social media update:

> Pneumonia, anemia ... *again. Back on IV antibiotics and two more units of blood. Sheesh. How about them Red Sox?

> Been thinking today: life is hard, so many of us are holding on to some kind of hurt. It's no wonder we lose our faith; we seek solace and comfort in this world--but it is only temporary. I'm so blessed to know what I know and feel what I feel. Wishing you love and peace today. I'm soothed when I listen to church hymns and popular Christian music.

March 17 St. Patrick's Day

The events of the past few days took their toll on Joe, and on me. I stayed home sick, rested on the couch, investigated rehab hospitals and missed Joe. My social media post the next morning indicated progress and promise:

> Finding hope where I can. Good Monday morning: miracle last night. In desperation because I was home all day with a sore throat, I called Joe's nursing station for an update. The nurse was too busy to speak with me (shift change?) but told me he had "a good night" after he sat up in the chair for a few minutes.

What I didn't portray in my social media post:

Terror- stricken after hearing Joe was out of bed, I stuttered "NO, no, no -- you have the wrong patient, my husband is Joe. Joseph, in Room 1050! He's not able to get out of bed! What is happening?? He just had surgery and the doctor said bed rest for ten to fourteen days!"

The nurse assured me she was speaking about Joe and called his room phone, handed it to him and he spoke to me. I wept, like I haven't wept since the first time I saw him in the ICU. "I lost you once, twice, three times already! The doctor said bed rest! I'm afraid you are going to put another hole in your bladder!" Sobbing. "Did you tear your catheter out again?" Sobbing. "I miss you!" More sobbing. "I can't take this anymore!" Still sobbing. "It's been two months...I want you to come home now! I can't lose you. I can't handle this. I can't."

So there was my sweet husband Joe, consoling me, his hysterical, blubbering wife, telling me it was only for a few minutes while they changed the bed because he spilled his ice chips, telling me he was fine, telling me there is no blood in his urine, there is no blood on his catheter, telling me everything is going to be okay.

After I calmed down, we spoke of our prayers. Father in heaven, my hope rests in you. Amen.

Joe remembers the large, muscular male CNA. He acted as if he liked Joe and was always kind to him. He had asked if there was anything he could for him. Feeling claustrophobic, but still struggling with neuropathy, Joe said he just needed to *sit up*. It was an almost impossible request. The CNA complied, lifting Joe out of the bed like a fireman would with one arm around his neck and one under his bent legs, and sat him in the chair. Joe remembers saying *Ohhhh this feels great*! Then I called and burst the bubble.

March 18

> Best news of the day: Dr. Ir told Joe he was the "most stable patient on the floor"! Wooo hooooo!

Urology team came to visit Joe and discuss his prognosis. I probed the question again of how Joe's catheter replacement caused bleeding, and how his bladder seemingly developed a hole. The female urologist apparently could hear no more of it; she crossed her arms and firmly told me "I'm sorry, you keep saying that the catheter was stuck to the mucous membranes, but *that just doesn't happen*. Think about it: they're called *mucous* membranes (she emphasized the word) – they're slippery with *mucous*."

I reminded the urologist that I was merely repeating what I was told by the nurse at the first rehab hospital. I was satisfied, however. I didn't need to press the issue any longer.

March 21

> Joe's discharge to a new rehab hospital was pushed to today, Friday – because of an insurance authorization delay. He is ready! Phenomenal care at this hospital, especially Dr. Ir, and the CNA from the 10th floor who came down to give a goodbye hug. We are blessed to have been in your care.

Joe's Discharge Summary notes, verbatim. We eventually would call attorneys to see if there was enough evidence for a malpractice suit against the first rehab hospital. There wasn't. Each attorney asked us the same question: what permanent damage has Joe suffered as a result? They explained that we might have had a case if a doctor removed the wrong limb or organ. (I would certainly hope so!) The bottom line is that pain, suffering and perforated organs are evidently not claimable in our state.

Discharge Diagnosis:

1. Gross hematuria likely secondary to recent history of Foley catheter manipulation
2. Extraperitoneal bladder perforation
3. Acute blood loss anemia
4. Adjustment disorder with anxiety features
5. History of chronic respiratory failure, status post tracheostomy
6. History of severe pharyngeal dysphagia status post gastrostomy on tube feeds
7. History of hypertension
8. History of colostomy with Hartmann's pouch
9. General debility secondary to multiple comorbidities status post recent hospitalizations.

This hospital's gifted urologists finally addressed the securing of Joe's catheter, including it in the discharge instructions for all of his following caregivers to employ:

1. Foley catheter must be secured to patient's thigh at all times to avoid any traction…this is especially important when the patient is mobile with physical therapy or otherwise.

The miracle of the past several weeks' events is that Joe finally received excellent care in the hands of caring, responsive and talented professionals at the third hospital.

Chapter 5

Progress

The new rehab hospital- the fourth hospital - is everything the old rehab hospital wasn't. His physiatrist doctor, Dr. L, saw Joe upon his admission. Therapists are lined up and ready to work *with* Joe, not *on* him. Our advocate, Barb, is overseeing every aspect of Joe's care, beginning with a summary of the care plan. Dr. L is a Hampshire Christian graduate – a fortuitous coincidence. He is a meticulous manager who coordinates Joe's therapy and makes swift work of removing of Joe's feeding tube and trach within the first few days of his arrival, as well as beginning to wean Joe off of his pain meds.

Joe is earning his nickname again, surpassing all therapists' expectations. Determined to go home, he consistently gives a little bit more than asked, and pushes himself harder.

Joe's swollen, arthritic knees are the most problematic impediment to his walking therapy. Despite losing seventy pounds, he's still a big guy – six feet one inch tall, two hundred and seventeen pounds bearing down on jelly muscles. Sore knees bear the brunt of his weight while standing and walking.

Speech therapy (swallow test) was not going well. Joe failed the test twice – the first was at the hospital before this one. We learned that this is not uncommon. Included among the atrophied muscles are those of the swallowing process. The esophagus cannot move food and liquids from the back of mouth to the stomach; coordination of movements that allow a person to breath, swallow and talk is complicated. Joe diligently practiced the prescribed laryngeal/pharyngeal conditioning exercises intended to strengthen the muscles of the neck, mouth and throat. Most times, he wheeled himself to the bathroom and practiced in front of the mirror. Aaaaaahh. Uuuugggggh. Grunt. He held his tongue and swallowed, lifted his head, ran his tongue over his teeth. Hearing this, his roommate Mick sometimes called out to him to ask if he is okay.

Blessings continued: An X-Ray technician from the first rehab hospital approached Joe while was working out in the physical therapy room. She asked him if he was a patient at that first hospital and told him that she thought she recognized him. Joe affirmed, apologizing that he didn't remember her. She expressed amazement that he was alive and doing as well as he was, and explained that she was Torrey who did the admission X rays on him. Torrey performed the barium swallow test X rays on Joe and came to check on him occasionally.

During one visit, Torrey intimated that she was a person of faith – a believer. Heavy duty conversation followed. She bore her soul to us, telling us that she was in the proverbial gutter before she found Jesus Christ. She shared her philosophy on life - Joe and I agreed: Most of the things we worry about are trivial; they simply don't matter in the grand scheme. She told us that Christ is the center of her life, and we agreed.

The feeling of joy under Dr. L's and other care providers was bittersweet. But the "system" once again would raise its incredibly disorganized, unprofessional head. Generally, though, we were looking forward to Joe's final discharge to home.

Late March

> Warrior walked almost 100 feet today with the walker. Enjoying time with childhood friends Big Cosmo and SJ. Good friends are a salve for the spirits.

Patrick's birthday today. I'm one thousand times more grateful for him, and for the experience of motherhood. I delighted in posting his baby pictures, and a picture of me and my giant belly just days before I went into labor.

March 27

> Warrior walked twice around the gym this morning with the walker. Downsizing his cannula which may be the last step before trach removal. Thank you Father in heaven for our church friends who are volunteering to rehab our bathroom to accommodate Joe's mobility needs. Demo begins this Saturday. How blessed we are.

March 28

> Warrior had his trach removed yesterday. Can you believe how he is progressing? Everyone tells him he is way ahead of schedule. That's my Joey! Demo begins on the bathroom tomorrow. I wouldn't be surprised if Joe would be there to help. Miracles abound. Thank you merciful heavenly Father.

Example of good intentions paving the road to you-know-where. Seeing progress, I figured Joe could use some incentive to continue, so I brought him a photo I'd taken of the red-winged blackbirds who had returned to the yard- a sure sign of spring.

> "Look, honey, it's going to be spring soon! The blackbirds returned!"

Instead of being encouraged, he cried a child's cry, "I want to go home now."

March 29

> Thank you, 101 year - old house, for keeping us warm and safe
> and dry. Honoring you and the hearts and hands who built
> you, the love that was shared here, the lives who came before
> us here. Thank you walls and floors and tiny bathroom.
> Pondering life in 1913 and appreciating the original owners
> who worked the dairy farm on this property. Feeling very
> much in touch with them today...they are here with us.

March 31

The International Court of Justice ruled that Japan's "scientific research"
whaling in the Southern Ocean was illegitimate. I was not encouraged:

> Celebrate with us today, as this is a tremendous milestone
> and accomplishment wrought by hands, hearts and minds of
> incredibly diligent and brave people. But be forewarned: Be
> watchful of the backlash! Mark my words! And let's not forget
> #Taiji or all of the captive cetaceans, all of the imperiled
> marine life worldwide, and catastrophic state of our ocean.
> Celebrate today - Yes. Take our eyes off the goal - *NEVER*.

April 1

> Waiting for Joe to return from his third barium swallow test.
> He is weak and sad today, wanting to give up. I did a cheer
> for him (Joey Joey he's our man, if he can't swallow, no one
> can!) and threatened to do a jump in his room, in my clogs,
> however they have a very strict slip and fall policy here.

> Joe's roommate, Mick, eats three times a day. Joe can smell
> the food through the closed curtain between them, and it's
> stimulating his appetite. I reminded Joe of the verse "I can
> do all things, through Christ who gives me strength." Please,
> Lord, can we change the status board to reflect the food that

he can eat, by mouth, beginning today April 1, instead of NPO (nothing by mouth)? Warrior needs this victory. Amen.

Later that day:

First meal! Small bites, turn head, hard swallows. Thank you Lord!

Joy would be interrupted. The rehab hospital made a doctor's appointment at an off-site location. The case manager asked me how I planned to transport him there. *Really?* More salt in a wound.

Social media rant:

> Dear people with jobs in health care: Is it too much to ask if you would actually *read* the fine details in the paperwork? This is your job, yes? Caregivers with loved ones in the hospital have already been through hell and don't need any more stressors or crises. And don't use insurance companies as an excuse for your imprecision (read: mess -up). No, I won't be transporting (driving) my debilitated, wheelchair-bound husband to his urologist for a cystoscopy, nor will I be transporting him back to his room. He is still *your* patient; YOU transport him, and make sure the insurance company pays, not me. PS I want a job like yours, where I can make mistakes and the only consequence is someone else's suffering. Rant for the day. Out.

More blessings from the hearts of children: PE, one of the daughters of dear church friends, insisted that she visit Joe. Since she is in a wheelchair and one of several children, her Mom had to make arrangements to set the time aside so that she and PE could travel. They visited with Joe for several hours. PE told Joe that she had challenged everyone at church while bearing her testimony to pray for him so that he would get well.

She is a bright spot in our lives. She never fails to bear her testimony about her beliefs. Her demeanor is fresh and innocent, humbling and inspiring. After several hours, her Mom told her it was time to go, but PE persisted. "No, Mom, I have to stay here and take care of Joe because he needs me.

I'm not leaving him." This made Joe cry. Her mother told her gently that Joe needed to rest and that the nurses would take good care of him.

PE's visit, along with visits by childhood friends Big Cosmo and SJ were highlights of stay at the final rehab hospital.

April 3

> Discharge date = Saturday! Took a selfie today post- catheter removal..first sunshine since mid-January. Blessings continue...

Thanks to Dr. L, Joe's expert physical therapists and Joe's grit, he will have been in rehab a short *fifteen days*, rather than three to five months as was originally estimated.

How is this possible?

April 4

Barb the advocate arranges for a team to install a railing at the front steps. My father generously handed me cash to pay for the job.

> Thanks to the carpenters for a pro job on the railing. Imagine Joey walking up these steps to home, finally..tomorrow!

April 6

> Saying good bye to the best roommate, Mick. Plans for a reunion day of fishing are on the horizon. Thanking our heavenly Father; Joe slept comfortably in his own bed last night for the first time in nearly three months. Hats off to all bedside nurses!

The most unexpected consequences of Joe's return home were his loneliness and depression; he missed 'round the clock care, doctors, nurses, friends and attention he received in the hospitals. He called Skylor and told her he missed her. I was feeling inadequate.

Chapter 6

Angels, and Mothering

April 7

Healing has begun. Enjoying the prayer shawl our friend Rita knit, Donald's guardianship and a blessed Sunday's sunshine and fresh air.

Can you believe it? 5 days out of rehab. Praise God.

April 13

Thank you Julie and Jack...delicious brunch, fantastic company and conversation, happy days. Love you and appreciate you for all the support and prayers.

April 17 Crowdfunding update:

Dear Friends, Family, Angels --Your generous donations are much appreciated. Joe is doing so well at home, exceeding everyone's expectations and surpassing goals. He has been working hard with the therapists on home visits, walking nearly 1/8 of a mile today with only the cane! Your contribution to this fund will help me to stay at home to help with Joe's rehab; neither of us is working, and I can't envision my working full-time for quite a while. Joe will need the ostomy reversal surgery in no less than six months, so it will be a long, long road before we are gainfully employed again. Our specific goal is to construct a handicapped-accessible seasonal room off of our back patio so that Joe has a sheltered location outside from where he can do gardening, therapy, etc. and not be stuck on the living room couch in our tiny 101-year old house. New England weather is always changing; we had snow here a few days ago and last night the temperature was 26 degrees F! Many thanks for making our dream a reality.

April 20 Easter, my favorite holiday – the celebration of Christ's rising from the dead

Sleepless, 3AM, walking the cats under moonlight; the leash snagged a thorny branch. Reaching to free it, I am pricked once, twice, thrice--and then-- I understand, and am humbled. Thank you, father, for allowing your blameless son to die and rise for us. Thank you, brother Jesus, for showing us The Way.

April 23

The wound is the place where the light enters you. -Rumi Posted by S M about the Bonneville Dam sea lions. So apropos. Another post that sustained me:

"Cry out to Him: I'm desperate for you. I'm lost without you. You are my daily bread, your very word spoken to me. I will love Him and adore Him. I will bow down before Him. ...my Prince of Peace." (Michael J. Smith "Breathe" Live) The violin in this song is chilling, and reminds me of our friend Emily who often played the violin at church.

On a visceral level, I understand desperation. I understand the fortitude that animal advocates must constantly summon to deal with incredibly horrific situations like the killing of sea lions for doing what sea lions do – eating salmon. I understand what the observers in Taiji must experience each time the killing boats return with a family of frantic dolphins or whales, herded into the killing cove and brutally slaughtered for food or selected for entertainment in aquariums around the world. I can't imagine what dedication and strength is required to stand as witnesses to this barbarism which goes on for six months every year. I am friends with two such witnesses. They are extraordinary human beings. I doubt I could do what they do. I wonder if they could do what I've done.

April 25

> Happy Birthday in heaven, Mom. You would have been 80 today. Having just visited with Joe in heaven, I thank you for being there for him, and for me. Love never dies.

April 30 From Charles on the occasion of our 8th wedding anniversary:

> *"I wed thee forever, not for now;*
> *Nor for the sham of earth's brief years.*
> *I wed thee for the life beyond the tears,*
> *Beyond the heart pain and the clouded brow.*
> *Love knows no grave, and it will guide us, dear,*
> *When life's spent candles flutter and burn low."*
> (Marvelous Work and a Wonder, 203). Elder Bruce R. McConkie

May 3

Joe's birthday. I'm thinking about his birthday in 2008; we snorkeled with manta rays in Kona, on Big Island, Hawai`i. Precious memories such as these comfort me and are available whenever I need to escape into reverie.

Joe is feeling stronger and slightly more independent, more able to care for himself. From the shower chair he calls and asks me to wash his back. Our days are settling into a fairly acceptable routine, our new normal. I've accepted the downsides of cleaning his ostomy bag. Not so bad since we learned a trick from one of the CNAs at the rehab hospital; adding mint flavored mouthwash to the bag before emptying it masks the odor. We've named Joe's stoma "Stan" and determined that he has a mind of his own.

We are thankful that Joe's bowels (and Stan) are working and look forward to when the ostomy can be reversed.

After Joe toweled off from his shower, he walked into the kitchen, naked. I saw his abdomen, bisected from sternum to groin, and the ostomy bag, not for the first time. I had seen his naked body every day in the hospital bed. I watched the nurses clean and dress his open wounds, and I saw his stage four decubitus (bed sore). I also cleaned his wounds, washed his back, massaged him from foot to head, did Reiki on him, rubbed coconut oil on him for months. Today was not the first time I had seen his body, but today felt like the first, and I gasped, and cried "Oh honey, what have they done to you?" and sunk down onto the kitchen floor.

I've been having a difficult time being Joe's full-time nurse. Since we became ill in January, I pushed myself beyond exhaustion. The rehab hospital wouldn't accept Joe without a discharge plan that included someone at home to care for him. When the representative first mentioned this, I said I couldn't be there for Joe because someone had to work, and it obviously wasn't going to be Joe. His admission was denied. A rehab hospital in Springfield, Massachusetts 30 minutes from home was suggested-a poor option. I relented, and told the preferred rehab hospital I would stay home to care for Joe, asking them to reconsider. His admission was approved, and thus began my career in at-home nursing and caretaking.

May 9

I've been nursing Joe full time for four weeks. Our Primary Care Physician Doctor K told me yesterday: "There is no shame if you have anxiety and depression. You have been through a lot! It's about time your body caught up with you."

May 11 - Mother's Day

We decided we would return someday to the ICU when Joe was more mobile and comfortable in a car. We thought Mother's Day would be a great day to do so. Joe was ready. He knew he wouldn't recognize anyone. We wanted to thank everyone for their awesome care, and give them all some reassurance that some people in the ICU do not leave there on their way to the morgue. I was ready. I needed to make some happy Mother's Day memories.

We first stopped in the lobby to use the rest room. As we rounded the corner to the lobby, C was pushing a discharged patient in a wheelchair to the exit. She caught a glimpse of Joe, stopped in her tracks and began to weep. Joe walked (with his cane) to her and hugged her. She was limp. Backing away from him, she stared at him in awe, saying, "I never thought I'd see you like this! You look so good!" The woman waited patiently in the wheelchair. We explained what had happened from the time he left the ICU in January until the present day. Wishing her a happy Mother's Day, we said our goodbyes and let her return to her duties.

Walking the same route with Joe through the hospital lobby where I vomited, up the elevator to the third floor, to the speaker behind the locked double doors was surreal. I pressed the button and when K's voice came through the speaker, I said, "Hi K, this is Aoibhyann, I have Joe with me. He'd like to…."

The door swung open. K walked briskly towards us, and gasped.

> "Joe, this is K. She has been my true support throughout your stay here. She was always available for me on the phone, she made sure I was comfortable when I was in your room, she brought me hot drinks and cared for me."

I missed her. Most of the hospital staff had become like family to me.

Joe hugged K as others started to gather around us. Each one stood in amazement, finally able to see the patient for whom they cared, standing, smiling, hugging, talking, and walking. For thirty three days, he was a lump in the bed, attached to tubes and gauges and monitors, comatose. For thirty three days, they watched me and many others watch him, and wait, and pray. They tended to his every breath. They followed his daily care plans, rolled him to adjust his head, arms, legs; they cleaned his gaping abdominal surgical wound, and then rolled him to care for his decubitus.

They shaved him, bathed him, brushed his teeth and moisturized his lips. They administered his meds perfectly. They monitored his vitals, greeted his visitors, updated me on his progress, watched me massage him and perform Reiki on him. They dealt with doctors, specialists, phones, charts, computers, alarms, intercoms and grieving visitors. Angels of mercy in supportive footwear, they were.

Joe told them he was happy to finally meet them. He thanked them for caring for him and for caring for me. There were tears and smiles and then one by one, they trickled back to their duties, caring for critically ill patients.

Crowdfunding update:

> June 5 marks eight short weeks since Joe's discharge from rehab. He continues to gain strength although progress has slowed considerably.
>
> Joe has been enjoying our yard and unbelievably gorgeous spring weather; many strings of perfect "10" days, clear blue skies, low humidity, cool nights. Our permaculture garden is shaping up due to Joe's planting and careful attention. He has accomplished so much, planting mostly everything we started from seed or purchased at a local garden: tomatoes of course, peppers of all colors, eggplant, cabbage, broccoli, celery (left over from last year and babied indoors all winter), mint, parsley, basil, plus many flowers which Joe loves to cut and arrange for gift baskets or in vases and flowerboxes.
>
> Doctor insists on continuing many prescriptions although we both had bloodwork done a few weeks ago with partial results showing all is well for Joe except that his folic acid levels are low. No big deal, considering, as doctor said, Joe was nearly dead a few months ago.
>
> Frustrated, but blessed, taking it slow, grateful for all of our friends, family and continued support.

This past month we have been getting out more...We had lunch with Jameson at a world famous pizza place, toured a restored whaling ship, and last week were blessed to have our first visit to the Food Bank in town. Humbling and joyful experience to stand in line with 189 others in need. We also had Dad, Pearl and an old friend over for lunch- Joe did all the grilling :). Last week we attended a concert by local shanty man and wife of the founder of the nonprofit for which we volunteer. We sang along to American folk tunes and sea shanties...my favorite is "windy old weather, stormy old weather..when the wind blows, we'll all go together..."

We have been slowly trudging through the mounting bills and applications for assistance; were approved for federal health insurance and town assistance through a government grant which was expected in 2012 (!)... This is a one-time grant of ~$500 to help with our mortgage. We were denied for workers comp and home health aide; one we may appeal and the latter we don't require anymore.

Joe is still walking with a cane. His stamina is somewhat improved however he takes naps every day and has been sleeping late in the mornings; has been having a difficult time falling to sleep at night despite prescriptions to help him sleep. He's changed them twice already.

I have returned to some part- time tutoring, but that will end mid- June...and I've been fortunate and blessed to be hired to teach part time summer school from early July to early August. We figure this will help pay our mortgage for next month as we have now depleted the generous donations sent through crowdfunding.

Originally I had set a goal of $6000 to help us through 3 months of expenses; we surpassed this goal by nearly double thanks to your kindness. It has been five months since this journey began and we want you all to know we would have been homeless and destitute were it not for all of your help. Sincerest thanks to you all. You are in our daily prayers. Wishing you a joyful June.

Early in June, Joe was finally fit enough to attend the first hour of church, the sacrament portion of the three hours, despite being anxious about all the commotion his return might cause. I suggested that we prepare a simple sentence as a response to everyone who would ask how we were. We were both physically uncomfortable sitting for the full hour, but we endured. The members did not expect to see us, and welcomed Joe as if he was back from the dead, which basically, he was. There were so many questions, hugs, smiles, tears. So much love. EP was giddy to see Joe.

We heard stories from parents of children who prayed for Joe. Here's one from the Mom of BC.

> *You and Joe were A's teacher at the time and we were talking about how sick he was - (probably at dinner or it could have been family prayer) We told the kids to remember him. So first we prayed as a family but B continued to remember him in his personal prayers. No prompting from us and he would frequently ask if we knew how Joe was doing as he was getting tucked in to bed at night.*
>
> *It was just so sweet to hear him pray for him every night and then ask - is he getting better? We told him he was - that he was getting strength each time he prayed and we just needed to continue to pray for him as long as it took.*

Once Joe heard that story, he would go out of his way to find B at church, wave to him and give him the thumbs up. B's face was precious, as if he were witnessing a miraculous answer to his prayers.

June 21 Crowdfunding update:

Happy Summer friends and family far and near! Five months since this all began; we are so grateful for the gorgeous New England weather and the change of seasons here. Joe has been spending more time outside tending to our garden, relaxing on our back patio, appreciating nature and God's green earth, blessed beyond measure for the bounty and comfort of friends and family like you. Roses are in full bloom here, (so are the mosquitos), birds are abundant, raccoon mommas and babies, skunks, possum grace us with their presence nightly. It's like National Geographic in our own back yard. Joe especially enjoys the goldfinches with their sweet song and spectacular colors. We have been looking for the silver lining in everything cloudy; Joe's car was voluntarily surrendered last Monday morning - tow truck arrived at 7:20AM. Silver lining=one less bill to pay. Joe needs two more surgeries; one to reverse the ostomy, and one to repair the hernia which has been growing where the surgeon removed Joe's umbilicus. Silver lining= Joe will be home and recuperating through next year. Life as we knew it is changed forever; silver lining= new life, new opportunities. Many thanks for your generous donations and support throughout these months. We are so grateful and while we know that we can never repay your kindness, we keep you in our prayers daily and hope you know how much you have helped. Joe is healing slowly, and we have a roof over our heads, food on our table, a comfortable bed, health insurance, great doctors, a merciful and loving heavenly Father, a savior, brother and redeemer and good friends and family like you. What more do we need? Love and thanks, Aoibhyann and Joe

Caption: Joe can't drive and we can't afford the payment. Thank you, wonderful Auto Financial Services, for allowing us to voluntarily surrender the lease without penalty.

June 27

Church friends (who happen to be professional craftsmen) finalized the rehabbing of our bathroom to facilitate Joe's mobility by installing a new door.

> Goodbye curtain-for-a-door...hello gorgeous new perfect door installed on our out of plumb 101 year old house by D and L C. I don't want to paint it, it's so pretty. Feeling blessed.

July Crowdfunding update:

> Happy July to friends and family far and near. As we enter the sixth month of Joe's recovery and new life, we wanted to update you and share our thanks and appreciation to you

for the continual flow of love and support and prayers and kindness. We are humbled and profoundly overwhelmed by everyone's thoughtfulness and generosity. Blown away, we are! Blessed to be able to meet our second grandson, born July 1. We enjoyed being in the hospital this time. Mom, Dad, big brother and baby all doing well*. Progress here is still slow, but forward. Joe walks without the cane briefly...but still enjoys the wheelchair when we have to walk for any distance. We have a renewed appreciation for the term "handicapped" and all that accompanies the condition. 99% of strangers who see Joe in public places are kind and considerate, opening or holding doors, giving him first place in line, stepping out of the way, even apologizing if they step in front of him. It's interesting to observe people's reactions. In my undergraduate first year (Special Education) one assignment was to go to the local mall in New Haven, in a wheelchair, and document accessibility and public reactions to a wheelchair-bound person. Unforgettable! This occurred in the very late 1970s on the cusp of the Americans With Disabilities Act, or handicapped accessibility in public places. It's encouraging to witness how far we've come and how much we've grown over the past 30+ years. Promised we'd share the garden with you as it grows. Hurricane coming up the east coast of the USA in the next few days. Praying everyone is safe and homes and gardens and lives are preserved. Blessings to you all ...wherever you are, please know you are always in our hearts and prayers. Love, Aoibhyann and Joe

*In the hospital room with daughter in law, infant son and Patrick. New mother is glowing, and beautiful as ever, hours after giving birth. Patrick is overjoyed with baby's arrival, but annoyed with an itchy shoulder. He lifts his shirt to show us. The skin is red and irritated, perhaps from his scratching? There appear to be hives or bumps on the surface. We are all thinking it's a result of nerves.

The itching and bumps worsen. Baby and Mom are home the following day. Patrick visits a doctor and is diagnosed with shingles – terribly contagious, especially to a newborn's nonexistent immune system. He is banished by his doctor to the guest room and instructed to have zero contact with his wife or baby for three weeks.

August Crowdfunding update

Friends, family, supporters near and far, seven months since our ordeal began, realization of a dream occurred on the weekend of August 9 when we attended annual Hampshire Christian reunion at the beach. The dream that inspired many of us to cheer Joe on to good health and recuperation became a reality. Two of the many highlights were the distribution of thank-you gifts for donations, and our hand - held circle reciting The Lord's Prayer- a larger circle than originally formed at Joe's bedside on February 7th, when Joe was critically ill and in a coma. For people of other faiths, I give you these holy words, straight out of the Bible.

Our Father, who art in heaven, hallowed be Thy name.
Thy kingdom come, Thy will be done on earth as it is it heaven.
Give us this day our daily bread, and forgive us our trespasses
as we forgive those who trespass against us, and lead us not
into temptation but deliver us from evil. Amen.

Attaching a photo of that joyful prayer. Notice the angels watching over us. This photo is untouched and was compared to several in a series taken with the same camera. No one smoking a cigar, no campfire or barbecue grill in the area. The light source is not through the trees or shown in any other photo taken at the same time in the same location.

Joe continues to enjoy a slow recovery, but is approaching October and the colostomy reversal surgery. It is unknown at this point whether this will be an invasive surgery or done laparoscopically. Doctor predicts at least a four to six week recovery period "depending upon how it goes." Following that surgery and recovery will be another to repair of his hernia (early next year?) naturally developed in the umbilicus post - incision from sternum to groin and because this surgical site was left open due to sepsis. Joe is still experiencing hearing problems, numbness is his feet, sleeplessness, anxiety and weakness, but generally feeling stronger every day.

Miracles never cease.

Due to your generosity and the enormous success of this website, we have a cushion of approximately six more months. I completed teaching summer school and will most likely return to part time tutoring for a local school system in a few weeks. Joe is pursuing social security disability, but the process is painfully slow. We have no idea if he will be granted the disability, and even if he does, it could be a year from now, with no income in the meantime. Even then, it may only be up to 60% of his pay which was meager to begin with. Obviously our financial situation is dire, and we have you to thank for keeping us in our home, with food on our table, bills paid, secure in faith and gratitude to you and a merciful heavenly Father who continues to bless us.

Know that your kindnesses have extended beyond our circle, and know that you will all receive blessings as a result of your tender hearts and warm spirits.

One of the most spectacular outcomes of Joe's illness was the outpouring of prayer.

Chapter 7

Prepare for Change

The best thing about the future is that it comes only one day at a time.
~Abraham Lincoln

Wednesday August 27

The return of summer weather and renewed compulsion to keep writing. Feel overwhelmed in the morning when I don't start the day out with prayers. I turn to email and social media and I'm tired before I even start. I must retool myself to looking to the eternal first, and let everything else follow in God's hands. Must not forget the lessons I am learning through Joe's illness. Feeling worn and weak.

Magically when searching the internet for ideas for church activity tonight I find it with two clicks, yet I have difficulty and feel confused when trying to build my brand or figure out how best to help whales. My house continues to be more organized and I will feel so much better when it is a "house of order" which the church advises for all. Peaceful feelings result from organizing and cleaning. The end result brings harmony and rest. I'm not there yet, but I feel the need, and that's a good start.

September 3

Jays are squawking this morning typically, noisy buggers they are. They usually communicate with the others with their staccato sharp calls, a cat in the brush, a hawk high overhead. Today Felicia figured out how to escape the camper, so I suspect that is the reason for the racket. But maybe they are on high alert. Yesterday just before dusk Joe and I enjoyed watching a crow chase a hawk directly above our yard; in and out of the treetops they circled, scattering squirrels in all directions. Bawk! Baawk! Cheer! Cheer! Ppeeee! are the crows' superior and more dignified reply.

Leaves starting falling last month. Geese have been practicing their southern migration for many weeks. August is far too early for them, but everyone is saying this is one of the harbingers of yet another early, bitterly cold and snowy winter. We shall see.

Neighbor informed me yesterday that her while her tree guy was out scouting the woods on the fringe of our property he found a fisher cat's nest; he told her he found carcasses of birds, squirrels and a hawk at the base of a huge uprooted tree felled by one of the wicked winter storms last year.

When I first endeavored to allow our property to revert to more natural woodland, I did not anticipate a fisher cat taking residence. But it does not surprise me, in fact I'm rather pleased. I want for all to feel welcome and nurtured and home here. These creatures were here long before we were. All things should be brought back to balance and harmony. In our utopian farm, nature works so that we don't have to. I try to bring my Reiki hands to my work.

Monday, September 15 Autumn

Spent a bit of time this morning attempting to capture a photo of the sunlight as it glistened on the grasses in the backyard. I was taking pictures with the IPad and despite the number of attempts I could not duplicate the magnificence accurately. I was in awe and wonder of God's creation and humbled by my feeble attempt to replicate or capture how the sunlight sparkled on the leaves like waves on water, the surface a blanket of tiny diamonds. With such splendor on the earth, how can anyone deny a grand designer?

An impression came to me on yet another picture perfect September morning in New England; bright blue skies, low humidity, leaves just beginning to change, wildlife acting differently-Canada geese have been practicing their southward journey for weeks, songbirds are less visible at the feeder, quiet. Why? Have they no need to sing as brightly now that they have found a mate and are attending to family?

Similarly, autumn is the season when our ducks calm down. Less competitive, fewer hormones raging through their systems, they forage side-by-side, rest side-by-side, lying deep in the seedy grasses. They behave more like brothers then competitors.

I'm thinking it's another blessing to witness this beauty on the morning following a Sunday spent investigating preparations in these latter days. Our testimonies grow in fits and starts, and nowhere is this more apparent than in the area of preparedness. I am trying to apply the dream in which our church leader cupped my face in his hands and said "My dear, it is time to get to the Temple and receive your blessings." There is no clearer directive than what comes to me in my dreams. Temple blessings are delicate and extremely personal. I know what I have to do regarding home, friends, family, church and Temple, but life gets in the way. I'm trying to taper my priorities. I find it difficult to multitask now.

Our church began construction on a Temple in 2013; the second in New England. The significance of a Temple near our home cannot be overplayed. Many posit that the adversary, the fallen angel Satan, is displeased that God's work and our church is advancing. They predict he will redouble efforts to beguile members and lead them away from the church. I don't doubt it. Many of our church members have been plagued by bizarre illnesses and circumstances. One of the members of the Temple committee very close to Joe was hospitalized with diverticulitis shortly after Joe came home. He suffered complications due to surgery and nearly bled to death. Many of us have spoken about the coincidence of these happenings and the imminent opening of the Temple in our area. Joe had several brushes with death before the flu fiasco. It seems the closer we come to doing what's right and living righteously, the enemy throws us a curveball.

People who know Joe and me tell us it's time we caught a break. I believe we are presented with these opportunities so that we can harden our resolves and choose the correct response. Our hardships help us prepare for even greater challenges and rewards.

These musings come on the heels of Lidia's departure back to her farm in Hawai`i. She has also been given a directive and inspiration to prepare for what is yet to come. She answered "Yes". It has not been a simple undertaking. She labors long and anguishes over her lack of energy and support to do what she has been prompted to do. She wonders how it is that people will be using her farm as refuge when the time comes. She feels unsupported.

She was the church gardening specialist and for two years, advising the wards to prepare gardens and become more self-reliant. She found it ironic that she had to counsel people about preparedness, with a year-round growing season, resplendent bounty and perfect conditions for gardening. Her repeated message alerted people to the fact that if the ships and planes stopped coming to Hawai`i, the grocery store shelves would be empty in six days. We cannot live on papaya and banana, she told them. It takes three weeks to grow a radish from seed, and radishes are cool weather crops. Radish, lettuce, broccoli, spinach, onion, carrot green peas, cucumber, pepper and tomatoes require between three to twelve weeks from planting to harvest. Many people heard her and acted on her counsel, but many did not.

Lidia feels she presented this message with such a sense of urgency that she turned people away with her zeal. She related a parable about a king who foresaw a great dragon coming to destroy their kingdom. The king issued directives to build a wall, and was unrelenting in his demands. The people obeyed begrudgingly, working without his inspiration, but only out of duty and obedience. The king continued his demands until slowly, one by one, the people of the kingdom said they had had enough, and quit. They told the king they had done everything he asked and still he was displeased because the wall was not high enough or strong enough. They told the king that his demeanor was harsh and unforgiving. They told the king that they did not see the dragon and did not share his vision and therefore were not as desirous to build a great wall.

The king realized that he probably could have directed and guided the people of the kingdom with more kindness and less drive, but he had seen the vision of the dragon and was trying to protect the people.

The dragon came and because the great wall around the kingdom had not been completed, the people were vulnerable to attack, and many perished. This was heartbreaking for the king as he anguished over the vision that he had received, and anguished as he drove his people to work mightily to protect themselves, and he anguished over their cries as the labored, and he anguished over their self-defeat and fatigue. Even more his heart broke as he watched the dragon approach the kingdom and destroy so many because he knew this great catastrophe was coming and felt a sense of failure that he could not inspire more to diligence and obedience.

Lidia and I speak about the weight and burden of being inspired. I have always had the gift of *dreaming*: the ability to transcend everything in my immediate environment and lift myself to a different plane, a different existence. I've spent a lot of time thinking about this and can only assume that this is a defense mechanism that I developed very early in my life to shield me from perceived harm. I do not understand the physio-neurological basis for this ability, nor do I feel the need to spend much time investigating it. It has always been with me and I can switch it on and off. Resiliency? Escapism? This ability has served me well. I'm often motivated more by my dreams then by worldly, temporal circumstances. I am happiest when I am nurturing my inner monk.

How is this is a burden? I'll try to make it real for you. I'm not a follower. I don't think like typical people think, I'm not driven by the typical compulsions; I shun the news, I require massive amounts of silence and privacy to think, to pray, to process, to dream. It is as with the air, water, breath, food, and movement, I do believe I would die if I could not dream my little dreams or act on inspiration. I imagine this is what artists feel, and I keep my artist friend, Jolie D, with me always because of this. I remember she had just made the difficult decision to devote herself totally to her craft before she became ill. I wonder now if she wasn't acting also on an inspiration-God and angels driving her toward becoming all that she was designed to become before she left this earth.

The world's noise disturbs me and hampers me from achieving my true potential.

I find great pleasure and satisfaction in cleaning, not in the obsessive-compulsive way, but in the way that allows me physical exertion and release, and gives my hands something to do while my mind spins. It's cathartic. It helps me to maintain an eternal perspective.

October 3

And with one tiny tilt of the planet, one equal day and night, autumn.

We felt the threat earlier, when summer sun and warmth held us, blissful, hopeful. Harvest time comes quickly. Too many tomatoes. Darker, damp, dewy mornings.

Ducks are molting serious winter plumage. Donald is cranky and can't fly to or from his window shelf, porcupine feather nubs emerging.

October 3 evening

Tapping meditation today, created a "tapping tree" roots, trunk, branches and leaves replete with old and tired negative self-image, self-doubt, the same old bad record playing in my head, without my permission. Add that to the message left on my phone that my blood work is normal. Ha ha. Tell me why I'm in constant pain, then, dear doctor. Therese insists I see a rheumatologist. More doctors, more wasted days. We spent three hours yesterday just getting our teeth cleaned. Listen to me whine, with insurance and doctors when so many have so little, (the mantra of my prayers). Thank you, Lord for all of our bounty and blessings when so many have so little. Who am I to have these troubles when so many can only dream about driving my car to and sitting in a plush doctor's office, reading glossy magazines and watching television or listening to easy listening light rock radio.

Still, I must honor and recognize the source of my frustration...and to compare myself to the rest of the world or anyone random, family, friend, sister, does not honor me or what the "I Am" presence in me is trying to tell me.

Tapping uncovered my nasty little secret self-destruct, my obnoxious compulsion to help others and ignore myself. Makes me think about that comedic routine when the actor whines "What about *my* needs?" When I'm not thinking about whom I can help, I'm praying for them, or I'm volunteering to save the whale, save the seal, save the bear, save the elephant in the circus, save the sea lions who are being shot at Bonneville Dam for eating salmon, save the turtles, save the birds, save the bees, save the corals, save the Taiji dolphins, protect Muslims, protect the environment, keep a river-friendly lawn. Say no to GMOs, no to releasing balloons into the atmosphere, no to plastic bags, no to straws, no to animal testing, no to fur, no to war. Copying social media posts: "If you really think the environment is less important than the economy, try holding your breath while you count your money." "Depression, anxiety and panic attacks are not a sign of weakness. They are signs of having remained strong for too long."

So much in need of saving, while my hair falls out and I continue to languish, unfulfilled, feeling unrecognized unappreciated, unrewarded, under compensated.

As far back as I have memories, I've been a champion of the voiceless-a wayward toad in the road, a squirrel struck by a car, a stunned bird on the double yellow lines, a stray kitten…then I graduated to saving the whales. I played alone in the woods as a child, fashioning a lean-to out of sticks, ice skating on a shallow pond frozen over, collecting ground pine for home-made Christmas wreaths, making tools out of found objects from the forest floor. My imagination saved me. My imagination moved me from place to place, transported me from present to anywhere but there. Deep grooves and paths and rows were harrowed, through which I often trod. It's effortless for me to transport myself in an instant to anywhere I choose, making myself a hologram here, or there, wherever, whichever way is less pain.

But back in the real world, I want to strip my house down to the basics, empty my boxes and bins of clothes and start over with a few essentials, preferably ones that I made by hand (there are none). Embarrassed to look at what I save, considering my lifelong dream of escaping to my cabin in the woods, at the top of a mountain, off-grid, where I can grow my own food, make my own clothes and dishes, commune with nature, and drop out of society.

Instead, to entertain myself, I dye my hair. Blondes can't possibly have more fun, they just look as if they do. Placed the dye in funky places with ultra-light blonde and then medium blonde which emerged as reddish orange, and carrot in places. Five attempts to get it right and of course the gray and black grows back anyway. I understand women who give up the fight and embrace the gray, but I'm not ready to surrender yet.

When I'm being more realistic and less dream-driven, I find myself in a difficult position, like a woman with no country, when I look to female friends for companionship. I can't talk about trivia. I'd like to, but I can't. I think about all that humans are doing to this planet, and I bite my tongue whenever a less informed, less aware, less active person says or does something that could impact the environment. I haven't gone so far as to exclude people who embrace a less environmentally-friendly lifestyle, and I don't judge, so I find it easier to avoid small talk.

There are extreme activists on both "sides" of the issue of captive cetaceans (whales, dolphins and porpoises). I did my graduate thesis on transformative dialogue, and yet find myself sandwiched in the middle of two sides of a tired argument, try to highlight the positives of both. I believe there has to be some middle ground. No one wins when we fight. No one wins over hearts and minds by accusing, pointing fingers, blaming. We humans are not programmed to learn if we are stressed, so how does it make any sense to yell and scream and hope that anyone will listen? The response to stress is fight, flight, fear or freeze, not open up and respond, "Because you yelled and accused I am so eager to hear what else you have to say!" It is my lifelong desire to bring people together, to the same table, to share truths and honor one another and learn from one another. How to bell that cat?

Without collaboration, we go nowhere. Stepping off the box now.

Crowdfunding updates

Dearest Ones, October 5 will mark six months since Joe came home from rehab hospitals to recuperate at home. It has been an upward climb, a long haul, and many other metaphors but thus far we are blessed to have survived and Joe is expected to make a nearly full recovery. He still suffers from hearing problems, dizziness, numb feet and left leg, plus fatigue and instability on his feet. He has fallen three times - thankfully no serious injuries, just bruises and injured pride. Doctors tell him this may be as good as it gets. Days have been full with doctors' appointments, phone calls with insurance companies, and creditors. Joe has been diligently attending to the mountain of bills and paperwork-he has completed applications for Social Security disability and early disability retirement. Colostomy reversal on December 3 and two surgeries thereafter. We are so grateful to you all for your continued prayers, support, love and concern. Thanks to your generosity, we have a cushion of about three more months. Our God is great! Patient, merciful and forgiving.

A.A.E. MURPHY

We acknowledge His hand in all things. Much love and thanks to you all, also. Joe and Aoibhyann

Evidently, the fountain of support was running dry. That, or people were comfortable that the crisis was nearly over, and didn't see an immediate need. This post was about me, and received no contributions, except for good old Dad who once again bailed me out of serious financial need:

Dear Friends, a Family, Supporters- urgent appeal followed by an update on our health. You may recall we were in a car crash in 2011 when we lived on Maui. Our car was totaled and we were both brought to the hospital by ambulance with neck and back injuries. We received therapy and rehab, and pursued litigation. Aoibhyann suffered whiplash, two protruded vertebra and a fractured SI (sacro iliac) the web of bone that connects the spine and pelvis to the hip. Joe suffered whiplash, trauma to his left leg and his back.

Opposing counsel insists that I return to Hawai`i for deposition. We have zero funds with which to book the flight. If we do not show for the deposition, they could dismiss the case.

Round trip for the flights totals $1200.00. Opposing counsel is paying for hotel, cab fare and meals.

We know you have supported us thus far in excess of our goal which has provided us a cushion for mortgage and living expenses since last January..and for that we are eternally grateful. If there is any way that you could help us through this we can offer to reimburse you when the case settles (and it will). Please indicate when you donate if you would like reimbursement.

Right now we have enough for two more months! This is great. I have been interviewing through a recruiter for special education teaching positions, certain that one will be offered.

So, this may be the last request as we may have a paycheck finally and again.

Now on to Joe's update: Joe has been fitted for hearing aids in both ears as he has suffered 65% permanent hearing loss, neurological in origin..we have been told this is a result of the paralysis (poly neuropathy) and coma. Thank heaven for insurance as the hearing aids are $5000! He continues to have numb feet and fatigue, anxiety, restlessness and sleeplessness. He completed a home sleep apnea study last week; this will affect the anesthesia during his upcoming surgeries. Colonoscopy scheduled for December 3, then the surgeon will schedule the ostomy reversal operation.

We don't enjoy talking about our issues anymore (not that we ever did) and we try to focus on the good and the positive, so for now let us close with gratitude to you for helping us and saving our lives once again. With love and gratitude.

October 15

Thoughts today as I near the end of this year: Breath is life. Hawaiians, people of the Arctic and Maori understand this. Swimmers, scuba and free divers know this. Yoga practitioners appreciate this to stay focused, self-aware and grounded in the present. First breath is baby's greatest change, indicating the transition from fluid to air in the lungs.

I've been practicing Reiki and working on earning my Reiki II certification. Meditations and prayer have provided stunning insight.

October 24

Became certified as a Reiki II Practitioner. Posted the achievement on social media. Not one "Like".

Crowdfunding updates

Dear Supporters,

Don't read this if you are searching for light and breezy. Don't read this if you are interested in only happiness and positivity.

I've decided that this will most likely be my final post about living with Fibromyalgia, judging by the "Likes" and comments my previous posts have received (scant). I found some support groups and it is there that I will turn, given the obvious-I can't expect people who do not live with chronic pain to understand. The support groups and under eye concealer are becoming my fast friends.

When I began journaling about my thoughts I did it to raise awareness about the syndrome. Not looking for pity or sympathy. As with any other debilitating condition, it is insane to expect people who have not lived the experience to relate or understand.

Still, I thought that by sharing my daily challenge with social medialand, I could reach a wide audience, and perhaps my struggle would resonate with others. If I could reach one or two, it would be worth it. I did, and so it is time to ration my energy and focus inward.

My thoughts are accelerating at a crazy rate, just as my symptoms seem to be worsening. Is there a bio accumulation thing with Fibromyalgia, just like PCBs or mercury in fish?

"Laugh and the world laughs with you, weep and you weep alone." -Emma Wheeler Wilcox 1850-1919

I remarked to Joe this morning that there is a cruel irony in our fates: he, rehabilitating and healing from a near-death experience, 33 days in a coma, months of rehabilitation, two surgeries in a year that have his abdomen bisected from sternum to groin and peppered from left to right with scars. Me, chronic pain and fatigue worsening by the day, with a diagnosis of Fibromyalgia for which there is no cure. Despite medications, meditation prayer and rest, I'm spiraling toward someplace I'm frightened to consider. Joe's healing, and I'm weakening.

Thank you for your prayers and support through 2014 and our catastrophic situation. I hope you find joy in every moment and appreciate your daily blessings. Spring is here! Believe it! Sending love and peace, Aoibhyann

Happy Autumn everyone! Thank you thank you for your support thus far. Quick update: Joe's Dad, Christopher, went to heaven to be with Catherine on Wednesday. Services will more than likely be Monday and Tuesday.

Joe began wearing his hearing aids yesterday...quite an adjustment, but we are blessed to have them. We were also fortunate to babysit our grandsons yesterday. Aoibhyann is applying for jobs and certain that hiring is on the horizon! We acknowledge God's merciful hand in all things.

November Thanksgiving social media update

We are giving thanks for you especially today! We are grateful for mercy, for life, for breath, for friends and family both near and far, for our bounty, for our blessings when so many have so little.

Please know that we thank our Heavenly Father for you, by name, and for your kindness, prayers, generosity, comfort, words, actions, thoughts and concern for us this year. God is great. May we give thanks for all things, in all circumstances.

How fortunate are we to have an endless list of those for which we are grateful?

Have a blessed Thanksgiving, Christmas, Hanukkah, Kwanzaa, and all other holy days where we give thanks to God, Spirit, Higher Power, Creator.

January 2015

Crowdfunding updates

January 27 marks one year since the catastrophe that began with the flu and nearly took our lives. Thanks and gratitude to everyone who has sustained us though the ups and downs this last year. The old chapter ends and a new one begins tomorrow, Monday, when Joe will undergo colon reconstruction and colostomy reversal surgery. Dr. R, Joe's original emergency surgeon, will perform this surgery, along with another expert surgeon on the team. This is no small surgery. Prayers are again needed.

Although he has been cleared by all his specialists for surgery tomorrow, Joe has been apprehensive and nervous since he learned of the surgery date. We knew this day would come, but there is a huge difference between anticipating the procedure and hospitalization --and being rushed to the hospital, sick and in pain and then waking up 33 days later, paralyzed with your abdomen cut open like the Grand Canyon and stitched together from sternum to groin, unaware of what happened or how he got that way. I recall Joe's one of first questions upon waking was "How did I get here?" The anticipation in this case has been a difficult pill to swallow.

We have decided to focus on a few long weekends and visits with friends and family over the next several months to give Joe something to look forward to as he prepares for, and then recovers from surgery.

Please know that we count you in our daily prayers, and consider ourselves blessed to have life and breath and friends and family like you. Wishing you all a prosperous and joyful 2015.

Joe is in surgery now. Very cool patient tracking board, like tracking a package in the mail, helps me to check his status. He is in good spirits and the team is awesome.

Wednesday January 21:

Another milestone today as Joe expelled air out of his new colon! "Because it's all about the gas, 'bout the gas, no burping"

We laughed at the joyful noise! Never did I think I'd rejoice at the sound of gas, but this was magnificent. Because this signals Joe's body's readiness to accept food, the hospital will be introducing clear liquids and watch his tolerance. He is already down at least ten pounds (as of Tuesday) because he hasn't eaten anything solid since last week.

Wanted to share the great news, thank you for your concern and prayers.

January 27:

January 27, 2014= H1N1 Flu nightmare. January 27, 2015= Blizzard Juno. No match. We're breathing, standing, walking and together at home, not in the hospital. Thank you all for your love, support and prayers this past year. Hoping you are warm and safe and healthy.

Dearest Friends and Family, I wanted to share a few pages from my Fibromyalgia diary, not because I want to rain on the happy parade of Joe's recovery, but because I think it's important to be realistic and honest with you all. Everyone remarks about how strong I am but that is probably because I never share my half of the story. This ordeal that began almost exactly one year ago has taken a toll on my body. I am not the same in body or in spirit. I have been compromised in so many ways, not the least of which are my vibrancy and zeal for life.

Again, I'm not whining. For those of you who are interested in the real story, stay tuned for the next update in which you will get a little glimpse of what it's like to be me.

February 2015 Fibromyalgia Diary Entry 1

Fibromyalgia Diary February 2, 2015 Ground Hog Day

Many nights, I sleep in my clothes. On purpose. The energy demand of undressing and redressing is astronomical at the end of a day, especially after a snow day spent cooking and cleaning (read: resting). I didn't like shopping for clothes as a child, and I barely tolerate it now if it involves trying things on in the dressing room.

This lack of energy and chronic pain has been an education.

February 16, 2015

Impressed by random and arbitrary nature of good fortune. We struggle, and others have the appearance of less struggle. Intuitively I understand that pain is relative, and outward appearance can be deceptive, but life and death and all the in betweens are random. I'm having a crisis of faith today.

I saw a video of my cousin yesterday, at her daughter's college lacrosse game. She danced in the stands, resplendent in her mink hat, dressed to the nines. We grew up together in different states, visiting each other often. Her older sister was closest in age to my older sister. Two of them, two of us. Sometime along the way our four lives diverged and rerouted.

I mourn the fact that I could not dance in the stands, or be so closely involved in my son's college life. I mourn the loss of active motherhood. Yes, mourning is a choice, but "they" say that embracing of all stages of grief is essential to emotional health.

Many have argued our lives are the sum total of our choices. I cannot scream loud enough in disagreement, even if I had the energy to do so. I did not choose Fibromyalgia.

I am actively processing the misfortune of Joe receiving the H1N1 virus, passing it on to me, our hospitalization, our near-death illnesses, his complete succumbing to the virus and diverticulitis, total organ failure and cardiac arrest as a result of the virus, months of agony, paralysis (critical illness polyneuropathy) rehab, and the utter fiasco that is the paperwork and system following hospitalization, billing, creditors, applications for services and aid, disability and social security. Sometimes I escape into lala land, a self-imposed dream state where I navigate through the days focused only on the immediate tasks at hand, and fantasizing about lovelier places I've been, more pleasant locations I've lived, warmer climes, fairer winds, happier moments. And the whales, seals, dolphins, turtles, birds, and porpoises who bring me joy. These are places to which I retreat, to help me though the days. I conjure the scene, feel the warm sun, the fair winds, see the endless skies and sunsets, and hear the whales blow and breach. I transport myself effortlessly to a more pleasant memory until I am ready to deal with the less pleasant reality.

After Joe was discharged from rehab, my workload ramped up, and I was dedicated to 16-hour a day nursing. 50% of my hair fell out. I stuttered, struggled to complete sentences and cried when someone asked me how I was after caring for Joe and helping with his rehab since April. Dr. K said there was "no shame in depression and anxiety" after what I had been through.

Yet, one year and a month later, we think about how our lives are so much worse off now, in many ways. We had no savings or assets before. We had no summer home, no fancy cars, no 401k or retirement, we had no opulent home or vacations, we had no disposable income...living paycheck to paycheck, struggling to make ends meet. But we had our health, and our family and friends. Now, Joe is unable to perform the duties of his job, has been denied twice for disability, and is wobbly and unstable with numb feet and 65% hearing loss in both ears, weakness, fatigue and depression with no income since last year. I developed Fibromyalgia, characterized by chronic and constant body pain, fatigue, depression. Some days my feet and legs ache so much I walk like I had just ridden an elephant (not that I would, sweet creatures – do you know how baby elephants are "broken"?). My hands ache and throb, fingers stiff and swollen. I am medicated, but still suffer confusion ("fibro fog") and have difficulty making some decisions. My back and legs ache from injuries sustained in an auto accident in 2011, coupled with hip and joint ache from Fibromyalgia; many nights, good, restful sleep is challenging. Maintaining a full time teaching job with a 45 minute one - way commute has been the marathon of a lifetime. I must work. We have no other income. We are further away from financial stability now as the bills continue to mount, our credit is shot, and my current contract expires March 1. And we are less healthy now than before.

So I ask all the critics, where did choice enter this situation? Certainly we chose our lifestyle and work; Joe chose to return home to work here, but was it his choice to contract H1N1? Was it my choice to catch it from him?

I am amazed by the arbitrary nature of chance: who catches a virus, who doesn't, who lives and who dies? In the month of February 2014 when Joe was in the ICU, comatose, struggling to breathe, three people died from H1N1 at the hospital. Did they choose to die? Did they choose to catch the flu? Flu shot or not, the flu will infect.

I dedicate my rant to those who have caught illnesses despite (or because of) immunizations.

Allow me some introspection, self-pity and doubt today.

Please know I understand how fortunate we are to be in a warm home, comfortable bed with food on our table. Not looking for sympathy and don't need to be reminded of all we have when so many are worse off than we. We pray several times a day, prayers full of gratitude and appreciation for all of our blessings. Comfort does not come through comparing ourselves with others, and does not honor our personal pain, relative as it is.

From *Desiderata*: "…If you compare yourself with others, you may become vain or bitter, for always there will be greater and lesser persons than yourself."

March 2015 Fibromyalgia Diary Entry 2

Now that I'm not teaching I have vowed to keep a routine for myself; I try to wake early, with the help of the duck alarm clocks. Marvel at the differences between each new sunrise, looking east across our back yard, patio chairs nearly submerged in snow, notice how the morning sun casts lavender shadows on the drifts and mounds. Spring is in the air, in the brighter, earlier mornings, in the raucous, festive twittering of birds, the return of the harbinger red-winged blackbirds.

How can there not be a grand designer?

And I pray prayers of thanks for the blessings the new day promises.

I fold the blankets, rearrange and punch the scrunched pillows, left from last night on the couch where Joe nests, to avoid the living room looking like a hospital room. I feed the fish, assist with the ducks' exit from the kitchen crates to the front steps; they quickly settle to bask in the morning sun, hunkered down over their yellow feet and legs - Donald on the railing we had installed to help Joe when he returned from rehab, still weak and wobbly and not doing stairs handily- and Pegasus the Alpha duck taking command of the warm, black welcome mat. As much as I'd like to think I have control over these two bachelors, I know our relationship is one of compromise. We pay close enough attention to them, study their preferences and behaviors to know who likes what, and try to provide them with comfort and stimulation. Much to our inconvenience. They have been overnighting in the house since January when the temperatures fell into the teens. This repeats last year's January, February and March, when

Joe was in a coma, in ICU, in rehab, in hospital again, and I was alone and too tired, sick, weak to walk over the icy path to the shed to tend to them.

Many mornings have been spent in reverie, comparing last year to this. The difference is precious life compared to near death, for both of us.

I think people misunderstand Fibromyalgia; I know I did. It helps to think of it in the same category as chronic fatigue syndrome, or clinical depression, still misunderstood but more common. It's not a new illness; it has been studied for two decades or more, but is now receiving more funding for research perhaps as it gains a broader reach.

I've begun to dislike mentioning that I have the diagnosis. I think it just falls wrong and awkwardly on the ear. Nearly everyone who hears that I have it has something to say about it, maybe because there are so many commercials for the drugs for it on television now? They tell me to try this and that, ask what prescription I'm taking, suggest a book or a diet or a remedy. It exhausts me to explain, and yet I understand I may be a source of good information for someone who knows someone who knows someone who has it, so I don't want to retreat into silence about it. What is most irritating however is the suggestion that I'll feel better once I just do x y or z. The pain is chronic. It doesn't go away despite my mood or activity. It doesn't go away with change in diet, rest, exercise. It doesn't go away because I taught full time, and it is still here now that my contract has ended, which is why I am determined to keep a schedule and not yield to it and remain in bed all day, which is where I would stay, covers over my head, depressed, tired, defeated.

I think of Fibro as any other condition that marginalizes and alienates until we find others who suffer with it. Cancer. Diabetes. Heart disease. Obesity. Death of a loved one. These, we can relate to. Fibro is vaguer, more obscure. There are more misperceptions and misunderstandings about it than not, I fear. Ironically, if there was a support group in the area, we'd probably all be too tired to attend the meetings. The same with caregivers!

I feel as if my body is tired and in pain on a cellular level. No amount of cajoling, counseling, encouragement, love or support changes that.

In 1991, an article I wrote about being unemployed was featured on state's newspaper magazine. I began by remarking that friends and family mean well by telling me clichés and comforting idioms such as "one door closes, another opens" and "there's a silver lining in each cloud" and "everything happens for a reason" but there was no comfort in these words, just as there is no comfort now for people who don't understand Fibromyalgia, with one exception-- the appreciation of the blessing of concerned friends and family. I'm certain there are people who suffer any number of maladies alone. I saw it when Joe was in ICU: I spent every day by his side, sick as I was. I would walk the halls on the way to the bathroom or cafeteria and notice all those poor patients with no one by their side, no one holding their hand, massaging them, no one to do Reiki on them, no one to monitor their gauges and medication, heart rate, vital signs, no one to speak gently in their ear or play music for them, no one to read to them, pray over them, no one to rub their weakened limbs with coconut oil, do daily oral care, apply lip balm, clean their teeth, suction their mouth, observe their heart beating visibly through the hospital gown. No one to watch the monitors and suffer through alarms while the nurses rolled the patient every two hours, as oxygen levels dipped dangerously low, "desatting". I wondered where the loved ones were. What tragedy, to suffer and die alone. I think of Christ.

I watched throngs of families, young ones, old ones, children tugged along down the long hallway leading to the dying one, down the hall they went, back the other way, in tears, down the elevator, back to the parking lot, out into the world they went, all carrying these broken hearted loads of sorrow. Different faces, same story. A world of hidden, hurting hearts.

Fibromyalgia Diary - Empathy and *Thank You, Feet!*

Hello dear ones my name is Aoibhyann--and I have Fibromyalgia. A long story led up to my diagnosis, and I'm sure you all have stories too. If you are anything like me you are finding the pain from Fibromyalgia to be the most difficult situation to manage in your life.

I'm here to tell you good news, I hope you will spend a few moments of your time listening to a quick story about how I deal with Fibromyalgia. My intent is that you'll find encouragement and hope in my message. I thank you for investing your precious time and energy. Don't we know about saving our energy for things that truly matter?

So, let me get started right away by admitting that when I was first diagnosed, thought I would be superwoman and beat the illness. I tried three different medications and suffered through the adjustment periods; wanted to give up and stop taking them, but was encouraged to see it through. I finally found one that reduces Fibro pain, and provides good relief from depression and anxiety, so I'm going to stick with it. I'm fortunate to have insurance and a very kind doctor! I know there are so many of you who don't even have that.

Even though the prescription helps, I still struggle with activities of daily living--and I have learned to ration my energy for the absolute necessities. It took me many days to prepare this message for you, and I'm thankful for the microphone which types for me because typing by hand is very tedious and painful as I'm sure you know. I used to be able to type 80 words per minute! Now, my knuckles and joints in my hands are so swollen I can't wear my wedding rings...and simple manual tasks like opening jars and medicine bottles are either too hard or too painful! Isn't that a cruel irony? Those childproof caps should be called Fibro- proof.

And holding a hairbrush and a blow dryer? Torture.

Are you like me-- do you ration your chores? Do you skip the shower or bath and opt for cat baths-- washing the most important body parts? Do you hold off washing your hair until absolutely necessary? Do you pile everything up and save them for one trip instead of walking from room to room one item at a time? If you walk at all.

I took some good advice and started walking again for exercise; every step felt like I was walking on broken bones. I discovered soaking my feet after walks helps enormously with the pain. Researched, read, consulted with experts and fellow sufferers, tried out different variations and recipes and now have one that soothes sore, aching, cramping, and screaming- with-pain feet!

I decided to share my recipe with some friends, and we have all been amazed at the relief and comfort we have felt. You may think that sitting for 20 minutes with your feet in a hot tub is more important than the product that you use for soaking and I wouldn't blame you, I thought so too! I was dazed and confused at all the products and remedies and suggestions out there for people like us! If you try soaking your feet in only hot water, I promise it will not be nearly as effective as using my foot soak. I know because I tried it.

What I've learned through all my research and trials, investigation, reading fine print, comparing products, ingredients, testimonials, (Yikes! it was exhausting) is that simple, natural ingredients and the correct procedure help us to find comfort and relief from Fibro foot pain.

One fact that makes Fibromyalgia so pernicious is that there are of more bones in the human hands and feet than in the rest of the body, combined! Or that reflexology claims there is a connection between every major organ and system in our body -- and our feet?

Do it for yourself. Do it for your feet, your sweet, underappreciated feet, the feet who have carried you through life.

Even if you don't have Fibromyalgia --Count your blessings--we are assaulted on a daily basis with toxins that accumulate in our bodies, and the magic port hole through which we can expel these toxins is our feet.

Chapter 8

ARDS and a Blue Moon

When Joe was in the ICU, comatose, on a paralytic, and near death his heartrate spiked whenever the nurses performed the every-two hour repositioning. When they even readjusted his pillow, the heartrate spiked. Was the response to being moved the reason for his increased heart rate? We found absurd humor in the fact that moving his pinky was enough to cause it. I cautioned the staff daily that Joe had arthritic shoulders and knees, and even on a good day, he experienced pain and stiffness. He was a college football player, I recited, you can see the scar on his right knee, I pointed. Maybe the pain from arthritis was the cause? They heard me, but they continued to go about their duties, tolerating me as if I was a potted plant in the corner; plants and flowers are not allowed in the ICU.

The Discharge Summary addendum, explaining why Joe developed such a gaping bed sore on his back, just north of his butt cheeks:

> *The patient has a stage III decubitus...we could not move the patient during part of the hospitalization because of his*

hypoxemia, ARDS with minimal movement. On 100% oxygen on a high ventilator support, the patient desaturated rapidly, as a result of which the patient could not be moved...

Many weeks later, I learned that the staff was at times equally as concerned for me as they were for Joe. He was comatose, and provided 'round the clock care. On the other hand, I rolled down the ICU hall on the motorized wheelchair every day, schlepping three bags (one with all documents and paperwork, the second, my purse containing the usual items plus water bottle, bag of nuts or fruit, and the third containing my oxygen tank and apparatus), pale, frail, and worried -- a physical and emotional mess. Often the nurses hooked my oxygen to Joe's. He and I shared so much, and this was no exception.

And again, when Joe was in the first rehab, I warned all caregivers that he had arthritic knees and shoulders, cautioning them to be careful when they moved him, when they propped his hot, swollen knees under pillows, when they repositioned him. He played football in college, and even when he wasn't sick, he suffered with chronic pain in his knees and shoulders, I repeated, like a flawed cd, stuck on the same annoying verse. Again, they heard me, but displayed no inkling of response or adjustment, proceeding to handle him as if I hadn't spoken.

After three and a half weeks, Joe emerged from the coma. His body had changed drastically, and visibly. Those in a coma for a week or longer develop muscular atrophy, referred to as Critical Illness Polyneuropathy. Joe's was extreme. He was capable of opening his eyes, drugged and half-moon, making facial expressions and mouthing words, but was unable to speak due to the tracheostomy. Fingers, hands, toes and feet woke up next. Within a day or two, he was able to reposition his legs.

With so many parts beginning to awaken, I paid little attention to the arthritis, and worried less about it. I could only guess the cause of the elevated heart rate.

Over a year later, when he was recuperating at home, we re-read the paperwork from Joe's employer, qualifying him for disability due to complications of Acute Respiratory Distress Syndrome (ARDS). We were baffled about why they ruled ARDS to be the disabling factor. He was still weak, but had mostly recovered from the disaster of 2014. The ARDS had subsided, his lungs plumped up and began to function again, pumping oxygen to his body. His organ failure reversed, he appeared to have regained nearly all of his functioning, both physical and mental. People commented, "You look great! When are you going back to work?" To look at him (clothed), if you didn't notice the hearing aids or the waddle in his walk, you would not believe his ordeal. Unless you were with him 24/7, as I was, you would miss his grogginess, his funny, subtle occasional use of words in place of correct words. He puts on his best public face, and can be a chatterbox if he chooses. He doesn't like to talk about the past, or his recuperation. He can be anxious and nervous, jittery and claustrophobic at times. Heat bothers him even more than before; in rehab, he typically asked for four ice packs; one for his head, one behind his neck, and two for his swollen knees. Sometimes cranky, testy and touchy with me, he presents as normal when we're not at home. Are these medication related symptoms? ARDS related? His trach scar is barely perceptible, a work of art. He has regained the 70 pounds he lost during the three months in hospitals and rehabs. His personality has returned; he seems to be his old self. So the question remained: what was so debilitating about ARDS? I thought perhaps the employer was reaching for a qualifying condition, but no, that couldn't be right—these were medical professionals as scrutinizing as insurance companies, so –no—certainly they wouldn't manufacture a diagnosis or condition. There had to be more to ARDS. I began to research.

Here's what I discovered:

According to the Mayo Clinic, Acute Respiratory Distress Syndrome (ARDS) occurs when fluid builds up in the tiny, elastic air sacs (alveoli) in your lungs. More fluid in your lungs means less oxygen can reach your bloodstream. This deprives your organs of the oxygen they need to function. ARDS typically occurs in people who are already critically ill or who have significant injuries. Severe shortness of breath — the main symptom of ARDS — usually develops within a few hours to a few days after the original disease or trauma.

Many people who develop ARDS don't survive. The risk of death increases with age and severity of illness. Of the people who do survive ARDS, some recover completely while others experience lasting damage to their lungs.

The mechanical cause of ARDS is fluid leaked from the smallest blood vessels in the lungs into the tiny air sacs where blood is oxygenated. Normally, a protective membrane keeps this fluid in the vessels. Severe illness or injury, however, can cause inflammation that undermines the membrane's integrity, leading to the fluid leakage of ARDS.

The most common underlying causes of ARDS include sepsis, a serious and widespread infection of the bloodstream. Joe was septic.

> ARDS is extremely serious, but thanks to improved treatments, more people are surviving it. However, many survivors end up with potentially serious — and sometimes lasting — complications, including: scarring in the lungs (pulmonary fibrosis); Collapsed lung (pneumothorax); Blood clots- lying still in the hospital while you're on a ventilator can increase your risk of developing blood clots, particularly in the deep veins in your legs; Infections; Memory, cognitive and emotional problems. 190,000 Americans die as a result of ARDS annually. Mortality is down from 50% to 20-30% in the past several years. [iv]

We researched further and discovered stories from people who had required joint replacement one to two years post-ARDS. Evidently, the lack of oxygen responsible for shutting down organs also wreaks havoc on bones and joints. We grew to understand that Joe's shoulder injury was exacerbated by ARDS, leading to further deterioration.

August 2 Blue Moon Musings

Joe and I were not feeling well this morning, slept late and missed church. We overdid it yesterday, acting as if we were normal, healthy people. We were paying the price. The day had a different vibe: unusual humidity-free, mid-80s with an eastern breeze, pleasant and post-blue moon. Perfect time for a conversation about where we are and what I can expect as Joe faces yet another surgery on Wednesday—a complete replacement of his right shoulder - webbed and locked with arthritis, bone spurs, bone-on-bone pain. We attributed his sleeplessness, anxiety and general malaise to chronic shoulder pain, seeing as he is long over the flu, hospitalization, critical illness polyneuropathy, and rehab. He's fairly certain his left shoulder and both knees are in similar condition.

I'd been soldiering on as a nurse, wife, taxi, homemaker, companion, fellow gardener, pet care specialist, landscaper, friend and caregiver who is sick with Fibromyalgia. I cared for my needy husband and handled nearly every responsibility for him and me while I struggled with my own illness. Rarely did I have the time or energy to look further into the future than the current day, but this day was different. Perhaps it was the blue moon making me sensitive to the sounds of our lives: the oohs and ahhs as we walk, stand, sit for too long, or do anything strenuous; the morning coughs, Joe's belching, his open-mouthed snoring on the couch, the moaning and groaning, and his peccadillos, for example, the way he whistles when he has finished a painful or difficult task like shaving or showering: a slowly descending- pitched exhale through pursed lips. PFffffWhoooEEEEEEEEheuuuuuuwwwwwww! His mother Catherine whistled the same way when was in her 80s. Joe is not in his 80s, nor is he in terribly ill health. That one sound grated on my last good nerve, and heartlessly, I spouted.

> "So, tell me, what the heck can I expect, Joe? What's in store for *me* in the next 20 years? You're 58 and have disability retirement. Don't you ever wonder why you are considered disabled? Why did your employer qualify you for disability based on ARDS? What is my life going to be like with you?

What does our future hold? Are you going to be a couch potato for the rest of our lives? Don't you feel too young to be disabled? Are you permanently disabled? Are you ever going back to work? Don't you want to do something else with your life?"

Then, unfairly, it slipped from my lips:

"You're a young man! My father is 82 and still working, just survived a car crash and is in better shape than you are!"

I peppered him:

"What do you think about when you're up all night, reading, praying, worrying, wandering, and walking around outside under the stars?"

He headed toward the couch.

"Don't you dare pick up that remote. Don't you dare. We need to talk about this."

"I don't want to. I'm not ready."

"I am! We need to investigate this, together. I need answers. I'm tired of not knowing. The doctors tell us nothing about your future. You survived, and now look at our lives. What comes next?"

"Dr. K told me when this was all over, 2014 would just be an ugly memory and I'd return to my normal life."

"Yah, that hasn't happened. Don't you want to know why?"

We were blessed to be having this conversation. It indicated hope for the future, together, on this side of the veil.

To be fair, Joe could have returned fire. My daily Fibromyalgia routine was probably equally annoying. I'm no prize, either, with my four-hour-long morning stupor and cough, my aches, pains and stiffness, my loss of vitality and verve, thirty pound weight gain, hair loss, brain fog, forgetfulness, the "bloat" that comes with fibromyalgia (making me appear six months pregnant), diminished enthusiasm for life and increasing need for quiet, to be alone, to sleep, to think, to pray and to write.

He didn't return fire. He said nothing, but I knew my words stung.

Chapter 9

Contention vs Fear vs Faith

August 11

For God hath not given us the spirit of fear; but of power, and of love, and of a sound mind. ~2 Timothy 1:7

For verily, verily I say unto you, he that hath the spirit of contention is not of me, but is of the devil. 3 Nephi 11:29.

... Weeping may endure for a night, but joy cometh in the morning. Psalms 30:5

Reflecting on our ordeal, I continued to wonder why we were spared death. Easy to advise me to "get over it" or "forget about it and move on", harder to do. I recognize that our issue was not as catastrophic as that which befalls others, but thinking "it could have been worse" or "I'm lucky" doesn't honor our difficulties. And, without a deep understanding of the nature of the experience of suffering, it is impossible to hone the skills required to achieve transcendence and healing. Raised in the Catholic faith, I was taught everyone has a cross to bear, but a tiny fraction of the one that Jesus bore – a humbling reminder of the inferiority of our suffering compared to His. I thought suffering was inherent in this life. I bore my crosses and compared my cross to other crosses. Early in life, I gravitated to those who were worse off than I, and felt compassion and a yearning to help those in need. I suppose this was a gift that engaged whenever I was in crisis: the ability to ignore my own personal needs and focus on those of others. Some would say this is unhealthy. I might concur, but it is a thread in the fabric of my being, one that years of therapy and counseling and prayer has not unraveled. Without the ability to overcome and forgive my own shortcomings or the hurt inflicted by others, I might have failed to thrive. Without the capacity to truly embrace despair and survive it, I might have become a wounded, shallow, selfish, faithless woman.

It would be dishonest to say that my faith had not been tested, although I never gave up believing that there was a merciful entity in control. It didn't occur to me that atheists are right, that we are collections of cosmic material, evolved into form over millennia, with little significance other than what we gain in this lifetime. But are the Buddhists right? Do our souls come and go through reiterations and reincarnations until we have achieved perfection or nirvana? How could Darwin's evolutionists be right? How could we be nothing more than macroevolved ancestors of the cow or hippopotamus? I'm reluctant to broach the subjects of God and faith, or perpetuate the argument about organized religion. I want my faith to be seen in my works. I don't want to talk about it. So much of life can be argued. We humans seem to enjoy the pastime. I'm not going to delve into the merits or shortcomings of belief in the divine. I'm not going to resurrect the classic dispute about Creationism or "Intelligent Design" vs Evolution, but I feel the need to explain what made me who I am and how I handled our crises.

Scientific arguments about Christianity can - and often do - lead to rejection of God. I have been told by people very close to me that there is no man in the sky, (likely because the existence of a creator cannot be proven?). The deduction is also understandable considering history and the atrocities committed in the name of God. Science, however, does not provide 100% proof of evolution. Fossil records are incomplete. The debate continues, yet I remain firm in my need to believe, and disciplined in the practice. As I have explained in conversations with those who aren't as ardent, I know what faith in God has done for me, and no one can diminish that.

Our church is an organized Christian religion established in 1830 based on the answers to a question asked by a 14 year- old boy. The church may seem contemporary but the book known as *another testament of Jesus Christ* chronicles a family of people dating back to 600 BC.

Membership in the church has been an incredible gift.

I've sought counsel from church leaders on a variety of questions, one of which is how to explain what I believe. One of the Bishops of our ward told me I didn't need to. His words comforted and affirmed me: "In order to believe, we have to take a leap from what can be proven, to what can't. This is the essence of faith." I knew this, but it helped to hear it from him.

From former President Jimmy Carter:

> *"What are the things that you can't see that are important? I would say justice, truth, humility, service, compassion, love. You can't see any of those, but they're the guiding lights of a life."*

Even love has been scientifically dissected into hormones and electrical impulses surging through the body. We can't see it, yet we can witness it and other virtues such as devotion, attention, loyalty, altruism in the human and animal kingdom. We can't see wind, but we know it exists because we see its effects as it rustles the leaves. Why should love be less valid?

I take comfort in expressions such as these:

Faith is the antidote for fear. ~ Russell M. Nelson

A happy life must be to a great extent a quiet life, for it is only in an atmosphere of quiet that true joy dare live. -Bertrand Russell

With all the hype and controversy that appears to dominate our tiny world, I need to seek peace, and often recoil from fighting and bickering. What is our compunction to win an argument, to be contentious, or to be right? Why do we feel the need to argue our deepest opinions? Haven't we all seen the effect of mean-spirited words and actions, of aggression and ego? Aren't we all guilty to some extent of contributing to problems, engaging in futile arguments instead of working toward solutions?

Further, what is the most effective way to change the mind and heart of a person? I have never known an argument to be won by the person starting with the statement "You're wrong." I've seen so many animal activists spew insults and derogatory comments toward humans, and then make an appeal to them to sign their petition or 'Like" their social media page or support their campaign. In conservationist movements, there is a widening gulf of acrimony between those who support the captivity of marine mammals-particularly dolphins such as the magnificent Orca, or killer whale, and those who don't. (Orca are actually the largest dolphin.) Both sides of the argument are valid. Anti-captivity activists believe that capturing, breeding, training and using captive dolphins is enslavement for profit, a business model that equates to human slavery. Emotions run wild among activists.

Recently my high school has been embroiled in a debate about the change of the mascot. Emotions are played out on social media by graduates from many decades ago. The majority seem to oppose the name change because of the way it which it was decided - by a small group rather than the alumni. Would it have been possible to achieve consensus if thousands had been polled? Highly unlikely, considering the backlash. The debate persists regardless of the fact that the name change is a done deal. Most fascinating to me is the number of challengers, perhaps scant compared to the number of alumni, but ample on social media. Has social media become the forest where the tree has fallen and everyone opines about it? Have the social media fora facilitated our evolution away from philosophy, or return to it? Has technology sidelined our connectivity to such a degree that we vault into opportunities to interact with one another when they arise, such as the change of the name of a high school mascot?

On one hand I applaud the discourse among my former classmates. It's great to see names and faces thirty-plus years after graduation, like attending a reunion, only better because the conversations are recorded permanently so we can review and ponder, and we can post our most flattering profile photos, the ones that flash our smiles and hide the wrinkles. We can scour the conversations and choose which ones to engage, and break off into private messages if we so choose. Online chatter is a brilliant example of democracy, where everyone has an opportunity to be heard and every voice counts. Validation is an integral component of transformative dialogue.

On the other hand, I'm a wee bit disappointed (again) in the process that led to the dissention. Surely there was a more democratic method to invite discussion before the mascot name was changed? Once again, the decisions of a few affect so many.

And on the third side of the coin is my fatigue over contentious discussions that fail to produce change. Presidential debates come and go; Presidents come and go; we alternate majority leadership and party governance and slog through societal ills and issues in the best way democracy allows, despite inherent toxins of greed, corruption and vice.

How flawed, to argue inconsequence. What a waste of energies, breath and bandwidth. Better to be grateful. Better to be gentle. Better to love. You may bristle at my attitude, considering the immense gains we as a nation and people have made through dissention and protest. Granted. But my pacifism is the fruit harvested "of a quiet eye."[v]

> *3 Nephi 29 For verily, verily I say unto you, he that hath the spirit of contention is not of me, but is of the devil, who is the father of contention, and he stirreth up the hearts of men to contend with anger, one with another. 30 Behold, this is not my doctrine, to stir up the hearts of men with anger, one against*

another; but this is my doctrine, that such things should be done away.

The foundational message belying many religions is love. Love is just a word. Words are cheap and meaningless. Love first requires choice, then action and commitment. Love begins with self, as Jesus taught:

"By this shall all men know that ye are my disciples, if ye have love one to another..."

When Jesus spoke these words, he had just washed the feet of his beloved disciples as an example of service and sacrifice, emblematic of His descending to this world, taking on human form and all the suffering that entailed. As Bruce C. Hafen explains in *Spiritually Anchored in Unsettled Times,*

> Christ's love is so deep that He took upon Himself the sins and afflictions of all mankind. Only in that way could He both pay for our sins and empathize with us enough to truly succor us—that is, run to us—with so much empathy that we can have complete confidence that He fully understands our sorrows. So, to love as Christ loves means we will somehow taste suffering ourselves—for the love and the affliction are but two sides of the same coin. Only by experiencing both sides so some degree can we begin to understand and love other people with a depth that even begin to approach Christ's love.[vi]

Fibromyalgia has taught me to nurture myself first, how to ration my energies, and the importance of attitude, choice, and committing action to those choices. Before I am fully wake, in that precious time, I make a decision: I choose to look at my life with fresh eyes, through the pain in my feet, ankles, wrists, elbows, neck, head back and hips so severe it is as if I was beaten. I choose to ignore fingers so swollen they won't accept rings, hands so sore, a cup weighs sixteen pounds. I choose to overcome the lethargy, tenderness and ache, and push myself out of bed.

I choose to be distracted; watching the wildlife is one of my favorite pastimes. It takes patience to see the miracles of nature – the business of bumblebees on the wild aster, the hummingbird hiding in the maple who eventually emerges and flits around the pink Rose of Sharon and the lavender butterfly bush. Watching whales is like that: long stretches of time bobbing around on the water and scanning the horizon like radar, punctuated by exhilaration when the whales surface, blow or breach. Babysitting Hawaiian monk seals is like that, too: hours and hours of sitting in the sand watching a seal snoozing rolling over, scratching, snorting or repositioning. Or watching and waiting for the silky black newborn to roll over and nurse. Which teat will s/he choose? For how long will s/he stay on that one? Is there a pattern to the nursing? Check off time and duration on the chart. How long do momma and puppy swim? Then we return to the salty solace of stillness in the sand.

In the morning, I choose a grateful rather than grievant heart. Humbly (although inconsistently), I list my blessings: the rejuvenation of restful sleep, the comfort of a bed, a warm, safe and dry home, the peace of my surroundings, the coziness of two sleeping kitties snuggled at my side, the godsend of my healing husband and our intact, eternal marriage, my son, his wife and their boys, my family, my friends, my students, my teachers and mentors, and all body parts which are not cramped or burning. Some mornings are easier than others.

I'm thankful for ancestors like my father's mother, who at sixteen years of age chose to board a ship in Ireland bound for the United States to seek a better life. I'm thankful I feel her intrepid spirit buoying me.

I say prayers of thanks for food on our table, a (mortgaged) home resembling paradise – a 102 year old gambrel at the very end of a cul-de-sac, an acre of flat yard and garden, fenced on three sides, wooded wetland border that swells to swamp proportions every spring, attracting wild ducks and Canada geese, early redwing blackbirds. Eyes open, the morning allows me to make a choice. Another gift, knowing there are no guarantees I will rise with the sun.

The promise of tomorrow is a lie, so I try to focus on today.

I am in a category of privilege - hashtag first world problems - but problems indeed. I navigate through the mornings with gratitude, in silence when possible, and in prayer. But it's not all bluebirds and rainbows; I have to chase away negative thoughts. Prone to depression, bitterness, self-pity and anger and selfishness, I have to talk and pray myself out of that hole. The past two years have taught me to rely on faith and hope rather than my own ailments, complaints, ambitions or drive.

We are living proof that life can change in an instant, and that hope lives.

> "Real hope keeps us 'anxiously engaged' in good causes even when these appear to be losing causes on the mortal scoreboard. Likewise, real hope is much more than wishful musing. It stiffens, not slackens, the spiritual spine. Hope is serene, not giddy, eager without being naive, and pleasantly steady without being smug. Hope is realistic anticipation which takes the form of a determination—not only to survive adversity but, moreover, to "endure ... well" to the end."
> ~Neal A. Maxwell[vii]

Wonders can be found when we believe they exist, and we choose to look for them. We can choose to see our little worlds differently, to look with the eyes of the heart. I try to view life as abounding with miracles, but the price is not cheap.

August 12 Saved by Faith?

...for it is by faith that miracles are wrought; and it is by faith that angels appear and minister unto men; wherefore, if these things have ceased wo be unto the children of men, for it is because of unbelief, and all is vain. ~Moroni 7: 37

Is healing fortified by faith and belief? Some answers have come to me through study and experience. I lean heavily on my Christian background and seek mentors who have overcome horrible things life throws at us. Jesus

Christ is the perfect mentor for me. He performed miracles for a variety of reasons, but what strikes me is the explanations He gave to those He healed. The implication was that faith healed them.

> *27 When she had heard of Jesus, came in the press behind, and touched his garment. 28 For she said, If I may touch but his clothes, I shall be whole. 34 And he said unto her, Daughter, thy faith hath made thee whole; go in peace, and be whole of thy plague.*[viii] *Mark 5:27, 28, 34*

> *22 A Canaanite woman from that vicinity came to him, crying out, "Lord, Son of David, have mercy on me! My daughter is suffering terribly from demon-possession." 23 Jesus did not answer a word. So his disciples came to him and urged him, "Send her away, for she keeps crying out after us." 24 He answered, "I was sent only to the lost sheep of Israel." 25 The woman came and knelt before him. "Lord, help me!" she said. 26 He replied, "It is not right to take the children's bread and toss it to their dogs." 27 "Yes, Lord," she said, "but even the dogs eat the crumbs that fall from their masters' table." 28 Then Jesus answered, "Woman, you have great faith! Your request is granted." And her daughter was healed from that very hour. ~Matthew 15: 22-28*

> *14 When they came to the crowd, a man approached Jesus and knelt before him. 15 "Lord, have mercy on my son," he said. "He has seizures and is suffering greatly. He often falls into the fire or into the water. 16 I brought him to your disciples, but they could not heal him." 17 "O unbelieving and perverse generation," Jesus replied, "how long shall I stay with you? How long shall I put up with you? Bring the boy here to me." 18 Jesus rebuked the demon, and it came out of the boy, and he was healed from that moment. 19 Then the disciples came to Jesus in private and asked, "Why couldn't we drive it out?" 20 He replied, "Because you have so little faith. I tell you the truth, if you have faith as small as a mustard seed, you can say to this mountain, 'Move*

from here to there' and it will move. Nothing will be impossible for you. "-Matthew 17: 14-21

In the book's Bible dictionary, miracles of Christ are described:

> *An important element in the work of Jesus Christ, being not only divine acts, but forming also a part of the divine teaching. Christianity is founded on the greatest of all miracles, the Resurrection of our Lord. If that be admitted, other miracles cease to be improbable. Miracles should not be regarded as deviations from the ordinary course of nature so much as manifestations of divine or spiritual power. Some lower law was in each case superseded by the action of a higher. They were intended to be a proof to the Jews that Jesus was the Christ. Many of them were also symbolic, teaching such divine truths as the result of sin and the cure of sin; the value of faith; the curse of impurity; and the law of love. The miracles of healing also show how the law of love is to deal with the actual facts of life. Miracles were and are a response to faith and its best encouragement. They were never wrought without prayer, felt need, and faith.[ix]*

Am I a rock-solid believer who never falters? Hardly. I yearn for escape. You know the feeling: When I'm driving, sometimes I want to keep going, to drive past the exit I'm supposed to take. When I wake up in the morning, sometimes I want to roll over and pretend my life is something else.

My fab four ways to escape are faith, dreaming/envisioning, focused breathing and Reiki. I have been a compulsive volunteer, but I'm working on peeling myself away from that. The expression "You can't give from an empty cup" resonates well with me. I've grown from being a protest sign-waving activist to one who embraces a more passive acceptance, surrender and stillness when all around me is falling apart. I fear my docile nature is misinterpreted as weakness. Beneath my calm, a storm often rages-a storm that can only be sheltered in faith. I know in my soul that the storm will pass. I can summon strength through my mustard seed-sized faith, and through the process of tending to my own needs first.

Friends have lamented that they wish they had my faith. Family has seen my faith in action. I assume my faith is a gift rooted in my upbringing: Catholic school, good and strict parents who attended church regularly and expected compliance. Healthy habits, taught when I was young, grew into a foundation of faithfulness. But my faith is tiny and humbling compared to that of others who helped me during this particular trial which has fortified my faith, brought me closer to Christ, and helped me to see more goodness in people. It's as if we were given these challenges to hammer us into being good examples to others, and to provide others the opportunity to help.

Several of my church friends explained it this way: it is a blessing to serve. If I had shut people out of my lives during the past two years, I would have been denying other people the blessings they could receive by supporting, nurturing, caring and praying for us.

As members of our church, Joe and I embrace faith as one of the starting points rather than the objective. Faith underpins everything we do, but is only one of the many tenets we strive to incorporate into our lives. While investigating, we were intrigued by the similarities and the differences between this church and other Christian churches. We learned how a young boy received an answer to his prayer about choosing a church; we learned the reason for the perfect organization of the church leadership. We learned the history of the buried, unearthed and translated plates which became a holy book; we learned about the everlasting nature of marriage – not "till death do us part" but forever, on this earth and into eternity where we can be reunited with our families. We learned about The Plan of Salvation, The Word of Wisdom and the restoration of the gospel. We learned the thirteen principles entitled the Articles of Faith, summarized by founding prophet as an answer to the question about what we believe, shortly before he died. Shortly after we joined the church, we traveled to the Palmyra, New York home; we walked in the sacred grove where he first received an answer to his innocent prayer. We touched the tools in the barn, walked the acres where he and his family worked and loved. We climbed the hill where the boy was inspired to uncover the records of the early people. I know the life and trails of the boy, who would eventually be martyred for his faith, is not a fairy tale.

We learned about the value of seeking records of our ancestors and family history. The church-sponsored website FamilySearch.org has 4,600 local facilities in 126 countries where anyone can access genealogical records and receive personal assistance with their family history.[x] Researching family history is a labor of love and devotion to our ancestors who have left this mortal realm. Soon after we joined the church, I received the calling to serve as the Family History Center Director for our ward. I knew little about genealogy and even less about the workings of the Center. I accepted the calling gladly, prayed, and learned. Our family tree grew and we felt indescribably reconnected to our family members who had passed.

We also witnessed events in our lives which can only be described as miraculous, too perfect to be coincidental. Joe's survival may be one of those events.

Chapter 10

Deaths, Victims, Hearts and Comas

Wherever you are, death will find you; even if you are in towers built up, strong and high… Quran 4:78

August 15: Three men in our neighborhood died of massive heart attacks last week. We had met one two weeks ago. Phillip was kind enough to transport the gas grill we had purchased from his perpetual yard sale to our home. Fit, with a head full of manicured grey hair, his appearance belied his age. "I'm 72 years old, no complaints" he revealed as he guided the grill off of his John Deere tractor. We told him our story; Joe flashed his scarred abdomen, and Phillip, shocked, told Joe how "lucky" he was. I don't recall if Joe took the opportunity to bear his testimony about his belief in God to Phillip that day. As he laughed at the ducks, Phillip circled the garden so he didn't have to back up the tractor, and drove down our little lane toward home, out of sight. I won't be able to get that last picture of him out of my heart. The second was a man who lived two streets away. The third man who lived in #73, the home directly opposite to the exit of our lane. He could often be found perched inside, looking out through square picture window. We took to waving to him as we passed. He always waved back.

Three deaths in the span of one week in our neighborhood is worrisome. Fear of death lingers with us. On the other hand, we believe that because we were spared death from H1N1 and resultant illnesses, we have jobs to do, and will not be called home until those jobs are completed.

Joe is no stranger to worrying about an early death; his biological father died suddenly when Joe was only 22 days old. High School teacher and coach collapsed while playing in a teacher/student softball game. Running to first base, he felt pains in his chest and arm. He left the game and drove himself to the doctor, who rushed him to the hospital, but was DOA. Cause of death was a massive heart attack at the age of 34. John left wife Catherine – nurse at the hospital where he died - with seven children aged 22 days to 7 years old.

Catherine married Christopher five years later; Christopher and Catherine had 3 more children.

The specter of premature death has remained with Joe since he learned the story of his father.

I am no stranger to illness or death, either. Historically I am prone to respiratory illnesses: pneumonia, pleurisy, bronchitis. I've completed (ten years of) menopause, but had endometriosis, adenomyosis, ovarian cysts, fibrocystic breasts, chronic earache, sore throat and fatigue, Erlichiosis, protruding L4 L5 vertebra and a fractured SI as a result of the car crash in Hawai`i in 2011, but other than that I'm a generally healthy person with an apparently decent immune system. I rarely catch a cold or the flu, so there was no onus to get a flu shot in 2014 just as there hadn't been in any other year. Even with the first pandemic H1N1 in 2009, I was not fearful; I was teaching middle school students in Hawai`i and felt somewhat shielded due to geography. The Hawaiian Islands are some of the most remote on the planet, and although tourists were welcomed during flu season, safeguards were in place for all inbound flights and cruise ships to mitigate the spread. We heard of a person or two having the flu, but the chance that the pandemic that hit the mainland would reach Hawai`i seemed as isolated as we were.

Joe outlived his father, and fortunately I didn't inherit my mother's constitution. Magdalena's life began in one of the most notorious periods of human history. She was born in Germany April, 1934, the same year that Adolf Hitler came into power. The day before her birth, Hitler set up the people's courts where judges were obliged to swear an oath of loyalty to the Nazis. Then in August 1934, hours after German President Paul von Hindenburg's death, Hitler announced a new law combining the office of Reich President with that of Reich Chancellor, transferring the existing authority of the Reich President to himself. After a nationwide vote and Hitler's dismissal of von Hindenburg's last wishes for Germany to return to a constitutional monarchy, this (illegal) law essentially granted Hitler absolute power.

Children: innocent casualties of war: my Mom was a victim long before she was born, raised in a country demolished by the First World War and headed into the Second. According to her big sister, Erika, Magdalena was frail, waifish, fussy and sensitive. The children didn't have much to eat. Erika remembers picking and eating grass which tasted like spinach when boiled. She recalls their little brother, Horst, lying on a cot, near death from malnutrition, begging for *fleish, fleish* (meat). Magdalena often spoke of the heartache of seeing her favorite pet goose, Peter, slaughtered for food, but repressed many other childhood memories.

When Magdalena was three, her biological mother, Heike, died from complications of appendicitis leaving husband Emmett, a police officer, and seven motherless children: three daughters at home and four other siblings who would eventually be rehomed. Heike Ludwig hailed from a wealthy family; her father was a Baron who disowned her for marrying a commoner. Erika remembers traveling to the Baron Ludwig villa to ask for support. The housekeeper met the family at the front door and announced Heike's arrival to the Baron. He coldly turned them away, telling the housekeeper to close the door.

Stories have been told of the family walking three hundred miles from Danzig (present day Gdansk) Poland to Germany to escape persecution which became severe in early 1939.

I remember my Mom's stories of Christmas in war-torn Germany. Pappa (father) was deemed ineligible for service with the Nazis due to the fortunate loss of two fingers on his dominant hand in an accident while making toys in the woodworking shop. Mutte (Stepmother) knit sweaters for a store in town. On Christmas Eve the three daughters Erika, Sabine and Magdalena were each asked to gather up their doll and surrender to Mutte. She lovingly bathed each doll, combed the hair and dressed each in a newly knitted outfit. Mom remembers the joy of finding a "new" dolly on Christmas morning. Mutti taught the girls how to knit and crochet; my Mom was never fond of it. I misunderstood why until much later in my life when I pieced together the story of her childhood and her memories of it.

Magdalena met and married my father who was stationed in Germany during the Korean War. Leaving her homeland and family when she was only twenty-two to accompany her husband and baby daughter Therese back to the states, she never quite assimilated into American culture.

She kept a meticulous home, raised two daughters, grieved the loss of a third daughter at only two days old, learned how to shop, worked jobs ranging from waitress to administrative clerk for the government, and was perpetually ill. In the span of eleven years during my adolescence, she underwent eleven major surgeries, three of which were exploratory. Her scarred abdomen resembled railroad tracks. She suffered a stroke when she was only thirty-four. We were having spaghetti for dinner; Mom and Dad were having a heated discussion. Mom said she didn't feel well and pushed herself away from the table. I watched the right side of her face melt, followed by the slumping of the right side of her body. Although she fully recovered from the stroke, perhaps due to her young age, she continued to neglect her health, even smoking until her death in 2007.

I often did my homework by the light of the hospital television, next to my Mom who was attached to tubes and gauges. I am not uncomfortable in hospitals or with people who are sick. I am not uncomfortable dealing with people who have health or emotional issues. During my childhood, my Mom was always in some stage of sickness or recovery, and this affected us all profoundly.

My sister Therese, four years older, became my mother when our mother was ill. Dad traveled extensively for work, and when he was home, he served in the military one weekend a month. He took evening college classes for many years. I cherished the time spent with my father and mother when he was home and she was healthy. Still, a pall hung over our family. My mother often remarked that she was "cursed". Continuous surgeries resulted in painful abdominal adhesions and scar tissue, and obstructed bowels necessitating medication and additional surgeries. The revolving door between home and hospital facilitated her reliance on prescription drugs, and my aversion to them.

Early on, I detested the human condition: how we hurt one another - perpetually. I resented being victimized by other people's choices and addictions. It's one thing to suffer the consequences of our own volition; this is the way of the world. It's an entirely different thing to be held hostage by someone or something else. There was a way out, but I was a long way from that door.

I saw what drugs did to my mother, and was tacitly determined to never allow myself to become addicted to anything. Rarely would I take as much as an aspirin for debilitating pain from endometriosis and ovarian cysts, surrendering only after I was incapacitated. When I was old enough, blackberry brandy provided relief unless the cramps snuck up on me. The endometriosis began in my early teens, and I wasn't diagnosed until years later, by way of a fortunate drama.

My parents separated when I was seventeen. Our house was sold. Dad moved to the Deep South; Mom remained in state and took an apartment in a town near to our old home. I declined a journalism scholarship to a college that was two hours away from Mom, opted for the closer state university, majored in special education and stayed nearer to my Mom – a quick thirty- five minute drive.

Freshman year of college: I'm taking a Music History mid-term exam, and I feel the twinge in my belly indicating my monthly is imminent. I'm focusing on the exam and trying to block the increasing pain, but it persists. I begin to rock in my seat, not to the music, but as a natural reaction to the pain - a sign that I'm losing control. I manage to ask the instructor if I can use the rest room even though it's not allowed during the exam. He grants permission. I find my way to a bathroom stall, sit down and resume rocking.

I woke up in the ambulance. My boyfriend told me that I was found passed out on the floor of the bathroom. I was brought to the hospital, treated with medication, and discharged. I followed up with my gynecologist who diagnosed the endometriosis and prescribed medication for pain. The following month, I suffered another episode. I called the pharmacy to check on the prescription. They told me that my Mom had picked it up. She denied it. Enter blackberry brandy.

So were the early years of dealing with pain, hospitals, doctors, and disease, and the admission ticket to the School of Opportunity.

Fast forward to Friday of Mother's Day weekend in May of 2007. Magdalena had been discharged the previous week from a rehab hospital to her little apartment located one town away from Therese's home. The visiting nurse who checked in on her finds her slumped over in her living room chair. She is rushed to the hospital where Therese works as a nurse; Therese in turn calls me once Mom is admitted. Mom's in a coma, and is in bad shape, Therese tells me. Joe and I head out at eleven o'clock PM to drive three hours to be with them.

When we arrive, we hurry to Mom's room. She is quiet, almost peaceful-- and comatose. Therese tells us that Mom has a twisted bowel, and the doctor has ruled that she is not a candidate for surgery. I don't understand it all, but trust my sister as the medical professional and conservator of Mom's last wishes. Mom is placed on "comfort measures" only, meaning nothing other than medication to keep her in a coma is administered. No food and no fluids. Doctors tell us that Mom will probably not last the weekend.

It was the horrible conclusion to a life plagued with difficulty.

Family is called from far and near; all of Mom's grandchildren come to say goodbye. Therese and her husband, Joe and I stay with Mom through the night, and the following day. We sleep in chairs and empty rooms, never too far from her. Hospice nurse arrives on Saturday afternoon to suggest that we all say what we need to say. She tells us that our Mom doesn't feel a thing, and has no awareness of what is happening. Nurses check on Mom regularly, and report her heart is just as healthy as can be.

We wait. We switch seats. We step out for lunch, for breaks, to go to Therese's house and shower, change clothes, and bring back pillows and toothbrushes. We turn the TV on and then off. We speak of memories. We laugh and we cry. Therese and I both watch Mom closely.

At some point on Saturday I have the feeling that Mom doesn't want to let go just yet. I think maybe she has unfinished business that needs finishing.

I figure she would have wanted to hear a goodbye from our Dad, her-ex-husband; maybe it would be good for both of them, if they spoke one last time. My Mom never stopped loving my Dad, even though their relationship was like oil and water. So I call him, explain the situation, and hold the phone to her ear. He speaks to her.

> "You've been a good mother, but it's time to let go now. You've been sick for so long. It's okay to go to heaven and be with God. There's no need to hang on any longer."

Her face appears to relax, but her heart rate doesn't change.

Hours pass. I'm wondering if her sister Erika who lives in Pittsburg would like to say goodbye, so I call her, explain the situation, and she speaks lovingly to my Mom:

Sis, you are so beautiful, I love you sweetie. You are such a good sister and mother. You've done such a good job. Go to heaven now. Go to be with Mutti and Pappa, and all our family. Save a place for me and get ready for me so when I get there, we can have a party. We'll eat potato salad and Rolf will play the accordion and we'll sing and dance! I love you my beautiful sister. Go to heaven now. I will see you soon. I love you sis, I love you!

I'm holding the phone to Mom's ear, and watching her face while my aunt is speaking. When my aunt mentioned a party and potato salad, my Mom's mouth seemed to turn up on one side. She smiled a little smile, deep in a coma. How was that possible?

Therese! (I whisper) Did you see that? She *smiled*.

I'm stunned. I had been told that my Mom felt no pain and had no awareness of what is happening. How could she muster a smile? I know what I saw, and it wasn't an accident or a flinch. Therese didn't see it, but I know what I saw.

Saturday night May 12, 2007. Mom's heart is still beating with vigor, even though she's being administered the maximum amount of coma drugs. We are bookends on both sides of her bed, watching, praying, talking to her and to each other. I run my hands atop her head and pat down her hair, trying to tame the tangled nest. Mom was always a sartorial splendor, with her cute pastel polyester pant suits, exquisite perfumes and salon-styled hairdos. She sported the beehive in the 60s and 70s; we used to joke with her and ask her if she kept her head on the bedpost at night because her hairdo was always as pristine on Friday as it was on the previous Saturday when she had it styled. She was a big fan of hot rollers in the 80s and 90s, and by the time she was retired from the VA and working her little drug store job, she was styling her own hair. Always particular about her hair, clothes and makeup, she maintained her class and dignity to the end of her life, to here, in the sterile bed where she lie, dying slowly.

I leaned in and spoke softly in her ear, "It's a good thing you're sleeping, Mom, because you'd be really upset if you saw your hair right now."

We said prayers, read Scriptures to her and spoke to her about things that were happening in the moment, told her who was in the room with her. "Bella's here, CJ is here, Shelly and Marie are here and Patrick is coming soon. We're here with you, Mom. We love you so much. You don't have to hurt anymore."

A set of Scriptures that brought Joe and me incredible solace came to our hearts, the same ones that were read to us the day we met the missionaries, the first time we had heard of this new church. We invited the two clean-cut young men in their white shirts and dark suits with signature nametags (both first names were "Elder" – we thought it odd!) into our home to hear what they had to say about Jesus Christ, just as we had invited Jehovah's Witnesses in to pray with us and study the Bible.

I thought it would be fantastic if the missionaries could visit Jolie D, who had just completed her fifth round of chemotherapy for ovarian cancer, and was home, resting and inviting people in to pray with her. Same aged as I, she had become my muse. We met in the late summer of 2003 as she stood painting on the shore of Heron Brook pond, across the street from the condos where Patrick and I lived. She was beautiful to watch, a brilliant artist, seamstress and designer, a sweet, lovely, funny and gentle soul. She was trying to improve on the *Plein air* style of painting ("in open air"), wherein the artist uses natural, changing light, and paints outdoors. She had recently quit her job to devote herself full time to her art. Heron Brook provided a rich backdrop with its late summer golden and ruddy hues reflecting on the calm pond waters, Canada geese and mallards splashing and squawking and taking flight. I spent a large part of my free time there on the banks of the pond, studying the ducks and geese, walking around the perimeter with my rescued greyhound, Boots. I knew the pond well, and I knew most of the people who visited the pond regularly. Jolie was new, and stood out immediately with her easel and canvas, a pretty woman who seemed to make the light brighter, the pond sparkle a little more just by being there. I introduced myself and complemented her painting, and our friendship began – a friendship that a mere three months later would have me investigating alternative treatments for cancer, inviting her to our home to heal and rest and take a break from her less than healthy domestic situation, accompanying her to chemo treatments, planning writing and painting workshops together, sharing our deepest fears and dreams.

The first time I accompanied Jolie D to her chemo treatment, she taught me a memorable lesson about suffering. Her shirt was lifted to reveal the port through which the chemicals were administered. I winced, and asked her if it hurt. Her response was priceless: she kicked me in my shin, and asked "Does *that* hurt?"

She had the cancer beat for a while, then the tumors returned with a vengeance. In the fall of 2006, she rested comfortably at home after chemo and felt peaceful when people prayed with her. I thought the missionaries would be a perfect fit. I asked them if they would go to her, and then come back later that day to tell me the rest of their story. They complied, agreeing to send their companions to Jolie's home. I told them that I would call her to tell her that they were coming so she could buzz them into her apartment.

After the missionaries made an appointment with us for later that day, I called Jolie. Her husband answered.

> "Hi Jeb, it's Aoibhyann, how are you doing? Listen I just wanted to let you know that I'm sending some missionaries over to pray with Jolie. I know when we spoke on Wednesday that she wanted to pray with people, and I just met these young men who agreed to come by. I wanted you to know so you could buzz them in when they came."

> "Aoibhyann, Jolie just passed."

When the missionaries returned later that day, I met them on the sidewalk, inconsolable.

"You can tell me all about your church later, but first, I need to know: *where did my friend go?*"

They came into our living room, and without hesitation opened the book to Alma, Chapter 40 verse 11 and 12:

> *Now, concerning the state of the soul between death and the resurrection—Behold, it has been made known unto me by an angel, that the spirits of all men, as soon as they are departed from this mortal body, yea, the spirits of all men, whether they be good or evil, are taken home to that God who gave them life. And then shall it come to pass, that the spirits of those who are righteous are received into a state of happiness, which is called paradise, a state of rest, a state of peace, where they shall rest from all their troubles and from all care, and sorrow.*

The words brought comfort when nothing else could. I had lost friends and loved ones before, and because I was raised as a Catholic, I felt I knew God, and believed in heaven and hell. Jolie's death caused me to ask the question *where did my friend go?* and receive an answer and solace that none other than the missionaries could have provided.

Sitting beside my Mom, Joe and I read Alma 40: 11 and 12 to her several times. We spoke to her with hopes that she could hear us. We tried to offer comfort when we felt powerless to do anything else. We knew the peace the words brought to us, and we were compelled to share them with her. Then, Mom cried. It was a weak tear, but undeniable. It streamed down the side of her face and drew out my own.

I panicked.

"Therese, she's *crying*. What is happening? She can hear us. Is she awake? What is going on?"

I was losing my composure. The nurses assured me that Mom wasn't feeling anything, and wasn't aware of anything. They told us she wouldn't last the weekend. We were expecting her to die tonight, or be gone by tomorrow, Sunday, Mother's Day. But there she lie, a smile here, a wince there, and then, a tear.

Therese cried too. She had seen her share of sick and dying patients, but now she was on the other side of the bed, as she put it, and watching her comatose mother die slowly was a completely different experience.

Mom didn't die on Saturday night, or on Sunday morning. Mother's Day came, and as the sun began to set, I became restless, unable to stand any more. Why wasn't she showing signs of dying? Why did the doctors say she wouldn't last the weekend? Why was she wincing every once in a while? Was she still feeling pain?

Why did she wince when I rubbed her feet that felt so cold through the blanket? Why, when I removed her socks, did I see black toes? What did that mean? (It meant she was dying, but it also proved that she was feeling pain.) Why wasn't there any more that could be done for her? She hadn't had food or water since Friday. Nurses say she was maxed out on meds.

"You know, Therese," I complained, "If this were a dog, hit by a car and laying by the side of the road, someone would put her out of her misery… but a person has to lie here and suffer like this? It's not right. I can't stand it. This is not medicine. This is *outrageous*."

I was in multiple states of denial, rage, anger, fear and frustration all at the same time, pacing back and forth like a caged animal.

Mom didn't die on Sunday night, either.

Monday morning came. Doctor and nurses check on Mom, and have a chat with us in the conference area. Doctor tells us she is very close to death. I see his mouth moving and I know he's saying something, but I'm fuming inside, and I can't grasp what's happening. We're all exhausted. We've been at the hospital for three nights and four days, waiting for Mom to die. I feel betrayed, and I can't believe I'm actually hoping for my Mom to die. I think I might have asked the doctor a question or two.

Monday afternoon comes and goes. We haven't seen a hospice nurse since Saturday. We show the black toes to the nurses – a sure sign of impending death says my sister – and Mom's heart appears to be slowing slightly.

Monday evening, 6PM: I'm pacing again. I'm beyond tired and numb. Did I want Mom to die so I could rest, or did I want her to die so she wouldn't suffer anymore? My thoughts are excruciating and they torment me. There are no words to describe this period of time after life and before death for the living, or the dying.

I spied the nurse's whiteboard on the wall below the television, walked over to it and started to pray. "Heavenly Father, please send angels to take Mom to heaven to be with you. She's had a horrible life and now, a horrible dying. Please send angels to take her. She's had enough, and we've had enough. Please don't keep her here anymore. Why is she still here? We've done what we can do, we've said what we needed to say. What else is there? Why won't you take her?"

I fear that Mom is stuck. I worry that she's not ready, that she doesn't want to die. I wonder if she is working out her trip to heaven. I can't understand what's happening, if she was so sick on Friday and yet still has a strong heartbeat? It makes no sense and I'm desperate for peace for my Mom, and for all of us.

I pick up the whiteboard marker, and draw a purple angel with a halo. It's what came to my hand.

I say a little prayer again. "Please God, please, please. Enough. Please. Please come take my Mom home."

I return to sit by Mom, and hold her hand. She is breathing more slowly than yesterday.

6:15PM: In walks a hospice nurse we'd not seen before. Therese doesn't recognize her. She has a full head of straight, shoulder-length gray hair, and is wearing a violet colored sleeveless smock over a white long- sleeved turtleneck. I was so taken by her pleasant demeanor and fair complexion for a woman of her age. She exuded calm and peace.

She introduced herself as the evening hospice nurse (also unusual). She asked us if we had told Mom everything we needed to say to her, and explained that she was very close to death. We told her the story of how she lie in the bed for four days and nights, how her heart was so strong, how her feet were turning black, and how she smiled and cried even though she was in a coma, etc. I felt at ease with her, and I felt as if she actually cared about what we had to say.

After she spoke to us, she moved to sit by Mom's side. She held her hand, and spoke quietly in her ear. She wasn't there for more than a minute or so. It was all so peaceful. We didn't ask her what she said. It didn't really matter; it was the manner in which she spoke to my Mom that was absolutely genuine and divine.

The hospice nurse in the violet smock said goodbye to us and exited the room. The nurse entered and checked Mom's vitals. Her heartrate is slowing, she said.

By 7:40, Mom was dead.

Therese opened the hospital room window, a superstition about providing the soul a way to depart. We sat by Mom's side for some time. I tried to freeze the picture of her in my memory, capturing the details in my head so as never to forget: her creamy complexion, even in death! The shape of her fingers, her hands, her tiny lifeless body. I stared a long stare, the one when we expect to see the chest rise and fall with breath, but there was none. The death that we wished for had come, yet there was no consolation. Even though she had gone to "paradise, a state of rest, a state of peace, where they shall rest from all their troubles and from all care, and sorrow", we were left behind without her.

Therese never saw the nurse in the purple smock again.

Chapter 11

Flus, Vaccines and Rabbits - Oh My!

*"The secret of life is to have a task, something you devote
your entire life to, something you bring everything to,
every minute of the day for the rest of your life.
And the most important thing is, it must be
something you cannot possibly do."*
~Henry Moore

Summer will fade. I'm reminded that winter and flu season are just around the bend. Corner pharmacies advertise warn us to get our flu shots. Television commercials encourage the flu shot, some even offering rewards and incentives such as a percentage off future purchases. At this time in 2014, Joe and I were not concerned about getting the flu. We never had it before. Joe became sick in January, the month when he transferred to our home airport, but we initially attributed his illness to the fact that he was run down.

Approximately forty states reported widespread influenza-like illness (ILI) activity by the third week of January, 2014. Our state remained in the moderate to low category through March.[xi] We began to wonder if Joe's constant contact with the public as a transportation security officer at the (international) airport had any impact on his contracting the flu.

Despite what we've endured "all because we didn't get the flu shot" as Dr. K chastises, I am still uncomfortable taking the shot. Even in light of flu and flu-related illness such as pneumonia 2015, I'm hesitant. In 2014 flu season the CDC warned doctors that the flu shot was less effective because the flu strain had mutated.[xii]

August 18: a 16 year-old in New Zealand dies of pneumonia, a complication of the flu as "flu epidemic sweeps the city."[xiii]

The Center for Disease Control (CDC) presents a simplistic and concise justification for immunizations, and compares the need to continue vaccinations even after a disease has been rarified to bailing water out of a leaky boat:

> *Why immunize our children? Sometimes we are confused by the messages in the media. First we are assured that, thanks to vaccines, some diseases are almost gone from the U.S. But we are also warned to immunize our children, ourselves as adults, and the elderly. Diseases are becoming rare due to vaccinations.*
>
> *It's true, some diseases (like polio and diphtheria) are becoming very rare in the U.S. … they are becoming rare largely because we have been vaccinating against them. But it is still reasonable to ask whether it's really worthwhile to keep vaccinating.*
>
> *It's much like bailing out a boat with a slow leak. When we started bailing, the boat was filled with water. But we have been bailing fast and hard, and now it is almost dry. We could say, "Good. The boat is dry now, so we can throw away the bucket and relax." But the leak hasn't stopped. Before long we'd notice a*

little water seeping in, and soon it might be back up to the same level as when we started.

Keep immunizing until disease is eliminated.

Unless we can "stop the leak" (eliminate the disease), it is important to keep immunizing. Even if there are only a few cases of disease today, if we take away the protection given by vaccination, more and more people will become infected and will spread disease to others. Soon we will undo the progress we have made over the years.

Opponents to vaccines object to CDC claims, the mandated vaccination schedule and the process by which the vaccines are approved, accusing them and other organizations of malfeasance, fear mongering and scamming the public into a vaccine schedule that is neither safe, necessary nor effective.

Influenza is the common term for respiratory illnesses brought on by influenza viruses. There are three types: A, B and the lesser-known C, but there are many different "strains" or variations of the virus. Flu-related illnesses vary in type and severity depending upon factors such as the strain (or variant) of virus, the patient's age and health.

The grand allusion of safety from flu and flu-related illnesses is rooted in the generalization that flu vaccines are necessary, safe and effective as other vaccines. Considered collectively, vaccines are customarily viewed as essential safeguards against disease. The list of vaccine-preventable illnesses from the CDC:

Anthrax

Cervical Cancer (Human Papillomavirus)

Diphtheria

Hepatitis A

Hepatitis B

Haemophilus influenzae type b (Hib)

Human Papillomavirus (HPV)

Influenza (Flu)

Japanese encephalitis (JE)

Measles

Meningococcal

Mumps

Pertussis

Pneumococcal

Polio

Rabies

Rotavirus

Rubella

Shingles (Herpes Zoster)

Smallpox

Tetanus

Typhoid

Tuberculosis (TB)

Varicella (Chickenpox)

Yellow Fever [xiv]

I noticed two features of flu vaccines that could warrant singular categorizing:

1. **Flu vaccines are recommended to be taken annually**, as opposed to those for other illnesses which are recommended to be administered for finite amount of doses and intervals. The CDC suggests annual flu vaccines for everyone six months and older, claiming it is the best defense:

> "An annual seasonal flu vaccine (either the flu shot or the nasal spray flu vaccine) is the best way to reduce the chances that you will get seasonal flu and spread it to others…" This recommendation has been in place since <u>February 24, 2010 when CDC's Advisory Committee on Immunization Practices (ACIP)</u> voted for "universal" flu vaccination in the United States to expand protection against the flu to more people. [xv]

CDC has published a brilliant forewarning, devoting a comprehensive section to people at high risk of developing flu–related complications:

"Most people who get the flu will have mild illness, will not need medical care or antiviral drugs, and will recover in less than two weeks. Some people, however, are more likely to get flu complications that result in being hospitalized and occasionally result in death. Pneumonia, bronchitis, sinus infections and ear infections are examples of flu-related complications. The flu also can make chronic health problems worse. For example, people with asthma may experience asthma attacks while they have the flu, and people with chronic congestive heart failure may experience a worsening of this condition that is triggered by the flu. The list below includes the groups of people more likely to get flu-related complications if they get sick from influenza."

Children younger than 5, but especially children younger than 2 years old

Adults 65 years of age and older

Pregnant women (and women up to two weeks postpartum)

Residents of nursing homes and other long-term care facilities

Also, American Indians and Alaskan Natives seem to be at higher risk of flu complications

The list is supplemented by those who have medical conditions including:

Asthma

Neurological and neurodevelopmental conditions [including disorders of the brain, spinal cord, peripheral nerve, and muscle such as cerebral palsy, epilepsy (seizure disorders), stroke, intellectual disability (mental retardation), moderate to severe developmental delay, muscular dystrophy, or spinal cord injury].

Chronic lung disease (such as chronic obstructive pulmonary disease [COPD] and cystic fibrosis)

Heart disease (such as congenital heart disease, congestive heart failure and coronary artery disease)

Blood disorders (such as sickle cell disease)

Endocrine disorders (such as diabetes mellitus)

Kidney disorders

Liver disorders

Metabolic disorders (such as inherited metabolic disorders and mitochondrial disorders)

Weakened immune system due to disease or medication (such as people with HIV or AIDS or cancer, or those on chronic steroids)

People younger than 19 years of age who are receiving long-term aspirin therapy

People who are morbidly obese. [xvi]

2. **Flu vaccines are regularly reformulated as viruses mutate and change**. The CDC explains:

People's protection from viruses depends on having their having been exposed to the virus before, through infection or from a vaccine for that virus. In either case, the immune system "remembers" the virus and creates virus-specific antibodies that will neutralize the virus when it next enters the body. But influenza viruses can mutate, or change, rapidly. Every few years, influenza viruses mutate enough to result in a new strain. This process is known as antigenic drift. People who have been exposed to a related strain of that virus will likely have some pre-existing immunity to it in the form of antibodies, and the illness that results may be mild. Occasionally, a major change in a virus produces a strain so different from the others before it that humans have little or no preexisting immunity. This antigenic shift, and it can result in widespread, serious illness.

An influenza pandemic occurs when a new subtype or strain of influenza virus develops from antigenic shift and spreads globally. Three pandemics occurred in the 20th century, all of them caused by antigenic shift in influenza A strains. A pandemic in 2009, less deadly than the 20th-century outbreaks, was the result of a unique combination of genetic changes. The 1918-19 pandemic is the event against which all other pandemics are compared because of its unprecedented death toll.[xvii]

While it is possible to survive the flu without major complications, the CDC is very clear about possible outcomes of the flu.

"Most people infected with influenza may feel ill for several days and then recover, although some may carry the virus without feeling symptoms. In some cases, influenza can lead to pneumonia, other complications, or death.[xviii]

The US debate about vaccines is not new. From Vaccines ProCon.org Early History of Vaccines:

In response to immunization laws, in 1878, the National Anti-Compulsory Vaccination Reporter stated that "the dangerous illnesses following the vaccine process are... on the whole... a greater evil to humanity than small-pox itself!" [7] The Anti-Vaccination Society of America was founded in

1879 in response to the states enacting vaccination mandates and with the belief that it "is undignified" to mandate vaccinations and that the "efficacy of vaccination as a disease preventative is a matter of individual opinion." [8] In 1882 the New England Anti-Compulsory Vaccination League was founded and in 1885 the Anti-Vaccination League of New York City was created. [7]

Contemporary proponents of mandatory vaccines cite grand benefits, answering the question "Should any vaccines be required for children?"

(1) Vaccines can save children's lives.
(2) The ingredients in vaccines are safe in the amounts used.
(3) Major medical organizations state that vaccines are safe.
(4) Adverse reactions to vaccines are extremely rare.
(5) Vaccines protect the "herd."
(6) Vaccines save children and their parents [sic] time and money.
(7) Vaccines protect future generations.
(8) Vaccines eradicated smallpox and have nearly eradicated other diseases such as polio.
(9) Vaccine-preventable diseases have not disappeared so vaccination is still necessary.
(10) Vaccines provide economic benefits for society.

On the Con side of the argument:

(1) Vaccines can cause serious and sometimes fatal side effects.
(2) Vaccines contain harmful ingredients.
(3) The government should not intervene in personal medical choices.
(4) Mandatory vaccines infringe upon constitutionally protected religious freedoms.
(5) Vaccines can contain ingredients some people consider immoral or otherwise objectionable.
(6) Vaccines are unnatural, and natural immunity is more effective than vaccination.

(7) The pharmaceutical companies, FDA, and CDC should not be trusted to make and regulate safe vaccines.

(8) Diseases that vaccines target have essentially disappeared.

(9) Most diseases that vaccines target are relatively harmless in many cases, thus making vaccines unnecessary.[xix]

Opponents' opinions and reactions to mandatory vaccines range from uncertainty to alleging it has "gone beyond regulatory misconduct to criminal negligence." (Doctors Speak Out About H1N1 Vaccine Dangers)[xx]

The Vaccine Debate

I will go in this way, and find my own way out… ~ Dave Matthews Band

If your compassion does not include yourself, it is incomplete. ~Jack Kornfield

In 1998, Dr. Andrew Wakefield wrote an article for *The Lancet* linking the Rubella virus in the measles, mumps, rubella (MMR) to autism.[xxi] Investigators accused him of falsifying medical records of children in his study because he was in the pockets of lawyers who intended to sue vaccine manufacturers and scare the public. Co-authors of the study wrote a retraction of interpretation[xxii] article in *The Lancet*. Wakefield made a statement in *The Lancet* in March 2004 refuting their allegations, claiming the clinical and pathological findings in the studies of children stood as reported. Editors of *The Lancet* retracted Wakefield's article in 2010 and in 2011, Wakefield's license was removed and he was barred from practicing medicine in the UK. Wakefield continues to assert that he and his colleagues "acted in the best medical interests of these children."[xxiii]

Wakefield has become the proverbial canary in the vaccine coal mine. Others have joined the debate.

Robert F Kennedy Jr. has written and spoken publicly about the Vaccine/Autism debate, authoring works such as *Deadly Immunity* (Rolling Stone and Salon.com) and *Thimerosal: Let the Science Speak*. Kennedy claims he is pro-vaccine, but points the finger at Thimerosal, a preservative contained in vaccines dating back to the 1930s. Alleging it is one of the most toxic elements – "one thousand times more neurotoxic than lead" - Kennedy asks why we think it is safe to inject it into babies, and makes a link to the rise in autism. He commonly states, "…Almost immediately after it was put in (Thimerosal), autism cases began to appear. Autism had never been known before.[xxiv] The vaccine schedule was increased [in the late 1980s] and nobody bothered to do an analysis on what the cumulative impact of what all that mercury was doing to kids. We are injecting our children with 400 times the amount of mercury than the FDA or the EPA considers safe."[xxv]

In a 2007 video[xxvi], Kennedy claims, "In 1988, one in every 2500 children had autism American children had autism, today, one in every 166 have autism, and one in every 6 children have other kinds of learning disorders, neurological disorders, speech delay, language disorders, ADD, hyperactivity… all related to Thimerosal ."

"..There are literally hundreds of studies that connect Thimerosal to these disorders. The science is out there."[xxvii]

Deadly Immunity was corrected multiple times within days of publication, and was retracted and deleted by Salon.com and Rolling Stone on Jan. 16, 2011. [xxviii]

Kennedy introduced the film *Trace Amounts Autism, Mercury and the Hidden Truth* in April 2015:

> "We ought to have policies that encourage and promote full vaccine coverage, but the way we do that is by restoring the integrity and credibility of the regulatory process…by making sure the vaccines are safe and efficacious and are not going to harm our children…Big pharma is a trillion dollar industry, the vaccine part of that is increasingly one of the biggest profit centers of that industry…so they can put anything they want in that vaccine, and they have no accountability for it. Statistics and molecules don't lie, but statisticians do. And…it's a biological product, so the patents

never expire…no advertising, no marketing required… people
are forced to buy it…"

Kennedy asserts that financial entanglements of those involved with the
vaccine schedule remove the essential function of that industry: public
health.

> "When I was a boy, I received five vaccines, my children got
> up to twenty-two, and today children receive up to sixty-
> nine vaccines…now, there are two hundred and seventy-one
> vaccines in the CDC pipeline…"

SB277

Public opinion against vaccinations is not new, but was intensified
following the outbreak of measles at Disney World in California. From
the California Department of Public Health website:

> In December 2014, a large outbreak of measles started in
> California when at least 40 people who visited or worked
> at Disneyland theme park in Orange County contracted
> measles; the outbreak also spread to at least half a dozen
> other states. On April 17, 2015, the outbreak was declared
> over, since at least two 21-day incubation periods (42 days)
> have elapsed from the end of the infectious period of the last
> known outbreak-related measles case.

> Measles is a highly contagious viral disease. It is widespread in
> many parts of the world, including Europe, Africa, and Asia.
> Measles begins with a fever that lasts for a couple of days,
> followed by a cough, runny nose, conjunctivitis (pink eye),
> and a rash. The rash typically appears first on the face, along
> the hairline, and behind the ears and then affects the rest of
> the body. Infected people are usually contagious from about
> 4 days before their rash starts to 4 days afterwards. Children
> routinely get their first dose of the MMR (measles, mumps,
> rubella) vaccine at 12 months old or later. The second dose

of MMR is usually administered before the child begins kindergarten but may be given one month or more after the first dose. For anyone planning to travel internationally, the California Department of Public Health (CDPH) strongly encourages all Californians to make sure they are protected against measles and other dangerous diseases before they go abroad.[xxix]

California acted with haste; SB277 was introduced in February 2015 by lead authors Senators Pan and Allen, and signed by Governor Jerry Brown in June, 2015.

These laws and mandates do not occur within a bubble. I'm reminded again of how the decisions of a few affect the lives of so many, not always for the greater good. A friend of a friend, "H", is living in California with her four year- old daughter who is preparing for pre-school. H is concerned about the vaccines mandated by law to be administered before children can attend school. Opponents of the bill/law claim it has significant impact on parents' rights to make medical decisions for their children, asserting it will require every child to receive all state-mandated vaccines before attending any school in California. Those who choose not to vaccinate their children do so with the notion that the complete course of vaccines would do more harm to children than the diseases they prevent. With SB277, California joins Mississippi and West Virginia as states having stringent vaccine laws. The law bans the "opt-out" feature, wherein parents were allowed to decline vaccinations for their child due to personal beliefs.

"The blanket policy of mandating vaccines is repulsive," said H in a phone interview. "It disrespects and is a huge infringement on parents' rights and religious objections, and denies people the ability and right to make educated medical decisions." H told me that the opponents to SB277 are unrelenting. "There were so many people at the Sacramento State Capital [Peaceful March for Parental Rights and Freedom] they filled the room to capacity, and the line of people wanting to get in ran around the block. The CDC should be acting as a watchdog, similar to the [Food and Drug Administration] FDA, not regulating vaccines and GMOs." H has a BS in

Science, a state certificate in wastewater management and two years of law school. She comes from a military family and is "not a hippie", referring to one of the many denouncements made by the pro-vaccine community about anti-vaxxers. She feels it's disgusting that wealthy parents can opt for homeschooling, yet poor parents have no option but to "poison their child" before they can attend school. H's final question drove the point home: "What if a vaccine was developed for AIDS? Should every child be mandated to take it?"

Text from SB277 Legislative Counsel's Digest:

> This bill would eliminate the exemption from existing specified immunization requirements based upon personal beliefs, but would allow exemption from future immunization requirements deemed appropriate by the State Department of Public Health for either medical reasons or personal beliefs. The bill would exempt pupils in a home-based private school and students enrolled in an independent study program and who do not receive classroom-based instruction, pursuant to specified law from the prohibition described above. The bill would allow pupils who, prior to January 1, 2016, have a letter or affidavit on file at a private or public elementary or secondary school, child day care center, day nursery, nursery school, family day care home, or development center stating beliefs opposed to immunization, to be enrolled in any private or public elementary or secondary school, child day care center, day nursery, nursery school, family day care home, or development center within the state until the pupil enrolls in the next grade span, as defined.[xxx]

"H" claims parents of school-ready children are planning evasive tactics such as finding doctors who will secretly falsify records of immunizations or provide record of medical exception. The number of individuals and groups of concerned citizens who are fighting to repeal SB277 is virulent.

CDC.gov website provides information on the 2015 Vaccine schedule in graph/chart form[xxxi] which is downloadable and fairly simple to understand.

Herd Immunity

The arguments which cause me greatest concern are those by the anti-vaxxers. I don't know why these individuals, scientists, parents of vaccine-injured children and the like continue to sound the alarm about vaccines. There is also the steady counter-argument by the vaccine industry regarding "Herd Immunity", the theory that indirect protection from infectious disease occurs when a large majority of the population has become immune to the infection, resulting in protection by "the herd" for individuals who are not immune. The foundation of herd immunity (according to the vaccine industry) is mass vaccination. Consider this, from Barbara Loe Fisher, Co-founder and President of the National Vaccine Information Center (NVIC):

> "The original concept of herd immunity is that when a population experiences the natural disease, and in childhood diseases it meant the childhood population experienced certain childhood diseases, natural immunity would be achieved. A robust, qualitatively superior, natural 'herd immunity' within the population that would then protect other people from getting the disease in other age groups.
>
> ... I'll just take influenza, for example. When you have enough circulating influenza of a certain strain in a population, the population achieves at some point a 'herd immunity' effect.... Because enough people have experienced it, they're protected naturally, and then that protection confers protection on other people. But the vaccinologists have adopted this idea of vaccine-induced herd immunity. The problem with it is... is that all vaccines only confer temporary protection, at least the vaccines that we have been using, only confer temporary protection. And pertussis vaccine is one of the best examples.

Whole cell pertussis, DPT vaccine, was used since the late-1940s, universally in our country. ... When you look at effectiveness of either the whole cell or this acellular pertussis vaccine, what you find is that there's a lot of problems with extended vaccine-induced immunity. So you have a very short shelf life, basically. And what is the reasons for that? Well, pertussis vaccines have been used for about 50-60 years, and the organism has started to evolve to become vaccine resistant...

... And I can read you the results of one study looking at what is the pertussis organism about now, B pertussis... 'Results showed that the progressive gene loss occurred in finished B pertussis strains isolated during a period of 50 years and confirmed that B pertussis is dynamic and continuously evolving, suggesting that the bacterium may use gene loss as one strategy to adapt to highly immunized populations.'

... Because you know what, every life form... wants to live. Wants to survive. Universal principle. And viruses and bacteria are no exception. And when you put a pressure on a virus or bacteria that's circulating, with the use of a vaccine that contains a lab-altered version of that virus or bacteria, it doesn't seem that it would be illogical to understand that that organism is going to fight to survive, it's going to find a way to adapt in order to survive. And I think that this is not something that's really understood generally by the public— that vaccines do not confer the same type of immunity that natural exposure to the disease does. [xxxii]

Barbara Loe Fisher's comments seem reasonable when viewed with the increase in antibiotic resistance.

With a firestorm of controversy swirling in my head over efficacy and safety of vaccines, I'm reluctant to take the flu vaccine. The other side of my brain is petrified to experience what I did in 2014. My rational self (and Primary

Care Physician Dr. K) insist that I take the shot. But the more I investigate vaccines, the more confused I become. Are the preservatives in the vaccine harmful as anti-vaxxers report? What's the difference between Thimerosal, ethyl mercury, methylmercury and mercury? What are formaldehyde/ formalin, aluminum hydroxide, aluminum citrate, aluminum phosphate, benzethonium chloride, fetal bovine serum, polysorbate 80, monkey kidney tissue, polymyxin, neomycin, yeast protein, cellular protein, soy peptone, MRC-5 human diploid cells, WI-38 human lung fibroblasts, insect cell protein, ovalbumin, egg protein, chick kidney cells, chick embryo fibroblasts, human serum albumin, phenol, monosodium glutamate, casein, porcine gelatin, guinea pig cell cultures and glutaraldehyde? What vaccines contain them, or were created using them? Are they present in the vaccines given at my local corner pharmacy walk-in clinic?

Why was the National Childhood Vaccine Injury Act established in 1986? There has to be some truth to public claims of vaccine-related injuries:

> By 2012, the U.S. Court of Claims had awarded nearly $2.5 billion dollars to vaccine victims for their catastrophic vaccine injuries, although two out of three applicants have been denied compensation.
>
> This historic law acknowledged that vaccine injuries and deaths are real and that the vaccine injured and their families should be financially supported and that vaccine safety protections were needed in the mass vaccination system. The law set up a federal vaccine injury compensation program as well as included legal requirements for vaccine providers... "[xxxiii] That number has now increased to over $3 billion.

If the historic law acknowledged that vaccine injuries and death are real, what does the government know that the general public doesn't? Do I need to consult with a lawyer to understand the National Vaccine Injury Compensation Program? Do I believe the assertions made in *Health Impact News* that "the flu shot is the most dangerous vaccine in America?"[xxxiv]

And the research continued, adding fodder to my confusion.

Do I need to be worried about Ebola? What about enterovirus d68? Is there a link between vaccines and the meteoric rise in autism? If there is, what can or will be done about it? Is there truly a media blackout about vaccine injuries throughout the world? Is my Fibromyalgia related to my receiving the TDaP (July) and flu (September) vaccines in the same year? Is there a connection between chronic illnesses and vaccines? Do I need to be worried about my grandsons, age four and eighteen months, or my great niece and nephew, age six and two, or my infant great niece?

Is it even conceivable that our trusted governmental organizations deceive the American public? If not, why are so many people distressed by vaccines, and the vaccine schedule?

Where there's smoke, there's fire. Does that apply here?

Whose studies do I trust? Is there merit to the assertion that some vaccines are produced using aborted fetal tissue?

I'm intrigued to know if the incidences of childhood diseases such as diabetes, obesity, ADD/ADHD, learning disabilities, food allergies, birth defects, autism, seizures and cancer is correspondingly prevalent in isolated US communities, the Amish for example.

After I did (more) research on isolated US communities, I came across this:

> People outside the alternative health community are often confused by the lack of autism in the Amish people. The Amish do not experience autism, or most of the other learning disabilities that plague our technological society. They live in a society that consists of outdated technologies and ideals, at least by contemporary standards.

> Their diet consists of eating organic, fresh, locally-grown produce, and of course, they do not follow the established vaccination routines. To the dismay of the mainstream media and the medical establishment, this has resulted in a healthier people, who are void of all of our chronic diseases.

> Heart disease, cancer, and diabetes are virtually non-existent in Amish villages. Equally non-existent are our modern, chemically-engineered medicines, enhanced (chemically engineered) foods, G.M.O. (genetically engineered) foods, and of course, vaccines. How is it that those who are without the so-called "miracles" of modern orthodox medicine are healthier? The truth about health, medicine, and how they both relate to the Amish has become an embarrassment to some rather powerful people.

> There have been 3 (yes three) verified cases of autism in the Amish, and two of those children were vaccinated. No information is available for the third child, who was likely vaccinated himself. The strong correlation between vaccinations and autism is becoming undeniable...[xxxv]

I found problems with this post initially, beginning with the statement that heart disease is virtually non-existent in Amish villages. Untrue. And then I found myriad counter arguments to the "Amish Anomaly", claiming the issue is complex and cannot be explained away by the vaccinated vs. unvaccinated dichotomy. I found statements by a doctor who claim to be *the* doctor for the group who cited the incidence of autism to be 1 in 10,000. I found refutations, rejections, and contradictions in data, opinions, claims and report. Deeper down the rabbit hole I went. I found videos such as *Trace Amounts Autism, Mercury and the Hidden Truth, Bought – The Truth Behind Vaccines, Big Pharma and Your Food,* and *Direct Order,* the documentary about soldiers who refused to take the anthrax vaccine.

I found a controversial, well-documented, heart-felt appeal to church leaders to review the church's policy on vaccinations. Comments written to the author were widely divergent, and I found this one supporting the author to be most poignant:

> "The [church Doctrine and Covenants] D&C says in section 89 that...In consequence of evil designs which do and will

exist in the hearts of CONSPIRING men in the last days… William Thompson of the CDC has admitted to fraud and coverups linking autism to the MMR vaccine. Is this not conspiring men, knowingly harming children and covering it up? Watch Brian Deer and the GMC, Selective hearing on [yo]utube. Andrew Wakefield never committed fraud and his partner was exonerated of committing fraud recently. He has asked to have a debate publicly, but nobody was willing to do that because he knows too much. He continues to help the parents and their children who suffer with autism. Satan is very deceiving. We need to be careful who we support and truly search for truth." xxxvi

I had to crawl out. I wasn't intending to open Pandora's Box of science and pseudo-science about the causes or occurrence of autism, or health in insulated communities such as the Amish in Pennsylvania and Ohio.

But I had.

However, there are ample testimonies of parents of healthy, "natural" unvaccinated children – too numerous to ignore. I wasn't interested in tackling the entirety of research at the University of the Internet to position myself to make a somewhat educated conclusion about the good or bad of vaccines, or about the connection between vaccines and illnesses, or about the veracity and legitimacy of the vaccine industry. I simply wanted to know if it was wise to get a flu shot this year, considering my evidently compromised immune system, Fibromyalgia, weakness, fatigue and general malaise. I simply needed to know if I would threaten my health by taking a flu vaccine. Research yielded no relief or answers and too many questions, taking me further down a rabbit hole, out of which I desperately wanted to climb. And stories continued to find me, like the one about the infamous Raggedy Ann doll's connection to vaccine injuries, created by Johnny Gruelle, father of only daughter Marcella, who died at age 13.

Down in the rabbit hole, I found the National Vaccine Information Center (NVIC), "… a national charitable, non-profit educational organization founded in 1982. NVIC launched the vaccine safety and informed consent movement in America in the early 1980's …the oldest and largest consumer led organization advocating for the institution of vaccine safety and informed consent protections in the public health system."[xxxvii]

Down the rabbit hole, I learned that October is Vaccine Awareness Month, and found *VaccineFraud.com*, Vaccine *Resistant Movement.org*, *Californians for Vaccine Choice, California Coalition for Health Choice* and social media groups such as *Nurses Against Mandatory Vaccines*, and *Know the Vax*, whose purpose is "…to share the side of vaccine education often not provided by doctors or covered in the media so that you can make a truly informed decision."[xxxviii]

I found *Running the Country.com*, where I watched Dr. Andrew Wakefield, (still going strong in Orem, Utah, March 2015), in *Feast of Consequences: Whistleblowing in the Public Interest.* I found celebrities Jim Carrey and Jenny McCarthy, and I heard the vaccine issue rear its gnarly head at the 2016 Republican presidential debate, to the probable dismay of doctors and health professionals.

I found Patrick Jordan, Dr. Russell Blalock and Dr. Rebecca Carly, and the term "weapons of mass destruction" in the same sentence as vaccines. I read about the assertion that intramuscular injections bypass the respiratory and digestive track and remain in the bloodstream (triggering an autoimmune response), the critical and overlooked connection to vaccine-related injury and illness.

And I saw the *Zika* virus on the horizon, and all the hysteria and finger-pointing and alleged connections to pregnant mothers and horrible childhood ailments like microcephaly - another virus for which we'll need a vaccine?

I needed to extricate myself. But how?

Regardless of whether I get the flu vaccine or not, I'll continue to be vigilant. I'll wear masks in public, beginning when autumn sets in, sunshine wanes, days shorten, and flu season begins. In the grey days of winter, I'll avoid going out in public as much as possible. I was never fond of shopping anyway, going out only for emergencies like cat food or toilet paper. This year will be no different.

I wasn't always one of those persons seen wearing sterile breathing masks in public, or disinfecting surfaces. I didn't believe in the value of a flu shot, thinking that I would get sick from it. I had been healthy, active, and health- conscious, carried and used germicidal lotion, washed my hands regularly, took vitamins, zinc and Echinacea. I'm not a smoker. I don't drink anymore. Exercise used to include jet skiing, swimming, jogging, walking, gardening, and small home maintenance. I felt my immunity was fairly strong; I taught for more than twenty years. That's twenty seasons of teaching sick kids – a great immunity builder. Despite pneumonia and respiratory ailments as a child, I was rarely sick as an adult. The source of major health angst was menopause.

Now, I run when I hear someone coughing or sneezing in the grocery aisle. I am the only one wearing a mask in the airport and on the plane. Why? My plane seat neighbor said I was "the smartest person on the plane." I'm not sick, I tell them, pulling down my mask so they can see my full face. I tell my story and hear the same excuses I used to invent, the same fears I embraced. They believe the flu shot is costly, or the preservatives are toxic, or the virus is alive and as a result, and they will be sick. These misconceptions are understandable and valid. I tell people that the advantages of receiving a flu shot may indeed outweigh the consequences of flu, but I can't be sure. Our lives can change in one instant, and yet I suppose the annual fear mongering has left us all weary, apathetic, confused, numb or complacent.

http://healthimpactnews.com/2014/government-pays-damages-to-vaccine-victims-flu-shot-most-dangerous-with-gbs-and-death-settlements/

Chapter 12

The Spectrum of Piety

The world is changed by your example, not by your opinion -Paulo Coelho

Joe and I were introduced in 2003 by our mutual friend. Our lives were similar; we were close in age and temperament, both divorced and raising teenaged boys. Our sons were our priorities. Single parenting of teenagers demands triple-time attention and vigil. Joe stood me up on three blind dates, claiming he couldn't leave his son home alone for too long. I declined the fourth date, but on the last chance at a double date, I relented. Earlier that day, a man with whom I'd been having a long-distance relationship told me he didn't want to pursue it any longer. I was heartbroken and whined to my friend on the phone, telling her I had been crying all day and was in no shape for a date.

> "My eyes are swollen, my nose is stuffed up and I'm in my pajamas. I couldn't look good if I tried. I'm in no mood to go out, let alone meet the guy who blew me off three times," I slobbered.

Ever-affable, she replied,

> "Listen: It's my freaking (she didn't use that word) night off. You can cry tomorrow. Now dry your tears and get dressed because we're coming."

Joe and I were married in 2006.

We had more than a little in common; we both were deeply spiritual and religious lapsed Catholics searching for answers to life's big questions: Why are we here? What is our purpose? Who or what controls our lives? What is our destiny? Fate? Karma? Self-determination? Where do we go when we die? What is on the other side of this life? Most importantly, we were both yearning for a relationship with someone who shared similar values, and someone who understood the necessity of having a third person in our relationship: God. We both acknowledged that the absence of God in our previous marriages contributed to the divorces.

As we dated, we searched for churches that soothed our souls. We invited Bible study in our home with Jehovah's Witnesses. We read the Bible, prayed our repetitive prayers, looked for relief in all the wrong places and in each other, in service, in family, and friendship. We church shopped, and always left the services agreeing we felt nothing. I stopped going to church altogether; dutiful Joe continued. Still, we felt there had to be *more*.

On Thanksgiving, November 2006, we had reached an emotional and spiritual low. In our empty house despite invitations to join us and an oven full of holiday food, I lamented to Joe over the football game on television, "Something has got to change. What is wrong with us? We are good people; why is our home empty on Thanksgiving?"

This prayer of sorts would reach the ears of God, and manifest two short months later.

When I first learned of the Church of Jesus Christ of Latter-day Saints in January 2006, I was fascinated, like reading a history book that had been hidden from me. The suggestion that there was a living Prophet other than the Pope who received revelation and inspiration from God was also intriguing. I felt left out, as if I had only been presented with half of a picture of history. Old rich white men wrote history books, a fact that I hadn't realized until I had completed my graduate degree in Education.

I never had the clout to question much while attending Catholic school, but deep within my true self was a rebel fighting to come out. For example, when I was in eighth grade, I ordered and wore a Vietnam War POW/MIA bracelet; US Air Force Major and his partner were carried as Missing in Action until the Secretary of the Air Force approved Presumptive Findings of Death for the Major on 29 Nov 1978. The remains were repatriated on 11 Dec 2000, and the government announced positive identification of the remains on 09 Aug 2002, 33 years to the day after they went down in Laos.[xxxix] I wore the bracelet for more than twenty years, and continued to work towards the causes of peace and justice. In February, 2003, I was frustrated that I could not find a peace and justice organization in my town. So, I created one. I recruited people to meetings in my home, organized candlelight vigils, walks and sidewalk gatherings to demonstrate a desire for negotiations before starting a war on Iraq. Our group presented discussions on cable television. We held hands with other local peace and justice groups across the bridge that spanned the main river, a show of solidarity and strength. I joined half a million people in New York City on February 15, 2003 to voice our opposition to war. During the local activities, I was spat on, yelled at, flipped off, nearly run over and insulted. I was told to go home to the Middle East. I was told I was not a patriot. I was accused of not loving my country. I countered every argument by explaining I loved our troops so much, I wanted them home, not in the middle of a pre-emptive war, and said that I felt God loved Muslim people, too. When the masses chanted or sang God Bless America, I wondered why God would not bless other countries, and could only conclude that He did.

I never understood the full effects of nationalism and xenophobia, perhaps because of my roots. My Mom was all German, and my Dad all Irish. I have living relatives in both Germany and Ireland. I've traveled to many US states and foreign countries, and believe I have a healthy world view. I don't believe that God loves any one country or culture more or less than any other. To do so would be in direct opposition to the concept of the love of God, at least the concept that I was taught.

But, it's understandable that people have lost faith and/or don't believe in God. When one views what that religious ardor has propelled, such as the Christian Inquisitions (Spanish, Roman, Portuguese); the Crusades; the Salem Witch trials; the rise of the Islamic State; political leaders thumping their chests and calling God's name in war, abuses at the hands of trusted church leaders, the rise of religious extremists, it is no surprise the principles of organized religion are questioned and faith may be doubted, shaken, lapsed or disappeared altogether. The dramatic rise of self-help, science and New Age practices are predictable.

The first book taught in the USA was the Bible. When settling the country, we rounded up and re-homed native people, took their children from families, sent them to boarding schools, disallowed them to speak their language or practice their faith, and taught the Bible in English. Considering what is currently occurring among those who do not separate religion from politics, it is no wonder why many in society are turned off by God/organized religion.

We blame God for the bad, and thank ourselves for the good. At the same time, many enjoy life without God, reaping abundance and success from heritage, hard work, good fortune or a whole host of other sources. Atheists deny a God altogether, and can live rich, full and contented lives. As Christians, how do we explain the atrocities we have waged on each other for more than two thousand years since Christ's life, death and resurrection? I learned the answer when I was forty-seven, when I found a new Christian church.

I was searching for a long, long time. While in my 30s I became fascinated with the concept of life after death, consuming numerous books I could about the topic; I was obsessed with angels, and stories about them. I had lost friends and family by death, but didn't truly understand the transition. I assumed good people went to heaven and bad people went to hell after they died. I didn't understand the Catholic concept of Limbo, nor could

I reason why innocent newborn babies like my sister, NJ, who lived only a few days after birth would be relegated to any other place but heaven. (Catholic doctrine teaches that we are all born with original sin which is cleansed by baptism.)

Not much made sense growing up Catholic, attending ten years of Catholic school, trying to be a good and pious girl, although I found peace within the stained glass windowed walls of church, and in the comfort of redundant prayer. I cried out to God in desperation, but rarely was there more solace than the belief that He was listening and watching over me, an invisible spirit in the sky. I was taught about heaven and hell, about the spirit which allegedly inhabits our souls, and the trinity of a heavenly Father, His son, Jesus Christ, and the Holy Spirit. I yearned for the notion of a God, higher power, Father, creator, divine entity who provided perfect love. We are taught as Christians that Christ, the only son of God, volunteered to inhabit an earthly body and come to us here to show us the way, to be the exemplar for how to live righteously in order to return to our Father in heaven after we die. We are taught that among all the prophets and leaders in history, Christ is the only one who, sinless, after his tortuous suffering, gruesome death on a criminal's cross and three days in a tomb, awoke from death and returned to demonstrate and embody life after death.

This one miracle – resurrection - distinguishes Christ as the singular prophet who conquered death to give us hope in our world and life beyond this corporal one.

Learning about and wanting to believe in angelic, heavenly beings who comfort, protect, warn, direct, and inspire us satisfied my thirst for evidence of an existence beyond our bodies. I noticed a pattern of similarities among those who had experienced near-death experiences (NDEs). Although the circumstances were as individual and varied as the people who reported, one thread connected the stories - the feelings of peace and love when meeting a divine presence. This was deeply embedded in my mind, and would eventually play an important role in my conversion to a different church, and to dealing with Joe's probable, impending death.

I am reminded life is not so much about my ambitions, or desires, however noble, as it is about following the teachings of the church, searching the Scriptures diligently with intent and listening for inspiration in order to bring this story to you, and make sense out of the devastation of our lives during and following our illnesses.

I had been struggling with direction of this story; every time I researched something deeply, it felt as if I got deeper and further away from the message. Perhaps that is part of the message – that healing catharsis required time and distance from the trauma. My focus is on sharing my history, illuminating the way for others who may be suffering a similar fate of loss, hopelessness, powerlessness, physical pain, confusion, spiritual, financial or psychic defeat or any combination of the above. I finally have the strength to relive the events and feel the emotions again. I'm appreciative of my and Joe's relative health nearly two years after our illnesses, and I'm mindful of others who are enduring tests and trials.

Lidia is such a case; she has so much power as a recovered (recovering, for it is not a finite process, as in one day you're victimized, and some day in the future, you're healed…it is as with grief: we may go through the stages of healing, but we are never the same. We don't return to our old selves) victim of ritual abuse as a child and the flood of repercussions. I believe her purpose is to *live* the survival, and share the steps she took to get there—scratch that—not steps, (what is a better word? Stages, strides, rungs of the ladder, measures by tiny degree, phases, periods, passages, travails, transformations, torment, agony, torture, distress, angst, sorrow, affliction, grief) that she bore to survive and to be where she is at her age. I believe her story resonates with us, and want her to share it, yet when I suggest this she recoils, still embroiled in the struggle. She needs to have some closure and healing before she has strength to dive in retrospectively to resurrect the ghosts of a tortured past.

Lidia and I are as close as sisters. She is further down the road of life experience than I, but we are both traveling the same path. Aren't we all? We recognized each other's spirits in the tiny Mauna meetinghouse on the north shore. She stood before our members at the podium and announced the annual talent show. Dressed in her signature style with an elegant Hawaiian print dress, adorned with a hand-made rudraksha, plumeria and kukui nut lei, she glimmered, and made us all laugh while describing some of the current entries.

I wondered where I had seen her before. The connection was so strong it nearly jolted me in the pew. I couldn't have possibly known her previously as we had just moved to Maui from Big Island, and it was only our second or third time at this chapel.

There is comfort within the walls and halls of our meetinghouses and Temples regardless of the location. We are family and home no matter where we are on the planet. Joe and I have lived in the continental US, United Arab Emirates and two Hawaiian islands, and always found solace and security among church members. Even after the culture shock I felt returning to Hawai`i from the UAE where I lived a life of modest dress, speech and action, bustling city with no guns, no sirens, no violence and prayer five times a day to bikinis, alcohol commercials on television, and crime, I felt safe within our church family.

The feeling of home attracted us to the church when we were investigating. Typically, when we visit a new ward, someone greets us at the door, or someone sitting near us will extend a welcome. Hello! Are you new? Welcome! Where are you from? The interior of a chapel is modest. Striking in its opposition to the statues, stained glass and generous ornamentation of a Catholic church, the meeting house chapel is bereft of a Christ figure on the cross hanging above an altar, exquisite in its simplicity. No gold chalices, no incense, no images of saints, no robed priests. Similar to Christian mass, we celebrate the sacrament representing the body and blood of Christ, symbolic of the Last Supper Christ held with his apostles on the night he was betrayed just as it is within other Christian sacrament services. But our lessons and talks are performed by members, presented at a podium (instead of an altar) and presided over by an all-volunteer bishopric consisting of elected priesthood. Missionaries taught us the reason for the humble motif: *members* represent Christ, not statues, crosses or engraved images. This was evident from the first moment we stepped into a meeting hall, and was reinforced wherever we traveled.

We were new to the ward, and yet I felt an instant connection to Lidia. She felt it, too. Early in our friendship, we spoke about it. Lidia explained that we surely were sisters in the spirit world, so our souls recognized each other when we met here on earth. I've had this feeling a few times in my life, but never as strong as with Lidia. It is often described as meeting one's "soul mate".

I understood the soul/spirit connection. Little did we know when we met how essential we would become to one another's survival. Our valiant higher selves fought for and transcended our earthly bodies and personalities. In the past, I had placed my friendships at the top of my priorities, just below my relationship with God, my duties as a single mother, my family and my career. I wrote a letter to Joe in the summer of the first year we were dating, explaining that I didn't want to hurt his feelings, but he was number six on my priority list. I had two long-term, intense friendships with female friends – one ended abruptly, and the other struggled - but my relationship with Lidia differed because God was in the center. Lidia and I comforted each other in the way that silence relieves clamor, or rain soothes drought. When endless words and conversations failed us, there was still reassurance knowing we were simply there for one another, far surpassing the obligations of friendship. This was the pure love of Christ flowing through us, to us..

Lidia's and others' examples would eventually teach me the meaning of Christ-like love in action, or charity, embodied in human form. Scriptures awakened me to my earthly purpose, explained well in <u>L. Tom Perry's October 2006 talk The Plan of Salvation.</u>[xl]

> *We are not left alone to wander through mortality without knowing of the master plan which the Lord has designed for His children. Many people wonder, "Where did we come from? Why are we here? Where are we going?" Our Eternal Father did not*

send us to earth on an aimless, meaningless journey. He provided for us a plan to follow. He is the author of that plan…

…Centuries ago Paul predicted: "The time will come when they will not endure sound doctrine; but after their own lusts shall they heap to themselves teachers, having itching ears; …And they shall turn away their ears from the truth, and shall be turned unto fables (2 Timothy 4:3–4)…We need not be confused. The answers to the puzzling questions regarding the purpose of life have again been given to mankind for our guidance…Jesus Christ, our Elder Brother, became the leader in advocating the plan designed by the Father…"

I'm blessed to be able to ponder these inspired words, blessed to be a member of our church and to have experienced hope. I wasn't always so certain. My faith and testimony were tested and stretched during Joe's and my illnesses. I admit I have had doubt about the purpose of my life, and the reason I was spared.

Chapter 13

Perception, and What Sustained Me

Much of the incentive for writing this story originates in these questions: Why and how did Joe and I survive? Did he will himself back to life, or was there more? What aggregation of forces orchestrated our recoveries? If we knew, what would we do with that information? What will we do with what we've learned from all that we've gone through? Prayer works. Belief in miracles works. Hope and faith and trust in a higher power and a higher purpose might have been the key to my survival. But how do I explain Joe's?

Joe and I did not take the flu vaccine before 2014. Given that Joe was run down and already sick with bronchitis, he may have been more vulnerable to the flu. Influenza A H1N1 was prevalent that season, reported by the CDC.

During the 2013-2014 season, influenza A (H3N2), 2009 influenza A (H1N1), and influenza B viruses circulated in the United States. 2009 H1N1 viruses predominated overall during the 2013-14 flu season…[xli]

Had we taken a trivalent flu shot, we would have received three viruses, according to the CDC:

> The 2013-2014 trivalent influenza vaccine was made from the following viruses:
>
> A/California/7/2009 (H1N1)pdm09-like virus;
> A(H3N2) virus antigenically like the cell-propagated prototype virus A/Victoria/361/2011;
> B/Massachusetts/2/2012-like virus.[xlii]

CDC recommended a quadrivalent [containing four viruses] flu vaccine which would have been ineffective in our case:

> It is recommended that the quadrivalent vaccine containing two influenza B viruses include the above three viruses and a B/Brisbane/60/2008-like virus.[xliii]

On the other side of the argument is the fact that many people who contract the flu did receive flu shots.

> CDC received reports of some people who became ill and tested positive for the flu even though they had been vaccinated. This occurs every season. There are a number of reasons why people who got a flu vaccine may still get the flu this season.[xliv]

Bottom line is that we may never know the answer to why, where or how Joe and I caught the flu. This is stuck in my craw, and I can't stop picking at it, or questioning how we survived.

Some survivors of catastrophic illnesses credit part of their healing to a positive attitude-not a new idea. Pioneers of this theory are abundant: Reverend Doctor Norman Vincent Peale (*The Power of Positive Thinking* and *Guideposts* magazine) Ralph Waldo Emerson, Dale Carnegie, Joe Vitale, (*Life's Missing Instruction Manual* and contributor to *The Secret*) Anthony "Tony" Robbins, Brian Tracy, Steven Covey and more too numerous to list. Many contributed to the discipline beginning as far back as the Declaration of Independence emphasizing the rights of "…life, liberty and the pursuit of happiness."

Sheer will doesn't answer the riddle of how I managed to survive H1N1 and bilateral pneumonia. Good medicine, luck, and a few other factors probably worked together in my favor. I'm forced to think about Jolie D., plucked from the prime of her life only after she found peace through prayer. She didn't tell me when she began to accept her inevitable death; my heart knew it. I heard it in the tone of her voice, felt her fight weakening. Selfishly, I judged her. I asked her why she was giving up. I imposed my needs on her, and she seemed to understand, gently explaining that she was tired. She may have consented to her fate early on, admitting that cancer ran in her family.

Since childhood, I've intuited that attitude plays a critical role in our health, but I didn't have the science to support that suspicion. Perhaps our illnesses and recoveries positioned me to search for scientific answers. Or are angels and miracles sufficient? Why can't I let it go?

It is purported that we can change our attitude and behavior by changing our perspective, or being "mindfully observant." In *Biology of Belief*,[xlv] Bruce Lipton's work about perception altering reality comes close to helping me understand the power of mindful observation. His presentation basically explains that we can change our behavior by changing our perception about a stimulus. Case in point: I can view the misfortune of Joe's and my illness as a disaster from which we will never recover—a reasonable and understandable response—or, I can view it as an opportunity for change and growth, despite the losses.

Dr. Lipton suggests that cellular behavior is changed by the input, and the response to that input. Behavior is related to signals, performing like a reflex. In science lingo, if you remove the antennae from a receptor cell, the cell does not move.

How this translates: If we remove a stimulus from our surroundings, we do not change relative to that stimulus. To illustrate, consider life in a desert, where rain is absent. If we don't understand or know what rain is, we don't worry about it. If we don't know what it's like to have to shield ourselves from rain, we don't carry umbrellas. If a stimulus is removed, we don't respond to it. We aren't changed by something that doesn't affect us. This is my very novice interpretation of Lipton's theory.

Dr. Lipton makes the conclusion that perception controls behavior. No DNA or genes are involved in this process, just stimulus/response. The difference in a cell is perception: what it sees determines how it responds. This can be extrapolated to our attitudes. What we "see" determines how we respond. It is also wonderful news in light of our ancestry. We don't necessarily have to perpetuate the mistakes, illness, sins or habits of our forefathers because these traits are not genetic.

Applying Dr. Lipton's view to my hospitalization with bilateral pneumonia and H1N1, I wonder if my desire and will to care for Joe contributed to my survival. Three people died from H1N1 at our hospital in February 2014. The flu was epidemic in the winter of 2014. Could my attitude about life in general have played a significant role in my healing and survival? Can a good attitude and desire alone to live be enough to overcome death? Doubtful, given the millions who die, wanting very much to live. I assume there is a divine confluence of factors which affect one's survival from catastrophe. In that light, I suspect this list of influences were essential to Joe's survival, in no particular order of importance:

1. There *is* a higher power in control of life. (What we can't explain, we attribute to the gods)
2. The subconscious/unconscious portion of our brain functions even when the conscious is in a comatose state: Joe heard us?
3. Simple statistics/odds: Joe is the 1/100 who survived his myriad illnesses.

4. Exceptionally excellent medical care provided by three out of the four hospitals and their staff.
5. Spiritual and emotional support Joe received from family and friends, and Hampshire Christian friends and teammates who joined hands and prayed The Lord's Prayer at his bedside.
6. Support Joe received while in the ICU, including Skylor's and my daily presence, advocating for him, reading to him, speaking to him, praying aloud for him, playing his favorite music, coconut oil rubs, amateur reflexology, certified Reiki and massage.
7. Visits by people from near and far, in four hospitals, and home.
8. Prayers, well-wishes and good energies sent by hundreds of people around the planet.
9. Joe's mission and work here on earth are not complete.
10. A combination of all of the above, and more that I don't know and will never be able to prove.

Stunned friends, family, and their friends and families prayed for us both. But there seemed to be something bewildering to our recoveries - more underlying, invisible, powerful forces at work. The atheist or scientist might argue it was luck, chance or numbers; we beat the odds. Not everyone who has the flu dies from it. The religious or faithful person might suggest that we still had work to do here on earth or that God's will was for us to live. I am a Christian, but I don't fully understand the reasons for our survival. I wonder if my will to live helped my chances.

Daily prayer, support from family, friends, social media and crowdfunding friends and contributors and church members sustained me. Particularly helpful were the bishop and priesthood who provided spiritual support and confirmation through their personal revelation that Joe would not die; Joe's Hampshire Christian support network via daily texts and phone calls from Joe's college roommate "K-Train"; Relief Society, family and friend angels who sent meals on a regular basis. The comfort of a home-made meal! Hot soups, casseroles, juice, and special requests, like my craving for mashed potatoes. Precious to me were visits by family and friends near and far; Joe's friend "Juice" who drove many hours from Vermont near the Canadian border just to visit Joe; LB and TR visiting three times from beyond New York City; Dane, the missionary who found us, driving four hours in a bitter winter snowstorm to visit Joe and assess his situation in the ICU, then visiting me later than night at home before returning to his family in New Hampshire. Dane was finishing his pre-med program. Joe and I love him like a son. He sat with me as I wept, and told me he didn't see anything that would indicate Joe was going to die. I didn't believe him, but I was grateful for his tender kindness. Dane and his wife returned again to visit Joe in the ICU.

More support: Dad and Pearl's daily phone check-in, visiting Joe (they were 80 and 78 years old respectively), paying bills, filling our home heating oil tank, bringing or making food, driving me when I couldn't, giving me a cellphone with unlimited text and calls so I could afford the endless hours of calls with family, friends, insurance companies, hospitals, visiting nurses, bill collectors; visiting me at home during bitterly cold weather, apparently making a crusade of caring for us. They exhibited enormous patience with me as I slowly fell apart and deteriorated mentally, physically and emotionally, evidenced by my brain fog, inability to make decisions and forgetfulness - although Dad light-heartedly teased me about it when we went out to eat. I'm rarely able to make a quick menu decision.

How do I show my father my appreciation and love for all he is, and for all he has done for me? The patriarch of our little family, he's shown enormous support for Joe and me throughout this craziness – a rock, as my sister refers to him. He's always been there for me, through the good and the not-so-pleasant. Same for my son, my sister, her children, their partners and spouses, for my cousins, my Mom's sister. After my Mom and he divorced, Dad was not far from Mom, buying her a car, lending advice, even speaking with her at my request while I held the cellphone near her ear as she lie in the hospital bed, in a coma, dying.

That's my Dad. And when I moved back to our home, he bought me another car, the first was when I lived with him in the Deep South, after his divorce.

"How the heck are you going to get around? What will happen when you get a job? How are you going to get there?"

Joe was living and working three hours from home, and driving a motorcycle. Our finances were limited. Our car was totaled in Hawai'i. I hadn't started teaching yet. So there was my Dad, thinking ahead, ensuring that at least I wouldn't have a car payment. He paid the first six months of my insurance, too. Dad doesn't just provide financial assistance; when he speaks, everyone listens. Retired from the military, 82 years young and still working (after retirement), he embodies a stellar example for discipline, loyalty, honor, decency, honesty and generosity. And he always smells and dresses as if he walked off the pages of a magazine. If you know my Dad, you know enough to give a firm handshake, address by his/her name, make eye contact, shine your shoes, be honest, arrive early, work hard, shut your mouth on the job, save your money and take your hat off when you are indoors.

Knowing Dad's expectations and living them are two entirely different things. At least we all have the blessing of knowing his standards.

Another saving grace is my only sister, Therese who took time out of her life to stay with me in the first days after my discharge. And Vera, Big Cosmo's wife, who sent constant affirmations that I was not alone; she suffered much of the same over the past decade with her husband. I joined the ranks of Vera, with Big Cosmo, and church friend Allie, with her daughter A, who has been chronically ill since birth. Allie at one time had maintained a blog about the vicious transition from victim to advocate. I relied on their strength, counsel and wisdom in ways that can never be repaid.

An abundance of ironies, coincidences and acts of kindness fortified and blessed us. Friends of friends recommended Barb as our Advocate, a miracle worker who happened to grow up in the same neighborhood as two of Joe's Hampshire Christian buddies. One checked in on us regularly and visited us, bringing lunches, and compassionate friendship.

Joe's childhood friends, some of whom he hadn't seen since second grade contributed to the crowdfunding campaign. When Joe became aware of all of the donations, he was "blown away" at the level of support, prayers and generosity. Some old friends traveled to visit him from as far away as California.

Hampshire Christian College teammates, roommates and friends were the most loyal and devoted group of grown men I've ever encountered. "Doc" rubbed Joe's feet when he visited him in the ICU ("I don't rub anyone's feet!"), "K Train", basketball player "Fern", "Duke", "King", "Ginzo", "Bumble" "Bee", lacrosse player "A-bear", "Hoobah", rugby player "Fat Dog", "Frenchie", "Juice", "Glennie Lou", "Elisabeth", JG, CL "Colonel", "Gerald" MC, and "A-hole" came often and regularly to visit Joe from long distances on terrible roads in bad weather.

Childhood friend SJ babysat for Joe the first week he was home from rehab so I could attend my niece's bridal shower. SJ was also instrumental in bringing Big Cosmo to see Joe in rehab; Cosmo hadn't been out of the house in a year - plagued by a decade of illnesses and injuries that rendered him bedbound.

Dr. L from the rehab hospital graduated from Hampshire Christian. Joe's trach was downsized on the first day he arrived. "How did that happen?" said one of his nurses. Joe was discharged from rehab after only fifteen days. His rehab was projected to require three months. Was his swift discharge driven by insurance, or some other constellation of forces?

More support came via a story shared by a church friend, another testimony about surviving the 1918 flu. Through this story, I realized I was not the only person to nurse a flu victim, or to write about it. The story was originally shared by Caroline Martinez regarding her mother, Arva Mitchell Watkins, about the faith of her mother, Caroline Hancock Mitchell.[xlvi]

LIVING TESTIMONY

My good mother tells me that when I was born in June 1918, the flu epidemic was raging. Mother says she had my older sister Emily and I wear a cloth mask over our face whenever we went anywhere so we did not contract the flu. Mama was a nurse before she was married to my father so she took special precautions with her two small girls.

However when I was about two and a half years old, the whooping cough was very hard on me. She said, "When May comes, I know she will get well", which I did. The next fall when I was nearly three and a half years old, mama had been up to Idaho Falls, Idaho with her three small children visiting with her sister Emily and family. Then we returned back home to Fillmore, Utah.

A few days later, mama says, I came down with a terrific headache, she did all she could, for me. Father was away at the time doing some trucking business. The next day mama took me to the doctor. After listening to her about my symptoms and checking me over he diagnosed my illness as infantile paralysis which shocked her greatly. By then both of my legs were stiff. Mama and the doctor rubbed my legs, the doctor loaned my mother a vibrator. I still remember it. Mama use to rub my legs frequently each day with the vibrator. Finally my legs responded and had movement in them but one leg was forever crooked.

Mama kept working with me and one day I could stand on one leg. Mama said she had put the chairs in a circle for me to walk around, soon I was using one leg well. With mama's faith that I could walk and her persistence and my determination, I finally walked after a fashion.

When I was perhaps four years old, mother said I was so bloated up she was almost afraid I would die, my father thought so, too. One day the Relief Society, sisters came over, when they were leaving our home, mama over heard one saying to the other, "they'll never raise that child"! Well in, desperation and because mama was such a "spiritual woman", mama went and knelt down at her bed. She ask the Lord what she could do for me. "Oh Lord, she cried, let this child be a living testimony of thy goodness and mercy". Soon after, mother had the strong impression to give me oranges. She sent my father to the store for a dozen, mama gave me half an orange twice a day; dividing some of the oranges with the other two children. Mama says that after the oranges were gone the bloat had left my body completely and a very thin child I was. But, now I was covered with a rash, the oranges had apparently take the poison out of my body. From then on mama says I began to get well. My dear mother, never gave up on me always doing what she could for me and her other children.

The school principal sent a letter home to my parents, stating, "You have a child by the name of Arva, who should be in school". Mama went to school and told them about my condition. The next year at age seven my kind and thoughtful older sister, Emily took me to school on her back, piggy-back style, when I felt like going. Later on my father went to the store and bought a coaster wagon for Emily to pull me to school until I could go on my own, (which was not for another couple of years).

To this day I'm grateful for my mother's love and my brothers and sisters.

I have a testimony of the gospel of Jesus Christ and know beyond a shadow doubt that Jesus lives and is the literal, Son of God the Eternal Father and that he does watch over us, his children. I know we do have a very special purpose in coming to this earth, our second estate, Amen.

by Arva Mitchell Watkins Sixteenth Ward, Kearns Real Pioneers. With permission from M. Pagani

Flu Statistics

According to the CDC,

> During the 2013-2014 season, influenza A (H3N2), 2009
> influenza A (H1N1), and influenza B viruses circulated in
> the United States. 2009 H1N1 viruses predominated overall
> during the 2013-14 flu season, though influenza B viruses
> became the predominant virus nationally later in the season
> and caused an increase in influenza-like-illness in parts of
> the northeast especially. After several recent influenza A
> (H3N2)–predominant seasons, 2013-14 was the first H1N1–
> predominant season since the 2009 H1N1 pandemic.

> …CDC received reports of severe flu illness among the
> young and middle-aged, many of whom were infected with
> the 2009 H1N1 virus. Nearly 60% of the flu-associated
> hospitalizations reported to CDC were 18 to 64 years old. A
> similar increase in hospitalizations among non-elderly adults
> was also seen during the 2009 H1N1 pandemic. These severe
> flu outcomes are a reminder that flu can be a very serious
> disease for anyone, including young, previously healthy
> adults.[xlvii]

The CDC acknowledges that the effectiveness of flu vaccine can vary, but
offers vaccination as the best protection, and recommends that everyone
6 months and older get an annual flu vaccine. They provide compelling
evidence to receive a flu vaccine:

> "We are committed to the development of better flu vaccines,
> but existing flu vaccines are the best preventive tool available
> now. This season vaccinated people were substantially better
> off than people who did not get vaccinated. The season is still
> ongoing. If you haven't yet, you should still get vaccinated,"
> wrote CDC Director Dr. Tom Frieden.[xlviii]

Still, I am hesitant to take the flu shot this year.

Why did I survive? Why did Joe? Some believers answered that question by asserting we have a purpose, that God has a plan for our lives. One of our dear friends who prayed daily for us knew that we would survive, saying "I knew if anyone would live to give God the glory, it would be you two." Some others shook their heads in disbelief when they heard our story, like when viewing a crumpled car and hearing the driver lived. We lived. Dr. K, our Primary Care Physician gave Joe a 1/ 100 chance of survival, and never thought he would meet him. We had made an appointment for our first office visit with Dr. K, and then we became ill. We didn't make it to that appointment but we had named him as our PCP at the emergency room, so he received every record and every report. As they continued to roll in, Dr. K asked his staff "Who is this guy? He's a dead man, I'll never meet him".

We lived.

Why did Joe survive, when any one of the illnesses he had was enough to kill? H1N1 Flu. Sepsis. Diverticulitis. Peritonitis. Burst colon. Acute Respiratory Distress Syndrome. Total body fluid overload. Organ Failure. Cardiac Arrest. Critical Illness Polyneuropathy. Perforated Bladder and Hematuria.

Doctors suggested some of the reasons contributing to Joe's survival were overall good health prior to the illnesses, relatively young age of 57, and history of athletics. He was a life guard and a paramedic. He played football since he was ten, and for Hampshire Christian (HCC) College before a career-ending injury sidelined him in his sophomore year. There, he earned the nickname *Warrior*; this character trait may have played a huge part in his recovery.

Joe began playing football in Junior Football league. He started and played every high school game in his career as an all- state middle linebacker, class of 1975. Captain of the undefeated freshman high school team where he played quarterback, he was the only sophomore to start varsity when freshmen were ineligible to play in the 1970s. People feared the tough All-State brothers, of which Joe was the third.

JG, class of '85 told Joe, "You and your brother were legends. We had to live up to them. We were supposed to play up to your yardstick." They did. Another brother was an all-state player and went to university on a football scholarship.

Oldest brother played every position on the field except quarterback. Joe felt he had to live up to, or exceed his brothers' reputations in high school, and in college, he had to match his father's, whose picture hangs on the HCC hallway wall leading to the indoor athletic field. Joe chose Hampshire Christian because his father played football there, but when he applied, he was offered a full ride football scholarship on the condition he improved his grades. He grabbed the chance to do so. Coming from a family of ten children, one does not pass up golden opportunities.

In the post-grad (PG) year at a college prep boarding school which claims to serve young men who have not yet fulfilled their potential, Joe's football team ended with a 5-3 record. Two of eight games ended in brawls. He played with tough city boys such as a skinny running back from Chicago, and "Mr. Mean" – (written in white athletic tape on his helmet) - a middle linebacker. Joe improved his grades and earned the scholarship to Hampshire Christian.

Warrior was an attraction from the moment he swagged into the freshman locker room in August 1976, lean and mean, wearing sunglasses, shorts, flip-flops and attitude. He spoke to no one, but made a remarkable statement. He was a year older than his teammates, and it showed. Some of them thought he might be a coach. He certainly knew how to make an entry. He admits the real reason that he earned success is that he was and is "just a little bit off center" – bent and determined enough to do what is necessary to achieve his goals. Mother Catherine used to say that Joe wouldn't listen to what he is told to do, rather, he did things his own way.

Does a 57 year-old male described as an athletic, off-center, productive, relatively healthy and optimistic who is in a coma and near death with critical illnesses have any control over his survival?

Influenza virus is an intelligent, indiscriminate killer. Joe's H1N1 morphed into H2N2, a subtype of the influenza A virus which has historically mutated into various strains including the Asian flu strain (now extinct in the wild), H3N2, and various strains found in birds. It is also suspected of causing a human pandemic in 1889 known as the Russian Flu, killing about one million people.[xlix] Dr. Ab, Infectious Disease specialist oversaw the administration of Joe's antibiotics totaling four at the same time for a few weeks. Joe's fever persisted, running from 99 to 104. He was given two courses of Tamiflu, the standard antiviral to treat H1N1.

Doctors pronounced he was not "turning the corner". The lungs and organs failed, he had total body fluid overload to the extent that the fluid began to seep out through " necrotizing tissue" on his forearms (maroon, split-pea sized pus-filled blisters), and eventually his heart failed.

How did Joe and I survive? Perhaps the more important question is why and how did Joe and I become so sick?

Many opponents to vaccines ("anti-vaxxers") report the best way to avoid sickness is to avoid ubiquitous assaults on the immune system, maintain a positive attitude, support ourselves by eating well, specifically organic and non-genetically modified foods, taking supplements and staying away from people who have been recently vaccinated. A challenge, albeit possible. One common assault on our immune systems is stress, a challenge to avoid or eliminate in our twenty-first century lives. But achievable. I've had nearly two years to contemplate the factors that may have led to the deterioration of our immune systems and our health, and I often focus on the good parts. The alternative (thinking about the negative) is counterproductive.

Chapter 14

Alternatives - Surrender to Fear - Rejoice In the Choice – Ho` Oponopono

After Joe left the first rehab where he suffered hematuria and a perforated bladder, I returned to concentrating solely on our healing. I wanted no part of anger, frustration or blame to become infused in my attitude, or to be defined by them. I didn't want to give any more energy to the rabid, wet hen I had started to become. I prayed to God to empty me of all judgment and to fill me with His love and forgiveness. I had been nurturing my inner monk for many years prior, so to continue in that role was not unreasonable. I practiced mindful breathing, daily prayer and I tried to incorporate and embrace mentalities I had learned in my travels around the world.

In Hawai`i, I learned about the practice of Ho` oponopono – an ancient Hawaiian prayer meaning "to make right" comprised of four simple statements:

I'm sorry. Please forgive me. Thank you. I love you.

When done correctly, it helps us to see with the eyes of the divine, and not the eyes of our memories. I helps us to forgive, to let go of the past, to take responsibility for ourselves and to love whatever our experiences are. Read them now, and repeat them. Go ahead. I'll wait.

Years ago, when I first considered them, I thought of it as folly. Absurd! Why should I ask forgiveness or apologize for something I didn't do? Why should I forgive if the other person isn't sorry? Why should I be thanking someone for hurting me? Why should I say any of these things when I had become a victim? I couldn't quite grasp the concept of universal consequences of our actions. Gradually, though, I tried to say the four sentences with meaning. I shared the concept at church. I shared it with my students. I told my friends about it. I mentioned it as often as I could, wherever it was appropriate. It's not something that can be thrown off the tongue easily. It has to be embraced and understood before it can be shared. No doubt, it moves people. It changes people.

Ho'oponopono helped me to understand that I am responsible for myself, for my actions, thoughts, and words. I cannot fully isolate myself from the world, as much as I would like to. I understand that I can appreciate each situation as an opportunity for forgiveness, growth, transcendence. I can respond to the world with love, gratitude, penitence, and humility. Or not. My choice. My consequences.

Ho'oponopono helped me deal with Joe's (and my) continued trials, including what we did to each other along the way, and how to accept the consequences of others' actions and choices.

After he came home and began to heal, I told him stories to fill the three-month hole in his memory. I showed him pictures and read him the daily social media and crowdfunding updates. I began to portray a picture of his illness and recovery, a picture that was veiled by coma and medications. Often, he wept, asking me to stop. He winced when viewing photos of him in the ICU, only viewing them quickly before turning his head. I didn't torture him with the stories and photos, but I did persist. I wanted him to know everything. I wanted him to gain the testimony I had about loving, caring, attentive, skilled and wonderful people – here and in the spirit world - who kept him alive and nurtured me. I wanted him to be able to thank those incredible people, and the only way I thought I could generate gratitude in him was to retell the stories. I wanted him to feel the peace that I felt in spite of the suffering.

Interestingly, he remembers some traumatic events post-coma with clarity. He remembers the night two huge men fought over him (about what he couldn't understand) and reinserted a larger trach after it had been downsized – something that I was assured would not happen. He remembers them pinching his throat and trachea with such force he felt they were choking him to death. He remembers fighting them, and thought maybe this was why there were two large men holding him down. He also remembers the trauma the night after his second catheter was removed, and his bloody urine, and the trip to the emergency room, and people arguing about where they were going to take him.

He vaguely remembers church friends who babysat for him in the first rehab so I could have a break. He remembers them being in the room with him, and having long conversations, but he forgets the content. No matter. The support and succor he received probably contributed to his recovery, despite the critical setbacks.

It seems in being discharged from the ICU and admitted to the first rehab hospital, Joe took one giant leap forward, and two back. The paradox of surviving death only to be jeopardized again in a new hospital where Joe was to have been rehabbed is remarkable, and pinched my soul.

This is not a criticism of western medicine, nor of those who endeavor so brilliantly to care for and save patients' lives. I don't mean to denigrate the people involved in the system. I understand some in the medical profession might take offense; none is intended. There is something amiss in the administration of the *practice* of western medicine; I can't put my finger on it, but I sense it has to do with the separation of western medicine from that of other cultures.

I was introduced to the power and value of herbal remedies when I was a child. Therese was asthmatic and often suffered episodes of labored breathing, wheezing and coughing. The remedy then was a vaporizer, and herbal tea sent by our German grandparents. I don't know if prescription medication for asthma was available back then in the 60s, but I know that the tea worked like a charm, and spared my sister innumerable trips to the emergency room. I'm thankful for this memory because it set the stage for me to recognize other "alternative" treatments, remedies and approaches to health challenges.

You gain strength, courage and confidence by every experience in which you really stop to look fear in the face. You are able to say to yourself, 'I have lived through this horror. I can take the next thing that comes along.' You must do the thing you think you cannot do.

~ Eleanor Roosevelt, *You Learn by Living: Eleven Keys for a More Fulfilling Life*

As we choose to follow the Master, we choose to be changed—to be spiritually reborn. Line upon line and precept upon precept, gradually and almost imperceptibly, our motives, our thoughts, our words, and our deeds become aligned with the will of God.

~ David A. Bednar, *Ye Must Be Born Again*, April 2007 General Conference

The understanding I've gained about surrendering to invisible forces and those over which I have no control has stiffened my will and fed my testimony.

Irony: The largest animal on the planet – the magnificent Blue whale – lives to be one hundred feet in length and survives on some of the tiniest organisms: krill and copepods, translucent shrimp-like creatures, measure only 1 to 6 centimeters long. Yet humans, with all of our ego, ambition and arrogance, with our wars, machines and weapons, with our intelligence, achievements, inventions, complexity, wealth, communication and science can be sickened and killed by the smallest virus. A typical virus is one hundred times smaller than a bacterium, and yet it behaves as intelligently and perfectly as the most sophisticated human creation - computer viruses.

Biological and computer viruses share many of the same traits; myriad similarities exist between the two. Essentially they are not considered to be living things because they cannot reproduce on their own, so they enter a host and use it to multiply. Just as computer viruses cannot reproduce unless they are injected or released into a computer system (for example email), biological viruses are not in and of themselves toxic without a host.

The problem of biological or computer viral infection is global; individuals, organizations and countries are equally susceptible. Implications of biological viruses are just as widespread and analogous.

The cost of disease and its prevention is astronomical. According to the CDC's 1999 Journal Emerging Infectious Diseases research article *The Economic Impact of Pandemic Influenza in the United States: Priorities for Intervention*, the estimated cost of the possible effects of the next influenza pandemic and of vaccine-based interventions in the United States would be $71.3 to $166.5 *billion*, excluding disruptions to commerce and society[l] Considering this estimate was made in 1999, we can assume the numbers have greatly increased after nearly 17 years.

Worldwide, the cost of damages due to computer viruses, spyware, adware, botnets, and other malicious code is likewise staggering. According to Computer Economics.com June 2007[li] article, the economic impact of damages from malware exceed $13 billion annually. Direct costs represented in the article are widespread but not all inclusive, defined as "labor costs to analyze, repair and cleanse infected systems, loss of user productivity, loss of revenue due to loss or degraded performance of system, and other costs directly incurred as the result of a malware attack." Important to note is that direct costs do not include: "preventive costs of antivirus hardware or software, ongoing personnel costs for IT security staff, secondary costs of subsequent attacks enabled by the original malware attack, insurance costs, damage to the organization's brand, or loss of market value."

Reflecting on the pernicious nature of viruses, how can we not conclude that we are vulnerable, fragile or doomed? With a broad world view, it might be easy to succumb to paranoia or depression. A bit of self-analysis is in order.

I've come to a place of surrender to events which I cannot control, and rejoice in the choice of how to handle them. Relying on faith in the word of God, theories I learned as an undergraduate in the study of Psychology, lessons learned during twenty-plus years of teaching and fifty plus years of life, and practices I've picked up during my travels such as Reiki and Ho'opnopono, I try to synthesize and utilize these concepts to deal with the apparent randomness of life.

The first: "Internal vs. External Locus of Control", set forth by Julian B. Rotter, one of the 100 most eminent psychologists of the 20th century[lii] within his Social Learning Theory. In the 1950s, Rotter theorized a continuum of behaviors people exhibit based on their perception of reinforcement for the behavior; those who were on internal locus of control end of the continuum felt that they had responsibility for (or power over) whether they received reinforcement for their behavior, and those along the external believed that forces other than their own such as luck, chance, or powerful people determine the amount of reinforcement they receive.

This concept grew from that of Sigmund Freud, the father of modern psychology. Freud's psychoanalysis, the preeminent view in clinical psychology at the time held that instincts determined behavior, and neuroses had their origins in deeply traumatic experiences that occurred in the patient's past. Individuals were seen as being subject to their unconscious impulses, and therapy required long-term analysis of childhood experiences. Rotter grew Freud's theory, suggesting that behavior was controlled by rewards and punishments, and that these consequences determined our beliefs about the underlying causes for these actions. Rotter proposed the law of effect, a principle that suggested people are motivated to seek out positive stimulation, or reinforcement, and to avoid unpleasant stimulation.[liii] This theory has been challenged and built upon, but its basic premise makes sense to me. I believe the vast majority of us have some choice or control over our behavior.

11 For it must needs be, that there is an opposition in all things. ~ 2 Nephi 2:11

My locus of control lies more on the internal side. I have seen what happens when I give in to depression, fear, despondency or helplessness, and it's all ugly. Applying Rotter's theory, I'm more motivated to seek out positive reinforcement rather than negative in order to avoid a less savory outcome. I absolutely do not take my leaning toward an optimistic attitude for granted. I appreciate that I have been blessed with agency (or the ability to choose) and can determine my disposition. Some people are not so fortunate. I've suffered bouts of clinical depression that went undiagnosed for some time. I empathize with people who struggle with personal demons. I'm thankful that I can choose to be thankful because in the past, my response to misfortune was black heartedness, and I know where that leads. Rotter would suggest I'm motivated by avoiding negative reinforcement, and he might be correct.

The second theory is Abraham Maslow's Hierarchy of Needs, first presented in the 1943 paper *A Theory of Motivation,* wherein Maslow suggests a progression of basic human needs often displayed as a triangle with the larger portion on the bottom representing basic Physiological needs such as air, water, food and protection from the elements. Maslow suggests that these basic needs must be met in order for the human to survive. I've seen this to be true continually in the past two decades as an educator; basic needs must be met before we can embark upon the tasks of teaching and learning, despite the learner's age. I've taught children in pre-kindergarten through grade twelve, students in community college and senior citizens, and one factor invariable affects success: hunger, thirst and shelter. I remember students as individuals who were in danger of not thriving or surviving due to basic physiological needs being unmet; a boy whose home was his mother's car; a girl who was locked in the basement of her home for the weekend so her father could go to the casino; endless students who came to school hungry and sick, regularly without breakfast. I understand the need for and support school breakfast and lunch programs. Regardless of their home lives, parental support or lack thereof, students must be adequately fed healthy food in order for them to be prepared to learn. My favorite response to students who refuse breakfast is to ask them what type of car they would be, if they could be one. The reply is usually something sporty or exotic like a Lexus, Lamborghini, Maserati, or Cadillac Escalade. I ask them what would happen if the car ran out of gas, or if we poured cola, coffee or donuts into the gas tank. Furtive pauses follow, then the light goes on.

Once these basic physiological needs are met, we can focus on the second layer of the hierarchy, where things become very interesting. On the Safety level, personal and financial security, health and well-being and safety from accidents or illness take precedence. War, economic insecurity, family violence, childhood abuse and natural disasters are examples of factors on this level. I think we all can relate to this. I've also seen the impacts of these factors at school: a boy who had been in sixteen foster homes in his eleven years of life; urban high school students whose parents had not received higher than an eighth grade education; the girl whose mother beat her in the face with an iron; the boy who came to school every day with a new bruise, claiming he fell while stepping off the bus; the girl who witnessed her aunt's murder in her own home; the diabetic girl whose father gave her candy for breakfast. The list is endless. I've seen ten lifetimes of sadness in schools.

Maslow's hierarchy is fairly popular and has numerous applications in educational and social institutions. As a teacher who understands that my students may not have eaten breakfast, I'm compelled to modify my expectations during classes held before lunch, or late in the day, or any time in between, depending upon the biology, physiology and psychology of the student. Or, I can bring a situation to the attention of my superior. Or, I can establish rapport with my students, or develop dialogue with them about their health and well-being. And, as a mandated reporter, all who suspect a child is in danger, or threatens to endanger someone else, must report to child protective services.

I will never forget my first student teaching assignment in 1990: my supervising teacher was a master special educator who managed her grade 1-6 self-contained classes like a pro. Each morning as students arrived, she would welcome them with sincere and diagnostic hugs while asking them how they were feeling. The purpose of the investigation was two-fold: first, to warmly welcome them and express genuine concern, and second, to ascertain if the students had pain or sore spots on their bodies. This could probably not take place in a classroom of 2016 with school policy clearly forbidding displays of public affection even between and among students, and the minefield of teachers displaying affection to students or vice-versa. Regardless, my supervising teacher left an enduring impression on me about the qualities of a humane and empathetic teacher, and about the need to consider a student as more than just a brain into which we pour information.

Needs on Maslow's pyramid are flexible and progress up or down the levels. Belongingness and interpersonal needs come next, followed by self-esteem and self-respect, and, if these are mastered, self-actualization and transcendence of self are the apex levels.

Maslow's theory, while appealing, has been criticized for overlooking societal and cultural perspectives, along with ignoring availability of resources, and age. Critics argue that the hierarchy cannot be one size fits all and that the needs of global societies are too diverse and ever-changing to categorize in a neat triangle.

Health in Maslow's Safety level however is one influence that affects us universally – and is the reason for this book. Using Maslow's theory, I could posit that many challenges in my life seem to originate with my mother's health (diminished because of war?), and Joe's illnesses resulting from the flu. I might infer that my poor level of safety and security beginning in my childhood may have affected my ability to achieve levels of self-esteem, achievement and self-actualization. And yet, it could be argued that I have arrived in adulthood with many of these milestones accomplished. How is that explained? Did Maslow neglect to factor in the invisible and intangible qualities of resiliency, faith, choice, volition and divine providence?

Perhaps man's delving into the human psyche through sciences such as psychology and psychiatry, biology, chemistry can yield only incomplete answers. Historically, we need more than science to explain the unexplainable.

I could not have changed my mother's upbringing. I didn't choose to catch pneumonia and H1N1 flu, and I didn't choose my husband's trauma, either. I didn't choose excellent doctors, nurses and caregivers; they came with the hospital which I did choose. I also chose the first rehab hospital where Joe suffered the hematuria and a perforated bladder. It could be argued that I chose to marry Joe who chose to allow his immune system to deteriorate, so essentially the choice to experience what I did was mine. Preposterous. This line of thinking would lead me to insanity, analyzing each second and each decision of each day for the probability of gazillions of possible outcomes. That would be "stinkin' thinkin". We chose to move around the world, but we didn't choose to catch the flu once we had returned home. We are coming to accept the unquestionable meaning in our suffering, although we haven't yet figured out what it is. But it's coming.

The year I taught in the Middle East, I joined eight hundred other teachers from around the globe. Originally I had applied to teach in Mexico, where I could speak the language and be with whales. The recruiter accepted my application but informed me that they were not placing teachers in Mexico at the time, asking me if I would consider the United Arab Emirates. *Where?* I prayed, fasted, discussed with Joe, investigated, dreamt and visualized our lives halfway around the world.

During the interview, recruiters examined our records and scrutinized our credentials, prior teaching experience and preferences for age and grade. We had some idea of which grade we would be teaching, but school and grade assignments were made once we had completed orientation. Two choices were available. I chose the more urban one because I was advised it would be easier for my husband to acquire employment there. Human resources contracted with hotel apartments and villas throughout the city for teacher housing, but we had to choose our housing before we were given our teaching assignments. I was fortunate to be placed in a third grade classroom, but the school was located an hour's drive from the city, actually closer to the neighboring Emirate. Some teachers were assigned to schools within a five minute walk from their apartment. Some in more rural areas, for example, carpooled with other teachers who lived in the same three bedroom villa apartment complex. The majority had fair assignments and decent apartments. Some, like me, had the expense of renting a car, (although gas was cheap!), paying for parking and insurance, and traveling the two hour round trip every day. Some, like me, were disallowed from leaving school even after the students were dismissed so we could travel back to the city to deal with endless paperwork in the main offices. Some, like me, were not informed that because we had not obtained drivers' licenses, we could no longer legally drive. Did we risk huge fines and possible imprisonment so we could teach? We adopted intrepid attitudes and wrote off our fates as the luck of the draw. It made no sense to whine about our placements or compare the quality of our jobs, principals, co-workers, apartments or lifestyles to others. But I whined, inwardly.

My life: wake at 4:00 AM to the song *One Love* - soundtrack of my life- on my mobile phone alarm, out the door at 5:00, pay the overnight parking (expensive), drive one hour depending upon traffic (horrible, like New York City) fog (equally horrible anywhere) or seasonal sandstorms (deadly) out of the city and across two islands, past the flocks of flying flamingos (flamingos *fly?!*), past the barren desert, teach for seven hours or more, attend meetings (sometimes in English, sometimes in Arabic), drive one hour or more home, park the car, prepare dinner, shower, (oh, the blessing of a shower), correct papers and prepare lessons for the next day, fall asleep buried in paperwork.

By the time Joe joined me, having been delayed three months due to Catherine's death, and botched travel plans, my driver's license had expired – along with my patience. Luckily, Joe was able to drive the rental car using his visit visa. Once a month we'd drive to neighboring Oman, cross the border so his passport showed he had exited the Emirates, and then reenter so he could stay for another thirty days.

Before he came, I was alone in a foreign country, navigating through limitless employment, housing, and travel details in a city that was growing at an explosive, unprecedented pace. It was said that at the time, one quarter of all the world's cranes were in the Emirates, and not one grain of sand was untouched. Maps were obsolete as soon as they were printed, and the ones were printed were in Arabic and meager English. I studied conversational Arabic for three months before arriving, so I felt confident with basics: *Do you speak English? Where is Al Hamra Street? I'm hungry, where can I find a restaurant? How are you? I'm fine thank you. I speak a little Arabic. No, I am not Syrian, I'm American.* Written Arabic was a different story altogether. Each time I signed a piece of paper, I said a little prayer that I wasn't risking my safety, my bank account or my future.

But there were so many happy times. The United Arab Emirates are spectacular jewels on the southern side of the Persian Gulf. The Muslim people with whom I lived and worked were beautifully welcoming, graceful, genteel and kind, although the drivers could use some lessons on manners. Joe drove me and two other teachers who taught at my school to and from work every day. Carpooling provided opportunities for venting, planning, sleeping, practicing Arabic, sightseeing and watching sunrises together. We threatened to place a sign in the car window: "Be nice to us: We teach your children." Joe was on the road four hours a day, making the two hour round- trip twice. In between, he'd cook, shop, search for jobs, work out or have lunch with the hotel sales manager, Mazon, with whom he had become fast friends. Joe would wait in the car outside school in the afternoon with bags of treats for us. My Muslim co-teachers viewed Joe as an oddity. Miss Sabah, seeing Joe waiting there faithfully every day:

"Miss Ave: This husband of yours, what does he do?"

"He drives us to and from school. He shops. He cooks."

"He *cooks*? What does he cook?"

I explained.

Disgusted, she said, "Tsk tsk. My husband, *he **sits**.* He does not move off of the couch."

I'm certain that Joe left a life-changing memory with her, and other women with Emirati husbands. I loved my fellow Emirati teachers, all covered in their floor-length, flowy, fancy abayas, showing not much more than their modesty, piety and dark eyes. Many months after I left, I finally figured out why I had felt so at home with them: they reminded me of the nuns who taught me in Catholic school.

My grade three girls – fifty six squealing, delightful uninhibited black-haired darlings – were sweet and funny and challenging. They tugged at my maternal instincts, my patience and my soul. They appreciated school. And they liked me. I adored them.

I learned as I taught. The girls taught me Arabic and I taught them English. They taught me about joy, as when, one warm morning during my lesson on the water cycle, their heads turned one by one toward the inner open-air courtyard. Rarely rude to me, they must have been witnessing something odd, so I stopped talking and turned my eyes in that direction also. Nothing happening. No one in the courtyard. What did they see that I didn't?

Then, I heard it: almost imperceptible at first. Ting. Ping. Ting ting. Did the girls feel it? Did they have that sixth sense? Ping ping ping ping. The raindrops touched the tile of the courtyard, evaporating as quickly as they fell.

By now, all of the classes had begun to gather at the doorways leading to the courtyard. Miss Mosa, the Principal, makes an announcement in Arabic over the loudspeaker. "Classes will assemble in the courtyard as we do for morning assembly," she instructs.

The gym teacher organizes an impromptu activity in the rain using a parachute-sized tarp. Classes circle the tarp, hold the edge and take turns waving the tarp up and down, bouncing one girl at a time. Wee! Up and down they squeal. While they are waiting their turn, the other classes are engaged in the simple merriment of being rained upon, some running with tongues sticking out, catching droplets as we do with snowflakes. I am in awe.

A.A.E. MURPHY

What I took for granted, living in lush places like New England and Hawaiʻi, USA, where precipitation is plentiful, and weather is something to endure or ignore.

One quarter of the eight hundred teachers left in the first few months.

The optimist believes where there are obstacles, there are opportunities for growth. The optimist accepts the inevitable. The optimist makes a choice to find the silver lining.

We learned about desert life, city life, Islam, customs, culture, Arabic oud, henna hand tattoos, Ramadan, 135 degrees Fahrenheit, modest dress, behavior and speech. We learned about Arabic wildlife, weather, environment, royalty. We met camels and falcons and sheiks. We swam in highly saline, crystal blue waters, snorkeled with fish so abundant they cast shadows on the rocks, and dug oyster shells the size of our forearm. We saw the tallest building in the world on the horizon, and by craning our necks at the entrance. We watched wild dolphins in the Gulf of Oman. We learned to love the song of the call to prayer and the ancient language. We delighted in warm orange sunsets and strange-starred night skies. We picked up trash everywhere we went, and it was everywhere. We learned how to drive, and how not to drive on the highway that links Dubai to other Emirates. We feasted on shawarmas. We blended into the eighty percent of ex-patriots who settled in this magical place to help build and educate. We respected our hosts and humbled ourselves as guests in a fairy tale land.

Did I choose my teaching assignment? Did I choose the overwhelming workload? Only by electing to sign a contract to teach in a foreign country did I choose. But others signed contracts too, and had an easier road than I. On the other hand, they may not have experienced the UAE as authentically as I. Would I make the same choice, knowing what I knew? Probably. I have few regrets.

After our return to the USA, a question nagged me: what was I going to do with all of the experience? How would I align the lessons I'd learned about people we had met, and cultures different from ours? I considered booking a slide show presentation at a local library about our lives in Hawai`i and the Middle East, but the busy-ness of life and then Joe's illness ate away at my time.

Chapter 15

Empathy, Mercy & Grace

Let us therefore come boldly to the throne of grace that we may obtain mercy and find grace to help in time of need. ~ Hebrews 4:16

We are "that couple" now. You know them: their reputation precedes them, the ones about whom everyone is talking and for whom everyone is praying. When you see "that couple", the first words that escape are "How are you feeling?" I hear my perpetually ill Mom's answer -"With my hands"- but stop the words before they leave my lips, fearing I would come off as disrespectful and flip.

Apparently, our story defines us, even though we try to change the subject when we're asked that magic question. We desperately want to talk about the weather, the local sports teams, the traffic, or anything other than the nightmare we've been through in the past two years.

Joe has suffered 65% hearing loss in both ears. He has hearing aids, but he dislikes them and frequently leaves them sitting in the drawer. (Does he really simply not want to hear me anymore?) He appears to have selective hearing; it amazes me that he can hear me grumbling in another room, but he can't hear me when I'm sitting next to him. We joke about it, but sometimes I groan with frustration when I have to repeat myself. Several times. Surely, I'm grateful that Joe didn't lose his hearing completely, but I assume it will worsen with age anyway. Dealing with a taste of early aging is the byproduct of the illness- for both of us. People who are older than we can commiserate with us, but our situation is not the same as natural aging. And of course we never forget that each day is a bonus- a gift from God, the Universe, higher powers. We live with a sense of urgency, having experienced death.

With lingering neuropathy in both feet, he is often unstable and uncomfortable standing, sitting, or walking for any length of time. His feet feel numb and cold at the same time, but socks restrict his circulation, so he often wears them loose and hanging half off his toes, like two limp tongues, or foot sock puppets. Two years later, he still takes medications for anxiety and depression. His world has changed. My world has changed. The flu and resultant illnesses transformed him from a virile, active, employed man to a disabled, retired one, deemed physically unable to perform the duties of his job. He cannot sit or stand for eight hours, walk two miles -prerequisites for an airport security officer. There are no "desk jobs" with his job. Imagine a man once active and engaged in life, now not so much, all because of a virus invisible to the naked eye. Everyone wants him to get back on the proverbial horse, to look for a job, to just put it all behind him. I think people want to see him as "normal" again, maybe because of the appearance of health. If he does find a suitable full-time job that he could perform, he jeopardizes his disability retirement. I don't think he's processed everything yet. I don't think he's ready to accept his new life, and I don't know how else to help him than by doing what I'm already doing – loving him through it, and remaining by his side.

We work on our marital challenges, seeking help, comfort and counsel from professionals and church leaders, visiting and home teachers. I feel as if this experience has relegated me to a lonely category; who can understand my challenges? Anyone can relate to some extent, if you've ever been sick, or known someone who has been hospitalized, or in a coma, or lost a spouse, or suffered with a chronic illness and the resultant systemic insurance quagmire or financial nightmare. Or if you've ever dealt with the fear of losing your livelihood, your loved one, your home, or your health. If you have been sick and needy for so long that you were forced to rely upon (and accept) the comfort and kindness of friends, family and strangers, you might understand our situation. I fear the support group I need – even if I were healthy enough to attend – doesn't exist. It's the colossal combination of all of these, and more, which draws me to the only one who knows the depths of my anguish. I've felt the grace of perfect love.

These earthly experiences can drive me to despair and privacy- my default personality - yet I know those reactions are not from God. I find inspiration from holy words to overcome the challenges wrought from the human body:

Romans Chapter 8: *5 For they that are after the flesh do mind the things of the flesh; but they that are after the Spirit the things of the Spirit; 6 For to be carnally minded is death; but to be spiritually minded is life and peace.*

Dealing with the changes in my life drives me away from society, and oddly, right back to it, obligated to turn the negative to positive, energized to share my story as an example.

Romans 8: 28 *And we know that all things work together for good to them that love God, to them who are the called according to his purpose...31... If God be for us, who can be against us?*

We are teetering on the brink of poverty, still "one paycheck away" from homelessness, not unlike so many other Americans and not unlike the way we were before this happened.

I acquired Power of Attorney for Joe when he was in the first rehab hospital to expedite the paperwork processes. To be honest, I was afraid that Joe would not ever fully recover from the polyneuropathy. I needed to make applications and decisions quickly to get the ball rolling on the notoriously constipated process of applying for Social Security benefits and Disability Retirement from his employer. Incredibly, Joe was approved for Disability

Retirement from, but denied twice for Social Security benefits (they claimed he is able to return to his job despite a letter from his employer stating he cannot.) We had been surviving on the $33K crowdfunding donations, but they dried up in the summer of 2014. Fortunately, I'm a teacher, so I can accept long-term substitute and tutoring positions when I'm not responsible for Joe's caregiving, or hobbled with Fibromyalgia.

Joe's had four surgeries in the span of two years: the original exploratory in January 2014 which resulted in removal of a portion of his burst colon and colostomy: the ostomy reversal in January 2015; total shoulder replacement in August 2015, and re-incision of the ostomy site in September 2015 because it didn't heal from the original reversal in January. He is facing one more surgery to repair a hernia that was created by the removal of his umbilicus during the original surgery. The hernia hasn't grown or caused Joe too many problems; his surgeon, Dr. R, is monitoring it and we feel safe for now. It is another fairly serious issue. According to the Mayo Clinic, the intestines can protrude through the herniated abdominal wall, become trapped and can no longer be pushed back into the abdominal cavity, or cause infection or tissue strangulation.

Time is quickly approaching when Joe will be weaned from most of his medications-not a simple process. One more challenge on his long list.

There is a church calling card of sorts with a photo of a man who resembles Joe and the words "Does God have a plan for my life?" (By chance, I saw the same card in a meme on social media wherein *plan* was changed to *flan*. Must appreciate humor.) We've placed the one with *plan* in the window above the kitchen sink so it can be clearly viewed and pondered. Answers seem to be coming.

Joe prays for several long spans of time, daily. He has never felt closer to our heavenly Father or His son, Jesus. He is more active with the church now, aptly completing his callings (volunteer jobs) as Home Teacher and recently as Family History Consultant, with me. We believe the assignment of callings to be divinely inspired. I agree that our calling to work on family history is divinely inspired, and part of The Plan for our happiness. By researching his family roots, Joe has discovered his ancestry leads back to a prominent family, one of the original settlers of the island where we lived, and further back to approximately 1020 AD. The significance and irony of this cannot be understated. Joe grew up feeling his father's presence, and acknowledges the presence of other spirits who guided him through this saga.

According to the main webpage, our church has the largest genealogical library in the world; fifteen million members are encouraged to research their family roots, driven by our doctrine that teaches that marriage and families can continue beyond this life. This can only happen when families are sealed together in one of the Lord's holy Temples around the world.

Finding Joe's ancestry linked to the history of those who bought and settled the island where we lived and worked, where we felt at home, was nothing short of astonishing. Researching our family history has brought us closer to each other, and closer to our ancestors. My commitment to Joe is grounded in the understanding that our marriage will continue after we both die.

He has time now to maintain the home as much as physically possible (not very), and help me with the domestic chores. He has taken command of bill paying again, a burden that was thrust upon me in January 2014 which I deeply resented. Joe spends far too much energy dealing with the "system" on the phone – a tangled knot of non-answers, runarounds, frustrations and dead-ends with customer service agents and insurance representatives. Having worked as a customer service representative for a health insurance company, I understand that people have jobs to do, but I also know that a customer can and should be treated with respect. Most of the time Joe keeps his composure and accomplishes what he set out to accomplish when he makes a phone call. Sometimes, an agent says something rude or inept to him, and Joe flips out. Not good for his blood pressure or his health. Not good for mine, either. We recently received a notice stating that a large bill was going to collections; this was for Joe's shoulder surgery which was pre-authorized. The joke of it is that we have carried two insurances for nearly two years. Some days it's all Joe can do to make a phone call, wait on hold for fifty-nine minutes only to be disconnected at the sixtieth minute, call again, wait on hold, finally speak with an agent to explain a situation, wait on hold again, explain the situation again, be told that he has the wrong department, or that agent can't help him... until he's done. Burnt out for the day.

Life was challenging for me before this happened. I struggled with back problems as a result of the car accident, had chronic fatigue, and menopause for the past decade, so even before this disaster I wasn't in outstanding shape. I often remarked that I'd gone through menopause, been divorced and taught in inner city public schools, so nothing scared me. Not so anymore.

My hair has grown back somewhat. I don't stutter, and I can finish my sentences when I speak. I'm not a tangle of nerves anymore. I still cry, but not daily, and not rivers of tears. Because of inflammation and weight gain I feel like I resemble Harry Potter's Aunt– the one who blew up into a balloon and floated out of the house.

I trust (most) doctors again, after a lifetime hiatus. I credit the talented teams at three out of the four hospitals where Joe was treated with saving his life. But there were incidents and events brought on by incompetence and neglect that nearly killed him, therefore, I'm plagued by lingering doubt in "the systems" of our earthly lives. On one hand I appreciate the medical profession more than ever before. I enlisted the advice and assistance of family members who are nurses throughout our ordeal, and trusted them implicitly. Barb the Advocate handled many situations with aplomb. And yet there were times when I stood at Joe's bedside, watching someone perform some medical procedure or action on him, and felt the imprecision, the subjectivity of it. I watched certified, trained, experienced professionals administer care in the best way they knew, and still felt a fragility, an absence of something. What was/is missing? How can I think and speak so arrogantly, so thanklessly, so faithlessly? My husband is alive due in large part to his caregivers, but I could have been writing this as a widow.

I acknowledge the excellent care and I'm humbled and grateful for it. I wonder how many people die of complications born of neglect, carelessness, mismanagement, human error and malpractice. Even if I knew, how could I reconcile their deaths? Time for inner peace and gratitude for what is, rather than engaging a tornado of doubt, fear and curiosity. Most days, I can ignore that tornado, but some days when I'm not feeling well, anger, bitterness and self - pity creep in and I am overtaken by despondency and grief. I understand these are the work of the adversary, the father of lies. I beat back the feelings as quickly as I can, but they exist, and I know they will return, never too far from me. Scriptures help me understand the difference between dark and light:

For behold…it is given unto you to judge, that ye may know good from evil; and the way to judge is as plain that ye may know with a perfect knowledge as the daylight is from the dark night… the Spirit of Christ is given to every man, that he may know good from evil…

…for every thing which inviteth to do good, and to persuade to believe in Christ, is sent forth by the power and gift of Christ; wherefore ye may know with a perfect knowledge it is of God…

But whatsoever thing persuadeth men to do evil and believe not in Christ, and deny him and serve not God, they ye may know with a perfect knowledge it is of the devil… after this manner doth the devil work, for he persuadeth no man to do good, no…neither do his angels, neither they who subject themselves to him… -Moroni 7:15-17

My prayer life is richer, improved through sincerity of heart. I have a more "humble and contrite" spirit now. My vision is more mature, my goals more realistic and centered on my core. I accept that I can't save the world if I don't first save myself. This comes with a cost.

I'm more dour, a little like Eeyore. I used to be sparkly. Perhaps it is the medication, or the chronic pain from Fibromyalgia, but all of this loss, all of these challenges have changed me. I don't believe we ever truly bounce back after grief, or return to our old selves. I think instead that after we've done the work and processed the losses, we become a scarred version of whom we used to be, scarred, and dulled. Some call this refining by fire, or polishing of the stone until it shines. I don't feel polished, purified or shiny - unless sloths can be viewed that way, (although sloths are gorgeous in their own way). Most days, I'm lucky if can slog through six good hours.

I still dream big: I've discovered the comfort and value of footbaths, and created my own brand which I call *Thank you, (Fibro) Feet!*

Fibromyalgia has stolen my attention, energy and motivation. I understand the line "Yes, I can do that, but it will take four days to recover." I often suffer migraines and bruise-like pain on my scalp so extreme I feel as if someone has taken a hammer to my head. This is not an exaggeration.

On days when a storm front is approaching, my joints and muscles throb. I see birds at the feeder, insatiable before a storm, and I grasp the fact that they must feel the drop in the barometric pressure too. How else could they predict and react to an impending change in the weather? But I doubt they hurt the way I do.

Birds are not the only animals to feel weather. When we were living in Hawai`i, two tsunamis struck the islands. They were of minimal impact to the `aina (land) but left an imprint on us. These were the first tsunamis we had survived, and because we lived on tiny remote islands, we were more connected to the island people than if we lived on the mainland. For example, we heard more about locals' reactions to the news of the impending tidal surge. Many who had survived hurricanes Ewa in 1982 and her fiercer cousin Iniki in 1991 scoffed at the forecast. Some gathered and partied at tsunami and hurricane evacuation points, one of which was located on the greens of our condos overlooking a 150 foot cliff. As it turned out, we "dodged the bullet" (never liked the expression, but it was common); the tsunamis failed to deliver a lethal blow, all that happened was a three - foot wave which affected the shores as if the ocean was breathing. A distant inhale sucked the waters out of the bays exposing rocks and seabed, followed by a slow, rippling return which filled the bays once again.

The most interesting response was that of the whales. A pilot flying over the island's north shore at the time of the tsunami reported seeing a large number of whales lined up in a row farther offshore, as if they knew to gather and stay safe. Following the 2004 Indian Ocean tsunami, abundant reports circulated about wild animals running away from the shore. Some rumor that animals have a sixth sense which makes them more sensitive to sounds, scents, vibrations and other atmospheric factors. Some claim that humans possessed this sixth sense, but have devolved.

I understand why the most common patients of Dr. Jack Kevorkian were Fibromyalgia sufferers. I try not to complain out loud in front of Joe, but when I do, sometimes he is kind and supportive and sometimes he tells me he doesn't want to hear it. I can accept this as a cruel response, especially considering what I have sacrificed for him and his ailments, or I can analyze it and be thankful for it. I don't want to become The Fibromyalgia Sufferer. The cliché is "I have XXX (insert illness here), but it doesn't have me." I don't want to take on the persona of a sick person. I've been too near to death to be debilitated by illness. Through Joe's caustic comment, I'm able to adjust my attitude and power through the pain.

Joe's ostomy was reversed, his shoulder has been replaced and his physical scars have healed, so I don't have to attend to him as I did two years ago when he was the new patient at home. Not having to change his ostomy bag is a huge improvement. He's more self-sufficient now, needing assistance and reassurance a portion of the time compared to when he first came home from rehab. It's nice to be needed less.

We were close before. Now, we share a rare experience that feels like fiction.

I take prescription medication now, something that I abhorred before. And I take supplements including D-Ribose, vitamin D, vitamin C, Zinc, L-Glutamine, Magnesium Oxide, a daily multivitamin, concentrated garlic, a stool softener and an herbal supplement called Blissful Joy. I changed my diet and my lifestyle. I am my own advocate. In the morning, after I've assessed which body parts are cooperating, after I feed and walk the cats, feed the fish and the ducks, after I make a cup of hot herbal tea and count my blessings, after I've done the dishes and swept the floors, after I say my prayers of thanks, after gentle yoga stretching, after I list my daily goals, I take some time to purposefully do what is important to me. This act is not to be trivialized. How many of us switch on to autopilot every morning? How many of us are blessed to have the choice?

I joined Fibromyalgia online support groups. Fearing that my preference to consort with other FM sufferers would offend family and friends, I wrote a social media post to explain my choice. I told my social media friends that I was not going to complain about FM anymore, that I didn't expect them to understand. I told them that I found good support among FM sufferers, and I apologized if I wasn't available for them. Even that post was misunderstood. It is taxing to explain myself and answer questions about FM. It's also a given that friends and family are concerned, and love me, and want to know what's going on in my life. There again my private nature comes into play. It must be infuriating for some to know what I'm dealing with and not be asked for help. Or is this my ego and arrogance speaking? Perhaps friends and loved ones have settled into acceptance of my situation and moved on with their lives. I don't blame them. The crises that Joe and I have endured are too much for us to handle, let alone others who may not be equipped. I equate our situation with divorce: divorcing couples can be treated like they're contagious: we're sad that they are divorcing, but we're thankful that it's not happening to us. Maybe that's a bad analogy because divorce is so common? When I was divorcing, I felt marginalized. I could only share my thoughts with those who were either divorcing, or divorced. When we suffer, we cannot expect others who have not suffered the same or similar strife to understand. Certainly people can sympathize, but sympathy and empathy are two totally different animals. Empathy requires a hand-in hand walk on the same burning path of coals.

While completing this book, I contracted shingles. Just when I thought I had a handle on Fibromyalgia, another virus joined the party. Nursing my wounds, I thought about my son Patrick contracting shingles on the day his second son was born. Patrick had to isolate himself from his family for three weeks. I sympathized with him because my sister has had shingles multiple times, and my stepmom Pearl had it twice; I understood on some level what they were enduring. I tried to offer suggestions to Patrick, such as applying pain patches to the affected areas. I checked in on him every few days, but he fought on. I felt helpless as his mother. When I developed shingles, I understood and I empathized.

When Jolie D finally died of ovarian cancer in 2006, I learned instantly and intimately about loss and grief, a lesson I wouldn't have chosen. Life (and God?) had other plans for me. My capacity for sympathy was renewed when she suffered, and my capacity for empathy was supercharged after she died. I understood loss. I understood love for a friend. I understood powerlessness and surrender. Grief drowned my spirit. Grief asked questions that I wouldn't have needed to ask. Missionaries answered those questions, planting a testimony about a great comforter. This testimony would serve as a foundation of faith and strength one year later when my mother died, five years later when I was injured in the car accident, and eight years later when Joe and I caught H1N1 flu.

For those who have lost a loved one to illness, or who have suffered/are suffering an illness or loss: this is your journey. No one but you can live your life. No one can make your choices for you. You are not the only one who suffers. You can seek out a hand of empathy to walk with you, but you are still the master of your attitude and will.

With faith or without, we are responsible for maintaining our temporal health to give ourselves a fighting chance against ruinous and random things like accidents, viruses and diseases. My mom, mistress of mixed metaphors, used to chide "God may feed the birds, but He doesn't throw the seed in the nest," a common quote with many (mis)interpretations, but mine is sure: life is work. My mother walked the walk. She spoke from experience, and carried her history into her future. Her example resonated throughout my life, as I'm sure most parents' examples do. She gave resilience a body and a voice. She taught me that life is difficult, sometimes through no choice of our own, and if we don't get up and fight, we will fall.

Then again, we have to put down the yoke sometimes. It has been promised that life can be joyful.

Adam fell that men might be; and men are, that they might have joy. ~2 Nephi 2:25

The wisdom we gain from suffering can be spread for goodness, or allowed to fester and toxify our souls. I lovingly challenge you to give it life and breath! Share. Tell your story. Don't worry about some who may not hear you. Honor your journey. It is uniquely yours. Certainly there are will always be those who suffer more and less than we, so comparing to another serves no purpose except to scrape the scabs of envy or pride.

The messages of prophets are clear: we are to do the work of life with humility, diligent service, virtue, knowledge, temperance, patience and love.

Jesus, the great exemplar, a brilliant teacher instructed us in various ways. He taught through stories, parables, words, works and miracles for all people, rich or poor, weak or strong, sick or healthy, young and old. He taught us how to live a simple yet abundant life in the body and in the spirit. In his second epistle, Jesus' apostle Peter admonishes us to shine our lights in dark places, knowing that the words of Scripture are divinely inspired, and meant to be shared:

According as his divine power hath given unto us all things that pertain unto life and godliness, through the knowledge of him that hath called us to glory and virtue:

Whereby are given unto us exceeding great and precious promises: that by these ye might be partakers of the divine nature, having escaped the corruption that is in the world through lust.

And beside this, giving all diligence, add to your faith virtue; and to virtue knowledge;

And to knowledge temperance; and to temperance patience; and to patience godliness;

And to godliness brotherly kindness; and to brotherly kindness charity.

For if these things be in you, and abound, they make you that ye shall neither be barren nor unfruitful in the knowledge of our Lord Jesus Christ. But he that lacketh these things is blind, and cannot see afar off, and hath forgotten that he was purged from his old sins.

Wherefore the rather, brethren, give diligence to make your calling and election sure: for if ye do these things, ye shall never fall:

We have also a more sure word of prophecy; whereunto ye do well that ye take heed, as unto a light that shineth in a dark place, until the day dawn, and the day star arise in your hearts:

Knowing this first, that no prophecy of the scripture is of any private interpretation.

When I allow myself to think about it, I miss my old life – the one without swollen knuckles, migraines and limping, when I was active and healthy and ambitious and cheerful. I miss the life I had with Joe before he became sick. Not that I'm resentful or jealous, but I'm weak sometimes. It takes too much energy to look back. Besides gaining perspective, there is little value in dragging the past into the present. But there are miles between knowing that, and having the tools and energy required to live like the obnoxious optimist I once was.

I struggle with a boatload of guilt -- which I have to dismiss. It's physically and mentally impossible for me to do what I want or need to do. On the other hand, I've rediscovered the sibling salves for guilt and self-pity: sympathy and empathy. I'm grateful for the perspective I've earned through my trials. I know more will come.

Joe and I continue to take pleasure in simpler things, together again. We're tickled when we combine leftovers to make our version of stone soup. Not that we starve—not even close-- but we enjoy the rewards of being thrifty and not living extravagantly. I practice good, old habits. I recycled and repurposed long before it was en vogue. Raising Patrick, I was managing a tight budget; he accused me of being Amish. He was not far off the mark. We re-wash plastic bags, use cloth napkins instead of paper towel, and boil water in a hotpot to wash dishes instead of taxing the ancient, oil-burning furnace. Joe and I maintain a "River Friendly Lawn" which really is an acre of weeds, but we've discovered dandelion, purslane and plantain. Our ducks give us eggs. As Rita's bumper sticker reads "My pets make me breakfast". Our cats bring us comfort and companionship. Our home is warmed by a cozy fireplace in the winter, safe and dry. We have loving friends and family, generous neighbors and church members who are always there for us, willing to help with our needs. We have health insurance and good doctors. And we have been shown the mercy and hope of second chances.

What more could we ask?

I've seen events in my life come full circle from strange to horrible to meaningful to wonderful. I choose to view these as blessings, or "tender mercies" from above.

The first friend I made in the UAE was Mazon. He made good on all his promises in a foreign land. He reassured me and offered me hospitality and trustworthiness when I needed it desperately. He wanted to meet my husband. I told him that Joe was coming, that his mother died the week we were issued tickets to travel. Weeks passed, and he hadn't arrived. Mazon became light-heartedly suspicious, "Where is this husband of yours, Miss Ave? I do not believe you have a husband."

My employers refused to re-book Joe's flight, causing me colossal grief and anxiety which was evident during a phone call in late October. He immediately booked his own flight.

Mazon's suspicion was finally suspended.

If you want to understand Arabic hospitality, think about this: Three wise men traveled on camels many miles across the desert to follow a star and bring gifts to a baby.

As fate, God, destiny or karma would have it, Mazon's son, Youssef, had always dreamed of following his father's path and studying in the US. We befriended him by phone and via social media when he arrived a year ago. We loved him because he was the son of a beloved friend. Youssef was trying to live here in the US alone, but was having difficulties. His timing could not be worse, with the crescendo of anti-Muslim histrionics. He was in need, and we opened our home to him. He has been a delight. Although he is only nineteen, he possesses wisdom and maturity rare to men his age. He's polite and mannered (Yes sir, Yes ma'am), helping us with domestic and physical chores with which we struggle. He makes us laugh, teaches us, cooks for us, carries our packages, cares for us, our home, pets and plants, and reminds us of all that was good in a Muslim country, and all that is good in the heart of a good Muslim.

And if Youssef wasn't enough of a gift, Joe's eldest son, Jameson, has come to live with us for a while. Joe couldn't be more grateful, bonding with his son again. On the day before Christmas, in our one-butt kitchen, they cooked side by side. About the holiday, the happiest in recent memory, Joe beamed, "I've been waiting for this for fifteen years."

I'm blessed to know that I can enact my agency, or freedom, to choose to live faithfully, simply, to shine my light and to recognize joy. I yearn to perfect humility, diligent service, virtue, knowledge, temperance, patience and love. A tall order. I want to be the new, strong bush that was once cut down by the master gardener. Logic tells me that while my body will not comply – wracked with chronic pain for which there is no cure (yet) – my spirit has been fortified to accomplish living with peace, gratitude and intention in the present, choosing hope for a blessed future here -- and in the next life. Each moment is a choice.

I know I'm supported by good friends and family here and in the spirit world, held in the arms of our merciful heavenly Father. I acknowledge

His hand in all things, therefore, I try to give thanks in all circumstances, and endure through whatever comes.

As I've taught my students, success can be found by focusing on realistic, manageable, achievable goals. I'm going to treat myself to a *Thank You, Feet* foot soak during which I'll listen to Spa music and dream about being with whales in some exotic place. I might then watch the sparrows on the feeder for a bit, and, when I have the energy, write some *thank you, I'm sorry, please forgive me, I love you notes* to everyone who put up with me while I was buried in my work. The first one will be to Joe, without whom there wouldn't be a story.

####

About the Author

Murphy was born and raised in New England, USA to a German immigrant mother and a second generation Irish father. Compelled to animal, child, political and environmental activism, she discovered the private joy and power of wordsmithing in her early years, before computers and digital media.

She holds a BS in Special Education MS in Education. Earning awards for Writing, Art, Photography and Grant Writing, she brought her gifts to a teaching career spanning over twenty years in a variety of venues including public, private and alternative, teaching students in grades Pre-Kindergarten through twelve, community college and senior centers.

Never forgetting her roots, her love for travel, world culture, transformative dialogue and cetaceans (whales, dolphins and porpoises), she has traveled to and lived in faraway places.

She shares her country home in the city with husband Joe and peaceful cohabitation with rescued animals including a retired racing greyhound, cats and ducks.

VIRAL Questions

1. Why did Murphy omit details about Joe's home rehabilitation and his surgeries in 2015?
2. How is wildlife significant to Murphy? Why?
3. Do you believe Murphy will continue to receive vaccinations? Why or why not? Should she?
4. Identify the theme(s) of the book, and cite examples:

Alienation

Betrayal

Birth

Coming of age

Conformity

Death

Deception

Discovery

Duty

Heroism

Escape

Family

Fortune

Generation gap

God and spirituality

Good and evil

Home
Hope
Hopelessness Love
Individualism Isolation
Journey
Judgment
Loss
Patriotism
Peace and war
Power
Race relations
Sense of self
Suffering
Survival

5. Why did Murphy choose VIRAL as the title? How is the concept exemplified in the book?
6. What motivated the main character to act the way s/he did?
7. How does VIRAL's setting contribute to the book?
8. How does the main character change throughout the book?
9. How does the main character interact with others? How would you describe his or her personality?
10. What is the turning point of this book? What was your reaction to that pivotal moment?
11. What was your favorite or most memorable passage in the book? Why did it make an impression?
12. What type of writing style does Murphy use? How does that affect your interpretation or impression of the book?
13. Generally, did you enjoy this book? Why or why not?
14. What is an assumption you made about the story that came to fruition, or didn't?

Endnotes

i   http://bionews-tx.com/news/2014/01/16/h1n1-flu-epidemic-fills-texas-hospital-beds-ers-chinese-avian-flu-expected-spread-north-america/

ii   http://www.nytimes.com/2014/01/28/opinion/brooks-alone-yet-not-alone.html?_r=0

iii   https://www.lds.org/scriptures/nt/matt/10?lang=eng

iv   http://www.mayoclinic.org/diseases-conditions/ards/basics/definition/CON-20030070

v   Austin O'Malley

vi   Bruce C. Hafen, Spiritually Anchored in Unsettled Times, (Salt Lake City: Deseret Book, 2009), 30).

vii   https://www.lds.org/general-conference/1998/10/hope-through-the-atonement-of-jesus-christ?lang=eng

viii   https://www.lds.org/scriptures/nt/mark/5.27-28?lang=eng#26

ix   https://www.lds.org/scriptures/bd/miracles?lang=eng

x   http://www.mormonnewsroom.org/topic/family-history-centers

xi   http://gis.cdc.gov/grasp/fluview/main.html

xii   http://www.cnn.com/2014/12/04/health/flu-vaccine-mutated-virus/index.html

xiii   http://www.goldcoastbulletin.com.au/news/gold-coast/liam-enese-16-year-old-gold-coast-sportsman-dies-of-pneumonia-as-flu-epidemic-sweeps-city/story-fnj94idh-1227487555520

xiv   http://www.cdc.gov/vaccines/vpd-vac/vpd-list.htm

xv   http://www.cdc.gov/flu/protect/keyfacts.htm

xvi   http://www.cdc.gov/flu/about/disease/high_risk.htm

xvii   http://www.historyofvaccines.org/content/articles/influenza-pandemics

xviii   http://www.cdc.gov/flu/about/disease/high_risk.htm

xix   http://vaccines.procon.org/

xx   https://www.youtube.com/watch?t=267&v=l1K74Tnrrok

xxi Andrew Wakefield, SH Murch, A. Anthony, et al., "RETRACTED: Illeal-Lymphoid-Nodular Hyperplasia, Non-Specific Colitis, and Pervasive Developmental Disorder in Children," www.theThe Lancet.com, Feb. 1998

xxii Simon H. Murch, Andrew Anthony, David H. Casson, et al., "Retraction of an Interpretation," www.theThe Lancet.com, Mar. 6, 2004

xxiii (Wakefield, Volume 363, Issue 9411 2004)

xxiv https://www.youtube.com/watch?v=zrIM2hwrLoc

xxv https://www.youtube.com/watch?v=zrIM2hwrLoc

xxvi https://youtu.be/zrIM2hwrLoc

xxvii https://www.youtube.com/watch?v=zrIM2hwrLoc

xxviii http://vaccines.procon.org/#background

xxix http://www.cdph.ca.gov/HealthInfo/discond/Pages/Measles.aspx

xxx https://leginfo.legislature.ca.gov/faces/billNavClient.xhtml?bill_id=201520160SB277

xxxi http://www.cdc.gov/vaccines/parents/downloads/parent-ver-sch-0-6yrs.pdf

xxxii A Special Interview with Barbara Loe Fisher By Dr. Mercola, http://articles.mercola.com/sites/articles/archive/2011/11/01/more-parents-waking-up-to-vaccine-dangers.aspx

xxxiii http://www.nvic.org/injury-compensation/origihanlaw.aspx

xxxiv http://healthimpactnews.com/2014/government-pays-damages-to-vaccine-victims-flu-shot-most-dangerous-with-gbs-and-death-settlements/

xxxv http://12160.info/m/discussion?id=2649739%3ATopic%3A1536735

xxxvi http://www.runningthecountry.com/the-mormon-church-and-vaccines-a-letter-to-the-first-presidency/

xxxvii http://www.nvic.org/about.aspx

xxxviii https://www.facebook.com/knowthevax?fref=ts

xxxix http://www.virtualwall.org/dg/GourleyLL01a.htm

xl https://www.lds.org/general-conference/2006/10/the-plan-of-salvation?lang=eng&query=plan+of+salvation

xli http://www.cdc.gov/flu/pastseasons/1314season.htm

xlii http://www.cdc.gov/flu/pastseasons/1314season.htm

xliii http://www.cdc.gov/flu/pastseasons/1314season.htm

xliv http://www.cdc.gov/flu/pastseasons/1314season.htm

xlv http://www.social-consciousness.com/2010/06/dr-bruce-lipton-biology-of-perception.html

xlvi Used with permission from Michele Pagani

xlvii http://www.cdc.gov/flu/pastseasons/1314season.htm

xlviii http://www.cdc.gov/media/releases/2014/p0220-flu-report.html

xlix https://en.wikipedia.org/wiki/Influenza_A_virus_subtype_H2N2

l Meltzer MI, Cox NJ, Fukuda K. The Economic Impact of Pandemic Influenza in the United States: Priorities for Intervention. Emerg Infect Dis [serial on the

Internet]. 1999, Oct [date cited]. Available from http://wwwnc.cdc.gov/eid/article/5/5/99-0507

li http://www.computereconomics.com/article.cfm?id=1225

lii •Haggbloom, S. J. et al. (2002). The 100 most eminent psychologists of the 20th century. Review of General Psychology, 6, 139-152. doi: 10.1037/1089-2680.6.2.139

liii http://psych.fullerton.edu/jmearns/rotter.htm

Printed in the United States
By Bookmasters